ACCORDING TO PLAN

THE UNFOLDING
REVELATION OF GOD
IN THE BIBLE

GRAEME GOLDSWORTHY

InterVarsity Press
Downers Grove, Illinois

InterVarsity Press
P.O. Box 1400, Downers Grove, IL 60515-1426
World Wide Web: www.ivpress.com
E-mail: mail@ivpress.com

InterVarsity Press® is the book-publishing division of InterVarsity Christian Fellowship/USA®, a student movement active on campus at hundreds of universities, colleges and schools of nursing in the United States of America, and a member movement of the International Fellowship of Evangelical Students. For information about local and regional activities, write Public Relations Dept., InterVarsity Christian Fellowship/USA, 6400 Schroeder Rd., P.O. Box 7895, Madison, WI 53707-7895, or visit the IVCF website at <www.ivcf.org>.

Cover illustration: Robert Holmgren/Getty Images

ISBN 0-8308-2696-3

Printed in the United States of America ∞

Library of Congress Cataloging-in-Publication Data

Goldsworthy, Graeme.
  According to plan: the unfolding revelation of God in the Bible /
Graeme Goldsworthy.
    p. cm.
Includes bibliographical references and index.
  ISBN 0-8308-2696-3 (pbk.: alk. paper)
  1. Bible—Theology. I. Title
  BS543 .G65 2002
  230'.041—dc21
                                                                            2002008870

P	17	16	15	14	13	12	11	10	9	8	7	6	5	4	3	2	1
Y	15	14	13	12	11	10	09	08	07	06	05	04	03	02			

CONTENTS

Preface 7

Introduction: How to Use This Book 9

PART ONE: BIBLICAL THEOLOGY—WHY?

1 The Leech Has Two Daughters 17

PART TWO: BIBLICAL THEOLOGY—HOW?

2 God Makes Himself Known 29

3 But How Can We Know? 37

4 Christ Has Made Him Known 47

5 And We Know Him Through Scripture 52

6 The Bible Is the Divine-Human Word 59

7 We Begin and End with Christ 71

PART THREE: BIBLICAL THEOLOGY—WHAT?

8 I Am the First and the Last 81

9 Creation by Word 90

10 The Fall 102

11 First Revelation of Redemption 112

12 Abraham Our Father 120

13 Exodus: Pattern of Redemption 130

14 New Life: Gift and Task *140*

15 The Temptation in the Wilderness *149*

16 Into the Good Land *156*

17 God's Rule in God's Land *164*

18 The Life of Faith *172*

19 The Fading Shadow *180*

20 There Is a New Creation *187*

21 The Second Exodus *195*

22 The New Creation for Us *201*

23 The New Creation in Us Initiated *210*

24 The New Creation in Us Now *218*

25 The New Creation Consummated *226*

PART FOUR: BIBLICAL THEOLOGY—WHERE?

26 Knowing God's Will 237

27 Life After Death 241

Subject Index 245

Scripture Index 247

A while ago an acquaintance of mine urged me to write a biblical theology for ordinary Christians. We were both aware that many theologies of the Old Testament or of the New Testament have been produced over the course of this century, but usually with one, or both, of two limitations. The more serious of these is the failure of so many writers to let the Bible speak with authority on its own terms. The other is the treatment of either Testament on its own, so that there is hardly any work which deals with the theology of the Bible as a whole. But even those works which have been written from the viewpoint of evangelical Christianity are usually written at a level which does not commend itself to Christians untrained in formal theological studies.

In this work I have attempted to do three things. First, to introduce the reader to an integrated theology of the whole Bible. Second, to write this introduction fully accepting the full inspiration and authority of the Bible as the word of God. Third, to write for ordinary Christians at a level that avoids unnecessary technicalities. Behind this endeavor is the conviction that learning to grasp the unity of the Bible, of its one overall message from Genesis to Revelation, is necessary for a right understanding of the meaning of any individual text.

In my first book, *Gospel and Kingdom* (Exeter, U.K.: Paternoster, 1981), the aim was to provide a basic Christian approach to understanding the Old Testament using the method of biblical theology. In my subsequent books *The Gospel in Revelation* (Exeter, U.K.: Paternoster, 1984) and *Gospel and Wisdom* (Exeter, U.K.: Paternoster, 1987) this method was applied to show the relationship of the Old Testament wisdom literature and the book of Revelation to the gospel of Jesus Christ. In *According to Plan* I have proceeded from the same starting point of the gospel as the means of opening up the message of the whole Bible. It is my deep conviction that every part of the Bible is given its fullest meaning by the saving work of Christ, who restores a sinful, fallen creation and makes all things new.

Graeme Goldsworthy

INTRODUCTION:
HOW TO USE THIS BOOK

This guide is written for those who have not had any formal theological education. Provided you have a desire to know the Scriptures, even if you have only achieved a very basic knowledge so far, this book is designed for you. Of course, if you have been to Bible college or theological college this book could still be for you. I believe that many preachers, ministers, Scripture teachers, youth leaders and the like will benefit from studying the basics of biblical theology. So, this is a beginner's guide in the sense that I have tried to introduce the subject without assuming much prior knowledge. I do assume, however, that you are a believer in Jesus Christ and that you have some basic understanding of what the Bible is all about.

This is also a beginner's guide in that I have kept the discussion to the essentials of the biblical message. By keeping the chapters short and by using diagrams and frequent summary statements, I hope to lead even the timid reader step by step through the paths of biblical theology.

FOUR PARTS

The main part of the book is part three, which outlines the content of biblical theology. I have included the other three parts in order to make the book more complete in its practical use. The four parts are as follows:

Part One: Biblical Theology—WHY?

Read chapter one first. Biblical theology is not an academic exercise but an essential part of understanding the Bible. The aim is to suggest some of the practical situations and problems in understanding and applying the Bible that need knowledge of biblical theology.

Part Two: Biblical Theology—HOW?

Read chapters two through seven next only if you think you are ready to consider questions of a more theoretical nature. But don't be too easily put off, and in any case you should read this section at some time. Here the concern is knowing how we can do biblical theology and be sure that we are dealing with the truth. You may have always assumed that the Bible is the Word of God, and that its essential message is clear, but can you give a reason for that assumption? What determines the method of biblical theology? Different people have used different methods and, for a lot of Christians, it is easier to ignore the question of method completely. It is important that we become aware of the things we have taken for granted, and that we recognize our own assumptions. But, if all that sounds too heavy, I suggest you read this section after you have read part three.

Part Three: Biblical Theology—WHAT?

Read chapters eight through twenty-five even if you read nothing else. This is the heart of the book. Remember that this book is not an exhaustive treatment of all the themes and materials found in the Bible. If some of your favorite characters or events in the Bible have not rated a mention, you may find that they are not as central to the biblical message as you thought, or that they do not add any theological concepts to those already dealt with. Obviously, it is not possible to deal with every part of the Bible, but I have tried to include the most significant themes of revelation.

Part Four: Biblical Theology—WHERE?

Section four has been kept to an absolute minimum in the interests of brevity. I did not want a beginner's guide to be so long that it would discourage beginners from acquiring and reading it. The practical application of biblical theology in the investigation of subjects vital to our Christian living really needs a separate volume of its own. But in order to show what kinds of issues can be researched profitably using the approach of biblical theology, I have included a couple of outlines which you may take up in greater detail yourself. The important thing is that you gain confidence in applying biblical theology regarding the questions that really concern you.

VISUAL IMPACT

To assist you to digest the contents of this book, I have used chapter subdivisions, summaries and diagrams.

In the second section of the book each chapter begins with a summary of the argument. This enables you to preview what the chapter is about and then, after you have read the chapter, to review it. Read these summaries carefully to get the general idea, then go on to the more detailed discussion in the body of the chapter.

In part three, each chapter begins with a brief summary of the biblical history relevant to the chapter, followed by references to the biblical books involved. Also in this section each chapter is headed with a selection of Bible texts. Note these Bible texts well. They are all taken from the New Testament and link the theme of the chapter to the person and work of Christ. They remind us of the way the Gospels interpret the whole Bible.

The subdivisions of each chapter are found under subheadings. I have aimed at some logical progression of ideas indicated in the subheadings. Most subdivisions conclude with a brief summary of its main ideas.

The end of each chapter of part three contains five main elements:

1. The heading summarizes the theme of the chapter as part of the total message of the Bible, which moves from the creation to the new creation.

   REGENERATION OF A NATION

2. A short summary of the chapter directs our attention to the idea of the kingdom of God as a central and unifying theme of the Bible. A diagram is used to show the way the theme of the kingdom is progressively built in stages as we move through the biblical story. It represents the three elements of the kingdom: God as ruling Lord, his people and the created order in which God and his people relate. By this means we can see at a glance how any given stage of biblical history reveals the nature of the kingdom.

   SUMMARY

   Mankind's rebellion against God results in the fall of the whole created order from its place in the kingdom of God

KINGDOM	GOD	MANKIND	WORLD
CREATION	GOD	ADAM AND EVE	EDEN
FALL			

3. The main themes of the chapter are listed. These are the building blocks of biblical theology, which shows the texture of revelation. In time you

should aim to become familiar with these concepts and with the way they are woven into the biblical story.

MAIN THEMES
Sovereignty of God
Creation *ex nihilo* (out of nothing) by the word of God
Order and goodness of creation
Image of God in man

4. Some key words are provided as a guide to the technical vocabulary of biblical theology. These words have been introduced in the chapter. If you find you cannot recognize any of them, perhaps a second reading is called for. Further research can be done using a good concordance and other reference books such as a Bible dictionary or theological dictionary.

SOME KEY WORDS
Creation / generation
Sovereignty
Image
Kingdom

5. Finally we briefly preview the path ahead. This important section reminds us that no significant biblical theme can be viewed on its own without linking it to its goal or fulfillment in Christ. This is a sketch of the development of major biblical themes and ideas from Old Testament to New Testament.

THE PATH AHEAD
Adam—last Adam, 1 Corinthians 15:45
Creation—new creation, 2 Corinthians 5:17
Heavens and earth—new heavens and earth, Isaiah 65:17; 2 Peter
    3:13; Revelation 21:1

STUDY SUGGESTIONS

At the end of each chapter it is up to you.

Study guides ask questions and set tasks to encourage you to rehearse the material. A beginner's guide cannot be read like a novel if you are going to get the best out of it. You need to think about what you have read and apply the concepts.

I recommend two books for you to read if you desire to build on the material of this book. The first is my book *Gospel and Kingdom*, which gives an overview of the kingdom theme. The second is *Biblical Theology* by Geerhardus Vos, which will amply reward careful study. At the end of chapters are other suggestions for related reading.

NOTES

To keep the format simple I have avoided footnotes. However, there are some circumstances which demand notes of explanation or acknowledgment of sources. These notes are placed at the end of the chapter.

Now read on, but please note concerning the word *man* that I am aware of the problems associated with its use in the generic, inclusive sense to mean "humankind." I have therefore used a variety of synonyms (*humanity, humankind* and *mankind*), but in some contexts these can be a little cumbersome. I have therefore retained a limited use of the generic term *man*.

ABBREVIATIONS USED IN LISTS OF BOOKS FOR FURTHER READING

BT   Geerhardus Vos, *Biblical Theology.* Grand Rapids, Mich.: Eerdmans, 1948.

GK   Graeme Goldsworthy, *Gospel and Kingdom.* Exeter, U.K.: Paternoster Press, 1981.

IBD   *Illustrated Bible Dictionary.* Leicester: Inter-Varsity Press, 1980.

KG   John Bright, *The Kingdom of God.* Nashville: Abingdon, 1953.

TNTC   Tyndale New Testament Commentaries.

TOTC   Tyndale Old Testament Commentaries.

ZPEB   *Zondervan Pictorial Encyclopedia of the Bible,* 5 vols. Grand Rapids, Mich.: Zondervan, 1975.

ABBREVIATIONS USED FOR BIBLICAL REFERENCES

The books of the Old Testament

Gen	*Genesis*
Ex	*Exodus*
Lev	*Leviticus*
Num	*Numbers*
Deut	*Deuteronomy*
Josh	*Joshua*
Judg	*Judges*
Ruth	*Ruth*
1 Sam	*1 Samuel*
2 Sam	*2 Samuel*
1 Kings	*1 Kings*
2 Kings	*2 Kings*
1 Chron	*1 Chronicles*
2 Chron	*2 Chronicles*
Ezra	*Ezra*
Neh	*Nehemiah*
Esther	*Esther*
Job	*Job*
Ps	*Psalms*
Prov	*Proverbs*
Eccles	*Ecclesiastes*
Song	*Song of Songs*
Is	*Isaiah*
Jer	*Jeremiah*
Lam	*Lamentations*
Ezek	*Ezekiel*
Dan	*Daniel*
Hos	*Hosea*
Joel	*Joel*
Amos	*Amos*
Obad	*Obadiah*
Jon	*Jonah*
Mic	*Micah*
Nahum	*Nahum*
Hab	*Habakkuk*
Zeph	*Zephaniah*
Hag	*Haggai*
Zech	*Zechariah*
Mal	*Malachi*

The books of the New Testament

Mt	*Matthew*
Mk	*Mark*
Lk	*Luke*
Jn	*John*
Acts	*Acts*
Rom	*Romans*
1 Cor	*1 Corinthians*
2 Cor	*2 Corinthians*
Gal	*Galatians*
Eph	*Ephesians*
Phil	*Philippians*
Col	*Colossians*
1 Thess	*1 Thessalonians*
2 Thess	*2 Thessalonians*
1 Tim	*1 Timothy*
2 Tim	*2 Timothy*
Tit	*Titus*
Philem	*Philemon*
Heb	*Hebrews*
Jas	*James*
1 Pet	*1 Peter*
2 Pet	*2 Peter*
1 Jn	*1 John*
2 Jn	*2 John*
3 Jn	*3 John*
Jude	*Jude*
Rev	*Revelation*

BIBLICAL
THEOLOGY—
WHY?

In this first section we ask why Christians should be concerned with biblical theology. We look at a number of the problems that we can meet when reading the Bible, and suggest some ways that biblical theology can help us in dealing with these problems.

THE LEECH HAS
TWO DAUGHTERS

Who of us does not find at least some parts of the Bible difficult to understand? It is easy to ignore the problems by keeping to the well-worn paths of familiar passages. But when we begin to take seriously the fact that the whole Bible is the Word of God, we find ourselves on a collision path with the difficulties. It is at this point that we need biblical theology to show us how to read and understand the Bible. What does a particular problematic passage mean? How can I tell a Bible story so that it speaks to us as the Word of God? How does the Old Testament apply to you and me? What does it mean to interpret the Bible? These are some of the questions that biblical theology will help us to answer.

THE BATTLE OF THE BIBLE-BELIEVERS

There's nothing like feeling that if something is enough of a problem to you, you become motivated to read about it. If the doctor tells you that you will probably die of a heart attack if you don't do something about your eating habits and lifestyle, the chances are that you will start reading up on heart disease, exercise and diet. You can probably also see the wisdom in getting the right information before committing yourself to buying a new car or going on a world trip. And when you've bought a piece of expensive equipment, such as a camera, a microwave oven or a video recorder, you usually feel the need to read the instructions carefully. You read the instructions so that you don't do some real damage, and so that you can get the best results out of your investment.

Every so often as we read the Bible we find things which are a problem to us. It might be something that appears to be very inconsistent with key truths found elsewhere in the Bible. Or it might be that a passage just doesn't make any sense to us at all. Some may just shrug this off and go back to familiar parts of the Bible that seem to present no problems. But the Christian who is serious about finding out what the Word of God says will not be content to take this easy way out. I hope that you are among those who would rather expend a bit of effort in order to gain a better understanding of the Bible as a whole. At this stage you may well ask, "What is biblical theology?" and "Why do I need it?"

As Christians we want to know that our faith and our commitment to Christ are soundly based. We want to know the truth about eternity and about the here-and-now. What should we believe, and why? How should we live, and why? What are the means of knowing the answers to these questions? Most Christians would accept the Bible as the primary source of our knowledge of the truth. How is it, then, that there are such differing views, even opposing views, about some matters of importance to us?

Some of the differences arise out of different perceptions of the authority of the Bible. If the Bible can be interpreted correctly only by an authoritative church, then it becomes subjected to a body of church tradition and teaching. If the Bible actually contains an admixture of truth and error, then some basis for discerning what is true within the Bible becomes a higher authority than the Bible itself. When Christians agree that the Bible is the highest authority, then the differences tend to emerge at the level of questioning what the text of the Bible actually says and how it should be interpreted.

A Seventh-day Adventist who likes a good discussion approaches a young Anglican curate at a railway station and says, "Excuse me, what day is the Sabbath?" Without hesitation the Anglican replies, "Saturday," which surprises the Adventist because he expects the answer to be "Sunday." So he nods and moves on. Both speak from an acceptance of the Bible as the final authority. The question as to why they differ about what day Christians ought to go to church doesn't come up. Were it discussed, it no doubt would illustrate the problem of how to interpret the Bible.

A forum is organized on the subject of speaking in tongues. A Church of Christ minister finds himself aligned with an Anglican against two Pentecostal ministers. There is no question regarding the supreme authority of the Bible, yet on the subject of the working of the Holy Spirit, very great differences of understanding are expressed. Each sees his position as consistent with the overall teaching of the Bible as the Word of God.

So it goes. Christians with the same or very similar convictions about the Bible disagree over what the Bible teaches on the subject of baptism, predestination or the second coming of Christ. "Bible-believing" Christians are very serious about this. Truth matters, and you have to defend what you believe to be true. Deciding to be biblical, and believing and acting upon what the Bible teaches, does not solve all our problems. We are never finished with questions of what the Bible says, how it says it and what it should mean to us. I am not suggesting that the differences in denominational beliefs are all going to be solved by biblical theology. But I am suggesting that any Christian who wants to understand the reasons for the differences, and who wants to develop a sound method of approaching the text of the Bible in order to find out what it really says and means, needs an understanding of biblical theology.

■ *The meaning of the Bible*
is not settled purely on the basis of our understanding of its inspiration and authority.

PROBLEMATIC PASSAGES

If I say, "The whole Bible is God's Word to me," how can I know what God is saying to me in any given passage? In what way is the word of a prophet to an ancient Israelite a word to me? How does the narrative of a bygone event touch my personal existence? And that is only the beginning of our difficulties. In the Bible there are many difficult passages, and many whose meaning seems to lack sense and consistency with what we believe the Bible teaches elsewhere. Some are quite plain as to their actual meaning, but they make no sense as God's word to modern people. Let's look at a few typical problems.

Remember the Adventist and the Anglican? If the discussion had proceeded, the following text would probably have come into question:

Remember the Sabbath day by keeping it holy. (Ex 20:8)

On the surface the meaning of the Sabbath seems plain enough. There would be no dispute over what the Sabbath day was for Israel, and the Bible gives a fair amount of information about what keeping it holy meant in ancient Israel. The dispute is over what that means for us today. A similar message from the same part of the Bible would present a different kind of problem for our two disputing Christians:

Do not cook a young goat in its mother's milk. (Ex 23:19)

Then there are those passages that use figures of speech, or images that are hard to grasp until we become very familiar with their background:

Dan is a lion's cub, springing out of Bashan. (Deut 33:22)

Your nose is like the tower of Lebanon looking towards Damascus. (Song 7:4)

Some passages are difficult because they are capable of a range of meanings and lack any clear context that might help us:

The leech has two daughters. "Give! Give!" they cry. (Prov 30:15)

Finally, we might mention passages that seem to present moral problems, or just seem hard to believe:

O Daughter of Babylon, doomed to destruction, happy is he who repays you for what you have done to us—he who seizes your infants and dashes them against the rocks. (Ps 137:8-9)

The sun stopped in the middle of the sky and delayed going down about a full day. (Josh 10:13)

But the Lord hardened Pharaoh's heart, and he would not let the Israelites go. (Ex 10:20)

He totally destroyed all who breathed, just as the Lord, the God of Israel, had commanded. (Josh 10:40)

These texts illustrate the fact that there seems to be many kinds of problematic passages in the Bible. Sometimes the problem is what the text actually means, and sometimes the problem is discerning personal application. The nature of the Bible is such that the way through these problems is to look at how the Bible holds together as one book with one message. Biblical theology is, in effect, the study of the unity of the message of the Bible.

■ *Biblical theology*
gives us the means of dealing with problematic passages in the Bible by relating
them to the one message of the Bible.

HOW DO I TELL A BIBLE STORY?

Bible stories can be told with great effect, whether to small children, a family-orientated congregation or a chapel full of theological professors. The art of story telling involves skills in creating drama with words, no matter what the source of the story is or its relationship to the truth. Even children telling ghost stories around a camp fire, or after lights out at a slumber party, instinctively realize the value of realism, suspense and surprise in their story telling. Bible stories can be told with attention to those elements that will breathe the life of drama and human interest into them, or they can be robbed of all liveliness and appeal.

Christians, however, do not usually tell Bible stories simply to entertain. We see them as vehicles of truth about God and ourselves. Sometimes we see this, not because the truth for us is obvious, but because the particular story is part of the unfolding drama that leads to its climax in the person and work of Jesus Christ. Such stories are mainly in the Old Testament. What, then, if I tell an Old Testament story with all the story-telling skills that I can muster? Is that all? Does the story then interpret itself, and does it then move people to act according to the truth? Mostly we would want to make some kind of application to the hearer so that what happened in ancient times is perceived to be the word of God at this moment. It is not enough to say that because it is in the Bible we know that it is the word of God to us. When Joshua had taken Jericho, do we see the meaning of this for us as self-evident? Since we do not find ourselves in the situation of attacking cities, we may discern a very general and rather bland lesson about trust and obedience to God's commands. Are Bible stories, then, mostly illustrations of faith or unbelief?

Sooner or later the relevance of the Bible story to the reader or hearer must be considered if we are to think about it as part of God's word to us. Biblical theology is a means of looking at one particular event in relation to the total picture. This total picture includes us where we are now, between the ascension of Jesus and his return at the end of the age. Biblical theology enables us to see ourselves in relation to the far-off events in the

Bible narratives. To uncover our relationship to a particular event is to uncover its meaning for us.

■ *Biblical theology*
enables us to relate any Bible story to the whole message of the Bible, and therefore to ourselves.

WHAT CAN I MAKE OF THE OLD TESTAMENT?

The Old Testament is more than just a lot of stories, although narrative history is the framework into which everything else fits. There are numerous problems that Christians meet when reading the Old Testament, but I shall mention only a few. First of all, the Old Testament is pre-Christian and never mentions the distinctives of the Christian faith. The people of Israel are not Christians and cannot be said to live "Christian" lives.

Second, the Old Testament contains a lot of directives that we as Christians do not observe. This is underlined by the fact that many Christians distinguish between a ritual law of Israel that no longer applies, and a moral law that is seen to be still in effect. A problem arises with a commandment such as the one requiring Sabbath observance, which some discard as ritual, while others hold to it as moral law.

Third, the prophetic view of the final saving work of God makes no specific reference to Jesus Christ, and is directed instead toward the national destiny of Israel. The kingdom of God centers on the restored temple in a rebuilt Jerusalem, to which are gathered all the previously scattered Israelites. Furthermore, the prophets do not really deal with the question of life after death or with the problem of the faithful who have already died by the time the kingdom of God arrives.

Fourth, if the Old Testament is somehow a preparation for the New Testament, as most Christians accept, why is the religion of the one so different from that of the other? The fact that the reading of the Old Testament in churches seems to be a dying practice only indicates that people perceive a problem with it. It is easy to say that the forms of the Old Testament religion are shadows of the New Testament religion, and that they are fulfilled by it. That, as a proposition on its own, could be said to argue for the discarding of the Old Testament once and for all. Yet there is something in the New Testament itself, as well as in the ancient traditions of the church, which prevents us from doing this. The Old Testament goes on being accepted as valid Christian Scripture and, as such, it demands interpretation.

Biblical theology examines the development of the biblical story from the Old Testament to the New, and seeks to uncover the interrelationships between the two parts. Prophecy, law, narrative, wisdom saying or apocalyptic vision are all related to the coming of Jesus Christ in some discernible way. Biblical theology is a methodical approach to showing these relationships so that the Old Testament can be understood as Christian Scripture.

■ *Biblical theology*
shows the relationship of all parts of the Old Testament to the person and work of Jesus Christ and, therefore, to the Christian.

THE BIRD'S-EYE VIEW

When you are close to the ground it is often very hard to see exactly where you are in relation to other places. A few trees, a dip in the ground, a couple of buildings or some other natural or man-made feature can prevent us from getting our bearings. That is why people build observation platforms on high buildings or on mountains, and why aerial photography became so important in war or in the peace-time making of maps. The bird's-eye view enables us to see things and places in relation to other things and places. A map is a representation of a bird's-eye view of a particular part of the earth's surface. It reduces an area that is too big for us to see at a glance to a model that is small enough for us to see all at once.

Some maps don't show spatial relationships because these are unimportant. Rather they show how different parts function in relation to other parts, or what their relative sizes are. Diagrams of electrical circuits or of a chain of command in the management of a business are maps of a kind, as are charts and graphs showing such things as a nation's imports and exports. Then there are descriptive word maps that do not rely on graphics and diagrams, but rather give verbal accounts. Biblical theology is a verbal map of the overall message of the Bible. In this book we shall also use some diagram maps to help us understand the way in which all parts of the Bible fit together into a coherent whole. Biblical theology assumes some kind of unity to the Bible, and that there is, indeed, one overall message rather than a number of unrelated themes.

■ *Biblical theology*
enables us to map out the unity of the Bible by looking at its message as a whole.

A QUESTION OF INTERPRETATION

The interpretation of the Bible is not always a simple matter. Some will not be convinced of this if their attitude is "I'm just a simple Bible-believer." However, we must recognize that written words are only signs or symbols that have meaning assigned to them by common usage. They represent sounds that we produce from our mouths to convey meaning to people. A word may have a number of different meanings in different situations or contexts. Similarly, a group of words may have different meanings depending on whether they are meant to be taken literally, metaphorically or symbolically.

The words in the Bible are no different in that they always need interpreting within their own context. Interpretation as a study in itself is referred to as *hermeneutics*, which is a word derived from the Greek word meaning "to interpret." Most commentaries on the Bible text concentrate on the meaning that the original writer or speaker intended. But we must go beyond this to the question of what the text means for us now. Once we understand what the biblical author was actually saying we look for its present meaning for us. This is what interpretation is about.

Biblical theology is essential for hermeneutics. The sound interpretation of the Bible presupposes some kind of biblical-theological understanding. Biblical theology makes the difference between the Bible as the Word of God to us now and as merely an interesting historical record. The ancient Babylonian king Hammurabi is famous for his code of laws. These laws need interpreting just as any words do if we are to understand their meaning. We may even ask how these laws have influenced modern concepts of law, if at all, and therefore have affected us. But when we look at God's laws given to Israel through Moses, we see them as part of the total revelation of God, which climaxed in the coming of Jesus Christ. As Christians we are therefore more deeply concerned to ask in what ways the laws of Moses have meaning for us now. Biblical theology provides us with the means of moving toward an answer for this question.

■ *Biblical theology*

provides the basis for the interpretation of any part of the Bible as God's word to us.

STUDY GUIDE TO CHAPTER 1

1. Write down some of the problems you have in reading and understanding the Bible.

2. Keep a record of difficult passages you meet in your Bible reading.

3. What lessons do you think can be drawn from the stories of Moses in the rushes (Ex 2), and David and Goliath (1 Sam 17)? Test yourself on other well-known stories.

4. Why is a "bird's-eye view" important for understanding any subject?

BIBLICAL
THEOLOGY—
HOW?

Can we really know God? If we can, what part must the Bible play in enabling us to know him? In this section we ask how it is possible to know God, and what are the sources of our knowledge.

As suggested in the introduction, some readers may find it preferable to move immediately to consider the content of biblical theology in part three (chapters 8-25) before reading this section. However, part two should not be considered an optional extra, and it is best read before part three.

2

GOD MAKES
HIMSELF KNOWN

How can we really know God? The answer starts with the fact that God knows us, and allows himself to be known by us. He has spoken to us and told us what he wants us to know of him. Not only can we know about him, but we can also know him when he draws us to himself and makes us his children through Jesus Christ. Theology is the word we use to refer to what we know about God. It can be used in a number of distinct though related ways. It does not have to be complicated. We can use the word to refer to every Christian's knowledge of God (Theos = God, logos = word, knowledge). Biblical theology is a way of understanding the Bible as a whole, so that we can see the plan of salvation as it unfolds step by step. It is concerned with God's message to us in the form that it actually takes in Scripture.

EVERY CHRISTIAN IS A THEOLOGIAN

The Bible speaks of us as knowing God and as being known by God. Both of these important facts are part of the theology that each of us builds up during the whole of our lives as Christians. Have you ever heard a person say (particularly in the middle of a discussion about the Bible), "I'm no theologian, but . . . "? My answer to that is, "Yes you are! All Christians are theologians, but some are more able theologians than others." Every Christian by definition knows God, thinks about God and makes statements about God. So, you are a theologian. Part of being a Christian is that we *do* theology. That is, we put together different aspects of what we understand about God, and we build it into some kind of coherent understanding of our existence as God's redeemed people living in the world.

There are a number of different ways that we can *do* theology, and in this book I want to examine one of these ways with a view to helping ordinary Christians to become more able theologians and, as a result, to become more faithful servants of Christ and his kingdom. So that we might better understand what biblical theology is, I will compare it to some other ways of doing theology.

SYSTEMATIC THEOLOGY

This sounds like something that is taught in theological colleges and schools of divinity. And so it is. But it is also of great interest to Christians who simply want to understand Christianity better. Systematic theology is so named because it involves the systematic organization of truths or doctrines under certain headings or topics. It is sometimes called *dogmatics*, signifying that it is the orderly arrangement of the teachings of a particular understanding of Christianity. It is concerned to state what Christians believe as a total system of doctrine covering all aspects of our religion. What do we believe about God, the death of Christ, the Lord's supper or the ministries of the church? Systematic theology is an attempt to answer the question, "What is the Christian faith?"

Systematic theology lies behind the confessions of faith that some denominations have drawn up at certain critical times in their histories. The Anglican churches have the Thirty-nine Articles of Religion (1562), and the Presbyterian churches have the Westminster Confession (1644). If you want to find the official doctrines of the Roman Catholic Church you must go to the Canons of the Council of Trent (1545-1563) and the decrees of the Second Vatican Council (1963-1965).

■ *Systematic theology asks:*
What should Christians believe now about any aspect of Christianity?
Its results: Christian doctrine.

HISTORICAL THEOLOGY

This is a historical study of the way theology has been done in the Christian church over the centuries. It looks at the emergence of key doctrines from particular points of time in the history of Christianity. It is interested in the struggles that have taken place in the attempt to establish true theology, and the inroads that have been made at various times by false teachings. Great Christian thinkers and movements, creeds and councils, breakaway movements and controversies are all part of the history of Christian thought and doctrine which is the concern of historical theology. It is closely related to the history of the church and also to systematic theology.

■ *Historical theology asks:*
What have Christians believed about their faith at any given time?
Its results: A record of the development of Christian doctrine.

PASTORAL THEOLOGY

As a distinct approach to theology, pastoral theology is a relative newcomer. Pastoral theology occupies itself with the way the Word of God touches people where they are and in whatever condition they are. It is concerned with the practical application of the gospel to Christians in every aspect of their life. At the heart of pastoral theology is a theology of ministry, its forms, gifts, function and authority. It must establish a biblical understanding of man in general and of Christian existence in particular. Its practical goals include healing, nurture and growth. Christians who grieve over the death of a relative, who suffer anxiety or depression, who see no reason to meet regularly with other Christians, who believe that forgiveness of sins allows us to go on sinning freely, who cry out for a more intimate fellowship than that which a formal church service can provide or who want to know how they should pray or make decisions, are all the concern of pastoral theology. It looks for the principles which are to be drawn from our knowledge of God and which may be applied validly to each of these candidates for pastoral care.

■ *Pastoral theology asks:*
How should Christians minister to one another so that they grow to maturity in Christian living?
Its results: Care and growth in the local church.

BIBLICAL THEOLOGY

Although we regard the Bible as our source book for theology, it is obvious that it does not present theology in a systematic way. If anything it is more like a historical theology which traces the history of theological thought in the people of God from the very beginning. Closer examination shows that this is only partly true.

There are some significant differences between the history in the Bible and the history of Christian thought. The Bible claims to be the very truth from God himself. Thus it contains a history of God's revelation to mankind rather than the history of people's thinking about God. It consists of a wide range of documents that claim to follow the process by which God both reveals himself to man and acts to save a people for himself. Biblical theology is concerned with God's saving acts and his word as these occur within the history of the people of God. It follows the progress of revelation from the first word of God to man through to the unveiling of the full glory of Christ. It examines the several stages of biblical history and their relationship to one another. It thus provides the basis for understanding how texts in one part of the Bible relate to all other texts. A sound interpretation of the Bible is based upon the findings of biblical theology.

■ *Biblical theology asks:*
By what process has God revealed himself to mankind?
Its results: The relating of the whole Bible to our Christian life now.

No one engages in any of these different approaches to theology without regard to some of the other approaches. Systematic theology will constantly make use of biblical and historical theology. Pastoral theology will probably draw fairly heavily upon biblical and systematic theology. Each kind of theology provides a distinct perspective on the one truth revealed by God.

EXEGETICAL THEOLOGY

Biblical theology is sometimes considered to be part of a wider discipline called *exegetical theology.* Exegesis is the process of getting out of a text what it actually says in its original setting. In order to exegete any text we must understand something of the way words were used in the time it was first spoken or written. We must also know something of the context into which they were spoken: the historical events and the revealed truths that surround the text in question.

Exegesis itself can be seen to involve a number of distinct operations, some of which the lay theologian will have to leave to the technically trained specialist. We can state these operations in the form of questions.

1. What is the text?

A comparison of two or three English versions of the same biblical reference will remind us that we are dealing with translations of ancient texts written in foreign languages. There is no one way of translating a text from one language into another. Translation is as much an art as a science. But in order to be able to translate we have to have a reliable text in the original language. Many people are unaware that the texts from which our English versions are translated are sometimes of rather obscure parentage. Textual criticism is a necessary task whereby the oldest known texts of the biblical documents are compared along with various ancient translations into other languages (called *versions*), and the history of these texts inquired into in an attempt to uncover the most reliable text of the Old and New Testaments.

■ *Textual criticism asks:*

What is the text?

Its results: Provision of the most reliable text possible from which our English translations can be made.

---

2. What is the source of the text?

Unfortunately, this question has become one of the major preoccupations of many biblical scholars who have approached the Bible with a greater or lesser degree of skepticism about its divine origins. Notwithstanding the negative and unacceptable aspects of such scholarship, many of the questions being asked are valid and relevant. This area of study is concerned with such questions as who wrote the document, when and where? It is also concerned with whether the biblical form is the original form or whether it involved the use of earlier traditions either oral or written. If earlier traditions have been drawn on, then in what way has the biblical author reworked them in the process of producing the final form? All these questions can be grouped together into that aspect of exegetical theology called *biblical introduction*. You will find references to these matters under the following technical terms:

   a. Literary and source criticism: Who wrote the document, when and where, under what circumstances and with what purpose?

   b. Tradition history: By what processes have various written and oral traditions come to be formed into the biblical document?

    c. Form criticism: How do the distinct forms of literary expression reveal something of the origins, history and meaning of the text?

    d. Redaction criticism: How has the author shown his own creativeness in reshaping older traditions to serve his particular theological purpose?

■ *Biblical introduction asks:*

What kind of document is this, where did it come from and how, who wrote it and with what purpose?

Its results: Provision of background information to the meaning of the text.

---

3. What is the meaning of the text?

Here we are primarily concerned with what the text meant *then*; what it meant for the original writer or speaker. The words must be understood in their own context. We should not invest the words with modern meanings but rather should try to feel our way back into the language and thought forms of the ancient writer. The context of the words includes not only the historical events surrounding them, but also all aspects of their being conditioned by the specific event, the language, the culture and the people themselves.

    Because we are concerned with the meaning of words (grammar) in their own historical context, we refer to this task as *grammatico-historical exegesis.*

■ *Biblical exegesis asks:*

What was the text intended to convey to those for whom it was originally written? Its results: Understanding of the intended meaning of the text.

---

4. How did the text come to be recognized as uniquely revelational and authoritative?

Our interest in the biblical text is quite different from the interest we might have in any other collection of ancient religious books. Of course, there are those who put the Bible on the same level as religious literature in general. But Christians cannot do that. We recognize the Bible as a unity not only on the grounds of the common themes throughout, but because it speaks to us as the word of God to man. When we consider the canon, that is, the extent of Holy Scripture, we are faced with the question of how and why biblical documents are to be distinguished from all other documents. Thus the question of their unique authority emerges. If they are inspired by God so as to convey his self-revelation in exactly the form he intends, then they have an authority which no other documents have. The existence of the canon means that it is the text as we have it in the Bible, rather than some possible prior text that we deal with as Scripture. This study of the extent of Scripture is sometimes called *biblical canonics*.

■ *Biblical canonics asks:*
What are the extent of the text and the nature of its authority?
Its results: Recognition of the whole Bible as the authoritative Word of God.

Exegetical theology, then, involves a number of different approaches to the biblical text in order to understand it as a part of a living process within history that resulted in the finished Bible. Its goal is the correct exegesis of the entire Bible so that each part of the whole is understood as it was originally intended to be. The last stage of exegetical theology is biblical theology, which examines the process or progression of God's revelation to mankind. Is biblical theology, then, purely descriptive? The fact that the last hundred years have seen the production of many differing, even opposing, biblical theological studies of both Old and New Testaments must make us wonder. Who or what establishes the ground rules of method for biblical theology?

These are matters we must consider in the next chapter.

STUDY GUIDE TO CHAPTER 2

1. What are some of the different ways of doing theology and their results?

2. How would you answer someone who says, "I'm just a simple Bible-believing Christian. I have no use for theology"?

3. Assign each of the following subjects to one of the branches of theology dealt with in this section, and give reasons for your choice:

a. Christian baptism

b. Latin versions of the Old Testament

c. The development of faith in children

d. The covenant with Abraham

e. Difficulties in the Hebrew text of Job

f. The sovereignty of God in salvation

g. Paul's doctrine of the body of Christ

h. Life after death in the Old Testament

i. Helping the dying to face death

j. Isaiah's theology of salvation

FURTHER READING

1. *IBD* articles on "Texts and Versions," "Biblical Criticism."
2. *ZPEB* articles on "Biblical Criticism," "Biblical Theology."
3. *BT*, chap. 1.
4. G. W. Bromiley, *Historical Theology: An Introduction* (Edinburgh: T & T Clark, 1978), pp. xxi-xxix.

BUT HOW CAN WE KNOW?

There are three main views of how we know what is real and true. The first view is that we are completely independent of God. It claims that we are in total control of the process of gaining all knowledge. God does not exist or, if he does, he is irrelevant. There can, therefore, be no knowledge of God but only knowledge of what people believe about God. We gain knowledge only through our senses and reason, and must decide for ourselves what is true.

The second view is that we are only partly independent of God. There is an area of truth that is beyond our human abilities to find out. Thus it can be known only by revelation. Knowledge that comes by revelation is simply added to the knowledge we gain by ourselves in order to complete the picture.

The third and biblical view is that God created everything and therefore knows everything. God also created humankind in his own image so that we know God from what is created. All facts, including those about ourselves, are facts about God, since he is the creator of all facts and gives them their meaning. Confusion enters because of sin. As sinners, we refuse to accept that the universe is God's and that we are God's creatures. We refuse God's interpretation of reality and substitute our own false interpretation. God justly gives mankind up to this folly and, as a consequence, we are no longer able to perceive the truth about God, which is everywhere around us and within us. But in his goodness, and in accordance with his plan of salvation, God provides a special revelation through his Word. He also sends his Holy Spirit to subdue the rebellious wills of his people so that they can perceive the truth of this revelation. By this means alone are we able to know truly.

KNOWLEDGE IS INDEPENDENT OF GOD (SECULAR HUMANISM)

Most people assume that in order to understand the world, we investigate it with our senses. We then use our reason to put together bits of information about things and to construct some sort of meaningful whole. The experiences that go toward the building up of this picture may be deliberately planned, as when a scientist designs an experiment and observes the results. Or, for most of us, they are the everyday experiences of life. We borrow from other people's experiences and we share our own. So we build up a picture of the world and of ourselves in which certain regularities exist that make life a continuous and meaningful thing. Today continues on from yesterday. And tomorrow I expect to be essentially the same person that I am today. I assume that the sun will rise and set, and that the "laws" of nature that I have grown used to will still operate.

This approach to knowledge of the world clearly works up to a point. Leaving aside the moral issue of how mankind has abused the possession of knowledge, there is no doubt that as a race we have learned a great deal about the world and the universe beyond. As a result, there have been great leaps forward in the care of the human body, in food production and in the technology involved in things like transportation and communications. I say this works up to a point because it cannot really handle matters that may be beyond the scope of our senses, such as life after death or the existence of God.

The assumption in this approach is that we as human beings are in control of the whole process of gaining knowledge. Of course, we haven't yet discovered everything there is to know. Insofar as we assume that reality is orderly, we recognize that every fact relates somehow to every other fact. Thus, all new facts discovered will in some way affect the understanding of old facts. Nevertheless, we assume that, given enough time and given access to all parts of the universe, we would be capable of knowing all there is to be known.

We may broadly describe this position as *atheistic humanism*. It is *atheistic* because it either asserts or assumes that there is no God who in any way can relate to our real world. God is simply ruled out as impossible or as irrelevant. There are those who claim belief in God but who succeed in keeping him completely out of their reckoning and their living. They are practical atheists because they think and act as if God were not there.

This position is *humanistic* in that it sees man to be at the center of the process and in control of his situation. This does not mean that we have always known where we are heading, nor does it mean that we have always been able to avoid disasters. It means that man is the only gainer of real knowledge, and that he alone can decide what is true and what is not true. In popular thinking, man is able to decide what is reasonable and what is not. But the slightest understanding of the history of civilization shows us that what was once thought to be unreasonable and therefore impossible frequently becomes the commonplace of human knowledge. What governs the "reasonable" in humanistic thinking is not the idea that we know it all now, but the assumption that man's knowledge-gaining is completely independent of any outside or supernatural help. The only world that there is to be known is the natural world which is open to our senses.

All forms of humanism make the enormous assumption that the human mind alone is the final judge of what is or is not true. When people present scientific "proofs" that something is true, it is rarely acknowledged that certain unprovable assumptions have to be made. It is assumed that the human senses and reason actually make contact with what is there, and that they are capable of assessing the meaning of what is there. In other words, man's experiences become the final point of reference for what is true. To the extent that man is free and in control of knowledge-gaining, any god that he might conceive of is not in control and is bound by the same laws as man and nature. The atheist eliminates the idea of God as irrelevant, and thus puts man in control.

Atheistic humanism

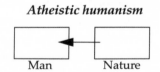

Man   Nature

There is no God, no revelation, no fall.
Man is in control and gains knowledge from nature.

KNOWLEDGE IS PARTLY INDEPENDENT OF GOD (THEISTIC HUMANISM)

Suppose we were to be visited by aliens from another world who are vastly superior to man in intellect and knowledge. We would want to learn as much as possible from them. They may be able to show us new and astounding things that could alter our understanding of all the facts that we have thus far learned. But, so it would be assumed, they could not alter the facts that we had already truly perceived. We would welcome these revelations of the extraterrestrial visitors as information from experts with greater knowledge than our own. We would, however, still see these experts as existing in our universe and as subject to its laws as we are.

There are some people who think of God as, to varying degrees, an extraterrestrial with expert knowledge to share with us. We may describe these broadly as *theistic humanists*. They are *theistic* in that they believe that a god or gods exist in a realm that is beyond our ability to know. If they conceive of this God in largely Christian terms, then they will probably believe that he had something to do with the creation of the world and that he has left the stamp of his character on it.

This position is *humanistic* in that it also sees man as able to control his knowledge-gaining. To the degree that he is really in control, he is independent of God. He investigates the universe and discovers facts, which he then organizes into a coherent body of knowledge. He does this without outside help, and he does it well!

But, so the argument goes, there is a realm of truth that we are not able to observe directly. If we are to know anything about this *spiritual* or *supernatural* realm, we must receive special or supernatural revelation. The theistic humanist sees this knowledge as filling the gaps in our naturally gained knowledge. As such, it will affect the way we see our natural knowledge because all facts are related. But it will not affect the essential truth of what we have already discovered; it has only added to what we already know. God, then, is the specialist who can add significantly to our knowledge. Since we already understand something of the nature of reality, the theistic humanist is likely to see God as being subject to the same laws of the universe as we are. Thus we are able to draw up rules by which we decide what is reasonable. It is inconceivable that God could say something to us that is contradictory to reason. Human reason will therefore sit in judgment on the Bible to determine what aspects of it can be accepted as revelation from God.

Theistic humanism

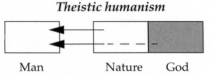

| Man | Nature | God |

God exists but is part of a general reality. The fall is insignificant.
Man is still in control and gains knowledge from nature, including some
knowledge of God. Added revelation from God is always filtered
through natural knowledge.

)

Knowledge Is Dependent on God (Christian Theism)

Let us now make some other assumptions that are opposed to those of the humanist. Suppose that the Bible is correct in what it says, and that the God of the Bible is real. The Bible presents God as quite distinct from everything in creation. He is not merely a part of a general reality but is the creator, sustainer and controller of everything that exists in reality. Furthermore, God as creator has stamped his character on the whole of creation. This he has done in a unique way in the creation of mankind in his own image.

Man was created to know God. Every fact in the universe speaks of its creator and is open for us to discern. In addition, the image of God in us means that we know ourselves only as we know God, and know God only as we know ourselves. God's eternal power and divine character can be discerned from nature, which includes humankind. Man in the image of God communicates by word, and this reflects the fact that God is one who communicates by word. The first word of God to man indicated the relationship that God established between himself and man and between man and the rest of creation (Gen 1:28-30). God spoke to Adam and told him what he needed to know about himself and his relationship to God. Thus, every word from God to man interprets the meaning of reality.

Christian theism
1. Man before the fall

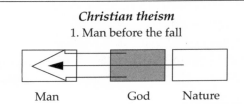

Man   God   Nature

Man receives revelation through nature and supernatural revelation through God's word. All natural revelation is interpreted through word revelation.

So far it may appear that we have presented a picture very like that of theistic humanism. There are some similarities, but there are two major differences. The first is that Christian theism recognizes that, even before sin entered the world, man was dependent upon the word of God for a correct interpretation of the world. God's act of creation was absolutely free. That is, God was not compelled to create by some force or necessity that he could not control. It was also a sovereign act in that the creation fulfills all God's freely determined purpose. What he wanted to happen did happen, and the history of the creation, including our human history, is determined by his sovereign will. On this basis God, and God alone, can interpret every fact in reality.

The second difference is that theistic humanism assumes that man's knowledge-gaining is not hindered by the fact of sin. To be sure, sin is seen as a cause of some confusion, but it does not alter man's ability to perceive the truth in nature. Sin does not in any real way remove man's freedom of will. Thus, free will is thought of as the ability to determine something that is not determined by God. God does not work everything in conformity with the purpose of his will, as Paul says he does in Ephesians 1:11, but rather he must wait upon man's decisions.

Against this view, Christian theism treats seriously the matter of sin. According to the Bible, sin brings death (Gen 2:17; Rom 6:23). This current state of death means not only that every living thing eventually departs from this life, but also that relationships with God are severed. In fact all relationships in the whole of creation are affected (Gen 3:15-24; Rom 8:20-22; Eph 2:1-3). The Bible also indicates that man suppresses the knowledge of God that is to be had through nature. He knows the truth but suppresses it in his wickedness. It is this knowledge of God that makes all people without excuse before God, whether they have heard the gospel or not. But in his consciousness, man can no longer admit that he knows God exists and that every fact in the universe points to him. Thus the sinner deliberately reinterprets every fact and gives it a meaning that fits in with his denial of God. Within him is the sense of God that belongs to the image of God. But in his thinking he has exchanged this truth for a man-centered understanding of the universe. The mind has become futile and darkened (Rom 1:18-25).

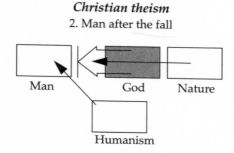

Christian theism
2. Man after the fall

Man   God   Nature

Humanism

Man suppresses the knowledge of God and substitutes atheistic humanism.

Christian theism thus understands atheistic and theistic humanism in biblical terms. All forms of humanism are expressions of the sinful nature of mankind's refusal to acknowledge the truth of God. They are futile substitutes for the truth.

If the sinfulness of man makes him unable consciously to recognize the truth, what hope is there? The Bible tells us that the deadness of man's heart and his hatred of God are overcome by the goodness of God. He gives a new and special revelation of himself, and he subdues our rebellious wills by his Spirit so that we understand and receive his revelation. The Holy Spirit convinces us that God's Word is the truth. Thus, the converted or believing sinner is being restored in his or her mind to receive the truth of God. Our restoration is not complete until we are transformed through our resurrection on the last day. During this life there is tension between the new life within us and the old life of rebellion against God. We never succeed in being totally consistent in our thinking and doing with what God reveals in his Word. But we are enabled to know things truly for what they are, facts interpreted by God.

How Can We Know the Truth?

This discussion is important for understanding how we do theology. We need some principles or rules as we come to the Bible to do biblical theology. I have considered three different approaches.

1. Atheistic humanism

This approach assumes that there is no God. The Bible is therefore not revelation from God but rather a record of certain religious ideas. The study and interpretation of the Bible is governed by these assumptions.

2. Theistic humanism

This assumes there is a God but, in common with atheistic humanism, asserts that man is in control of gaining knowledge. He gains true knowledge from nature through his senses, and reasons on this basis what is the correct approach to the study of the Bible.

3. Christian theism

This position recognizes the dependence of man upon God for true knowledge. The Word of God must instruct us in the various details of what God has said and done to rescue us from the consequences of our rebellion. It must also instruct us in the method by which we read and understand the Bible. There is no self-evident logic discernible outside the Bible; no naturally discerned rule as to what is possible or impossible. God as creator must interpret every event and every fact in his universe.

Each of these positions has chosen its own starting point, which is assumed to be true. If the starting point is false then everything that is seen to follow from it will also be false. These basic assumptions are called *presuppositions*.

PRESUPPOSITIONS

Presuppositions, then, are the assumptions we make in order to be able to hold some fact to be true. We cannot go on indefinitely saying, "I know this is true because . . ." In the end we must come to that which we accept as the final authority. By definition a final authority cannot be proven as an authority on the basis of some higher authority. The highest authority must be self-attesting. Only God is such an authority.

The presuppositions we must make in doing biblical theology are those of Christian theism. The alternative to this is to accept the presuppositions of some form of humanism. Either we work on the basis of a sovereign, self-proving God who speaks to us by a word that we accept as true simply because it is his word, or we work on the basis that man is the final judge of all truth. The Christian position, to be consistent, accepts that the Bible is God's Word, and that it says what God wants it to say in exactly the way he wants to say it.

Thus, when the biblical theologian sets out to describe the theology that is in the Bible, he must understand the presuppositions that he accepts as the basis of his method. Many of the biblical theologies that have been written over the past one hundred years have been shaped by the presuppositions of humanism. In such cases the Bible is not allowed to speak for itself, but is subjected to a continuous assessment on the basis of human reason, which is seen as quite independent of God.

The presupposition of an independent and self-sufficient human reason has resulted in the writing of biblical theologies that tend to be descriptions of the supposed development of religious ideas among the biblical people. Such descriptions are complicated by the refusal to accept the Bible's own testimony of the history of Israelite faith. When evolutionary philosophy was popular it was applied to the biblical documents to test their historical accuracy. The assumption was that religious ideas undergo a natural development from simpler to more complex forms. The possibility was excluded that the God of the Bible actually exists and reveals himself in the way the Bible depicts. Man is in control of the whole process of knowledge-gaining and God is only a religious idea that many people hold in varying forms.

Not all theologians who employ humanistic presuppositions are such extreme skeptics when it comes to assessing the Bible. What we have called humanism is, according to the Bible, the expression of our sinful rejection of God. As Christians we are still sinners and the tendency to humanistic thinking is always with us. Even if we start with truly Christian presuppositions it is difficult to remain totally consistent with them in our thinking about the Bible. Biblical theology should be done with a constant self-conscious effort to be consistent with biblical presuppositions.

■ *The presuppositions of biblical theology*

1. *God made every fact in the universe, and he alone can interpret all things and events.*
2. *Because we are created in the image of God we know that we are dependent on God for the truth.*
3. *As sinners we suppress this knowledge and reinterpret the universe on the assumption that we, not God, give things their meaning.*
4. *Special revelation through God's redemptive word, reaching its high point in Jesus Christ, is needed to deal with our suppression of the truth and hostility to God.*
5. *A special work of the Holy Spirit brings repentance and faith so that sinners acknowledge the truth which is in Scripture.*

STUDY GUIDE TO CHAPTER 3

1. What are the main assumptions made by atheistic humanism?

2. How does theistic humanism differ from atheistic humanism?

3. From the point of view of Christian theism, what are the defects of both atheistic and theistic humanism?

4. Read Romans 1:18-32 and summarize in your own words what Paul says about the effects of sin on our knowledge of God.

5. What are the presuppositions of Christian theism?

FURTHER READING

1. D. M. Lloyd-Jones, *Romans: The Gospel of God* (Edinburgh: Banner of Truth, 1985), pp. 366-394.
2. Colin Brown, *Philosophy and the Christian Faith* (Downers Grove, Ill.: InterVarsity Press, 1968), chap. 4.
3. Colin Chapman, *The Case for Christianity* (Tring, U.K.: Lion Publishing, 1981), esp. sections 5 and 6.

4

CHRIST HAS MADE
HIM KNOWN

Theology is not just knowing about God, but knowing him. To know him we need to be restored to friendship with him. In other words, we do biblical theology as Christians, not as neutral observers. Through the preaching of the gospel we have been brought to faith in Jesus Christ. Christ conquers our rebellious hearts and minds so that we worship him as Lord. Our only knowledge of Christ comes through Scriptures, and they give a united testimony to him. Christ is proclaimed as the one who reveals God to us; he is the Word of God. The Bible is the book about Christ that is inspired by the Holy Spirit. God has ensured that the Bible gives an infallible testimony to Christ. Biblical theology thus centers on Jesus Christ as the revealer and savior. To understand the Bible, we begin at the point where we first came to know God. We begin with Jesus Christ, and we see every part of the Bible in relationship to him and his saving work. This is as true of the Old Testament as it is of the New.

THE THEOLOGIAN IS A BELIEVER

The Christian is a believer in Jesus Christ. That obvious fact should not escape us! The word of the gospel takes hold of us and, by the Holy Spirit's power, turns us from darkness to light, that is, turns us to Christ. The gospel is the message of the kingdom of God as it comes through the person and work of Jesus of Nazareth. The gospel centers on the birth, life, death, resurrection and ascension of Jesus as God's way of saving us from death and of making us members of his eternal kingdom.

As we begin the Christian life by placing our whole trust in the Christ of the gospel event, so in the same way we continue in the Christian life. The gospel not only brings us to the new birth and faith as Christians; it is God's means of saving us totally. The gospel is the power of God for salvation (Rom 1:16), and this means the whole of salvation for the whole person. Thus the gospel converts us, the gospel sustains us in the Christian life and brings us to maturity and the gospel brings us to perfection through our resurrection from the dead.

An important part of salvation is having our rebellious minds and wills changed so that they become compliant to the Word of God. The Christian can no longer think like an atheistic humanist. The truth-suppressing mind is overcome by the Holy Spirit, who brings it to accept and believe the gospel. This renewing of the mind is a continuous process (Rom 12:2), and it means that the Christian develops the mindset of Christian theism. Since our perfection is not reached in this life, we all retain some measure of humanistic thinking. We must continually strive to overcome this evil through the power of the gospel.

As biblical theologians, we not only believe, but we also understand and accept the word of God as self-attesting. We will do more than simply describe what is in the Bible. We will sit under the authority of God's Word and seek to describe what we know to be the content of one unified and self-consistent Word of God.

Unfortunately, the biblical theologian may compromise the principle of the self-attesting Word of God, and apply unbiblical criteria for assessing the nature of the Bible and its message. He will then rearrange its parts, reconstruct its history, remove the texts which do not fit his particular philosophy and reinterpret the whole in the light of his own presuppositions which are the product of God-denying thought. Many biblical theologies have been written in which the biblical presuppositions have been rejected in favor of humanistic ones.

TRUTH IS RESTORED IN CHRIST

Jesus not only saves us from the effects of our sinful ignorance; he also informs our minds of the nature of the truth. We cannot separate the saving and revealing work of Christ. We are saved that we might truly know God and live in fellowship with him. The truth is restored for us in Christ. In everything Christ was and did during his earthly ministry, he was revealing to us the truth about God, ourselves and the whole created order. Thus, part of our salvation is to be saved in our minds. When the Holy Spirit of God applies the gospel to the sinner so that faith ensues, there is a new birth, which includes the renewal of the mind. From that point onward every fact in the universe is seen as affirming the reality of God. The Christian mind is being restored to its correct function of interpreting all things by God's Word.

This mind-restoring work of Christ in his gospel derives from his eternal role as the agent and purpose of creation. Paul says that all things were created in Christ, through Christ and for Christ (Col 1:16). This signifies that the meaning of the universe is found in the gospel. God created all things with a view to their redemption in Christ. The gospel is God's forethought, his blueprint to creation, not a mere afterthought because of sin.

Now, part of being saved is learning to do theology correctly. I'm not suggesting that this take priority over all other aspects. I'm not saying that the intellectual side of salvation takes precedence. But it *is* important. I am saying that the way our minds are saved and renewed is by the Holy Spirit conforming our thinking about all things to the truth in Jesus. This is part of what it means to say, "Jesus is Lord." If we will obey him in the moral actions of our lives so that we actively combat God-denying, sinful actions, so shall we obey him in our thinking. We must combat thinking that does not conform to the truth revealed in Jesus.

Christian theism
3. Man redeemed in Christ

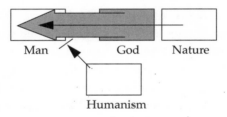

Man   God   Nature

Humanism

Christ reveals and interprets all truth about God and everything created.
The Christian resists the mindset of humanism.

CHRIST INTERPRETS THE WHOLE BIBLE

The only way we know who Christ is and what his gospel means is through the Bible. Jesus withdrew his bodily presence from the world. In its place he left the Holy Spirit and promised that this Spirit would lead the disciples into all truth (Jn 16:13). But Jesus himself was that truth (Jn 14:6), and so he promised that the Spirit would testify of him and glorify him. This ministry of the Spirit in which he points to Christ led to the preaching of the gospel by the apostles, and to the making of a reliable record of their witness in the New Testament. This means that what the Bible says is what God wants it to say. The Bible is infallible in the sense that it is the Word of the God of truth and it will not lead us astray.

Every word of the New Testament comes from the Holy Spirit's testimony to Jesus. The New Testament records the central facts of the gospel and explores the implications of the gospel for the lives of God's people. It shows us that the gospel is God's one way of bringing sinners to perfection. All the problems and imperfections that we experience are failures to be conformed to the gospel. The only remedy that the New Testament prescribes for our problems is to bring our lives to conform to the gospel.

Likewise, the one problem we have in the interpretation of the Bible is the failure to interpret the texts by the definitive event of the gospel. This has its outworking in both directions. What went before Christ in the Old Testament, as well as what comes after him, finds its meaning in him. So the Old Testament must be understood in its relationship to the gospel event. What that relationship is can only be determined from the witness of the New Testament itself.

Jesus, then, is God's Word to us:

In the beginning was the Word, and the Word was with God, and the Word was God. He was with God in the beginning. Through him all things were made; without him nothing was made that has been made. . . .

The Word became flesh and made his dwelling among us. We have seen his glory, the glory of the One and Only, who came from the Father, full of grace and truth. . . . No one has ever seen God, but God the One and Only, who is at the Father's side, has made him known. (Jn 1:1-3, 14, 18)

He is God's Word for the "last days" who brings the word of the Old Testament prophets to completion (Heb 1:1-2). He is the end of God's saving acts in the history of Israel (Rom 1:1-4), and thus fulfills all prophecy (Acts 13:32-33). The real meaning of prophecy always lies in the person and work of Jesus Christ (1 Pet 1:10-12).

This apostolic witness only restated what Christ himself said when he claimed to be the content of the Old Testament (Lk 24:27, 44; Jn 5:39). On this basis, he opened the minds of the disciples to understand the Old Testament (Lk 24:45).

The relationship of the Old Testament to Christ
Some New Testament assessments

Old Testament	Christ
Prophetic word	⟶ completed (Heb 1:1-2)
All prophecy	⟶ fulfilled (Acts 13:32-33)
David's line	⟶ ended (Rom 1:3)
Promise to David	⟶ fulfilled (Acts 2:30-31)
Old Testament tells of salvation	⟶ in Christ (2 Tim 3:15)
Whole Old Testament	⟶ concerns Christ (Lk 24:27)

STUDY GUIDE TO CHAPTER 4

1. Why does a biblical theologian need to be a believer?

2. How can you account for some of the differences in the way biblical theologians approach their task?

3. What does Christian theism teach about how the sinner can come to know the truth?

4. Look up the passages referred to in the last section of this chapter. What kind of relationship between Old and New Testaments do they indicate?

FURTHER READING

1. John Calvin, *Institutes*, book 1, chaps. 1-7.
2. John Wenham, *Christ and the Bible* (Downers Grove, Ill.: InterVarsity Press, 1984), esp. introduction.
3. *GK*, esp. chap. 9.

5

AND WE KNOW HIM
THROUGH SCRIPTURE

According to Jesus, the Old Testament is the Word of God, the Scripture which cannot be broken. Jesus also claims that he himself is the subject of the Old Testament. His teachings constantly point to the Old Testament as that which he fulfills. Thus the Old Testament does not stand on its own, because it is incomplete without its conclusion and fulfillment in the person and work of Christ. No part of it can be rightly understood without him. In this sense it is about Christ. God's revelation in Scripture is progressive, moving by stages from the original promises given to Israel, until the fullest meaning of these promises is revealed in Christ. While we come to understand the New Testament in the light of what goes before it in the Old Testament, it is God's fullest revelation and final word in Christ that gives meaning to all things. Thus Christ, and therefore the New Testament, interprets the Old Testament.

THE OLD TESTAMENT IS THE WORD OF GOD

Jesus and the apostles were positive about the supreme authority of the Old Testament. They honored it as God's way of speaking to his people. They saw it as the faithful record of what God had said through his servants the prophets. Thus, Jesus never expressed any doubts about the truth of Old Testament history. In fact the events of Israel's history were seen as part of the one history in which Jesus himself played the decisive role. The New Testament interpretation of the person and work of Jesus of Nazareth makes no sense if there is no substance to the historical claims of the Old Testament.

Moreover, Jesus regarded the Old Testament as the authority for truth from God. Theological disputes were settled on what was written, and error was seen as a result of refusing what is in Scripture. When the Pharisees put him to the test over the question of divorce he referred them to the Scriptures, that is, to the Old Testament:

"Haven't you read," he replied, "that at the beginning the Creator 'made them male and female,' and said, 'For this reason a man will leave his fa-

*ther and mother and be united to his wife, and the two will be one flesh'?"
(Mt 19:4-5)*

In a dispute with the Jews over his claim to be the Son of God, Jesus referred to a passage of Scripture and added, "and the Scripture cannot be broken" (Jn 10:35). The Sadducees received the same treatment over the question of the resurrection:

Are you not in error because you do not know the Scriptures or the power of God? (Mk 12:24)

In the time of his testing by the devil, Jesus attacked every temptation with the authoritative "It is written" followed by a quotation from the Old Testament (Mt 4:1-11; Lk 4:1-13). In the context of this awesome spiritual struggle between the son of God and the prince of darkness, Jesus understood the word of the Old Testament to be his most effective weapon because it carried the authority and power of God himself.

■ *Jesus taught:*
What the Old Testament says is what God says.

THE OLD TESTAMENT IS THE WORD OF GOD ABOUT CHRIST

Central to our understanding of the Old Testament is the fact that Jesus, the apostles and all the New Testament authors saw it as in some way a book about Jesus Christ. A number of key passages point to this, although we are not bound to a few proof-texts. The overwhelming testimony of the New Testament is that Jesus fulfills the Old Testament, which is another way of saying that the Old Testament is about Jesus. To take a few examples:

He said to them, "How foolish you are, and how slow of heart to believe all that the prophets have spoken! Did not the Christ have to suffer these things and then enter his glory?" And beginning with Moses and all the Prophets, he explained to them what was said in all the Scriptures concerning himself. (Lk 24:25-27)

He said to them, "This is what I told you while I was still with you: Ev-

erything must be fulfilled that is written about me in the Law of Moses,
the Prophets and the Psalms." Then he opened their minds so they could
understand the Scriptures. (Lk 24:44-45)

"You diligently study the Scriptures because you think that by them you
possess eternal life. These are the Scriptures that testify about me, yet you
refuse to come to me to have life." (Jn 5:39-40)

■ *Jesus taught:*
The Old Testament is God's Word about Christ.

THE NEW TESTAMENT INTERPRETS THE OLD

Such statements show us that the Old Testament does not stand on its
own. Of course, we can reach an understanding at the historical level of a
long series of connected events. We can even reach a certain theological
understanding of the then unfulfilled promises of God to his people. But
it is impossible from the Old Testament alone to understand the full meaning of God's acts and promises that it records. Yet a number of things seem
to work against the relationship of Christ to the Old Testament, being perceived and acted upon by the Christian. Not only is there a gap of some
three centuries between the Testaments which creates a break in the historical continuity, but also the Hebrew language of the Old Testament gives
way to the Greek of the New.

Over the years Christian scholars have developed specialization in either
Old or New Testament studies. The trend has been toward a study of the Old
Testament in and of itself. This is not a Christian approach to the matter.
Christians in increasing numbers have written books on the Old Testament,
which hardly even mention the fact that the New Testament exists. It has be-
come a common feature of theological and Bible college curricula that the
Old Testament is dealt with in complete isolation from the New Testament.
One result is that the standard of preaching and teaching from the Old Testament often leaves much to be desired. There seems to be a failure in allowing
the New Testament to determine how we relate the Old Testament to Christ.

As Christians, we must return to the principles of Old Testament interpretation dictated by the New Testament. When Jesus says that he gives
the Old Testament its meaning, he is also saying that we need the Old Tes-

tament to understand what he says about himself. Jesus drives us back to the Old Testament to examine it through Christian eyes, teaching that it leads us back to him.

In doing biblical theology as Christians, we do not start at Genesis 1 and work our way forward until we discover where it is all leading. Rather we first come to Christ, and he directs us to study the Old Testament in the light of the gospel. The gospel will interpret the Old Testament by showing us its goal and meaning. The Old Testament will increase our understanding of the gospel by showing us what Christ fulfills.

The following two diagrams illustrate the differences between the approaches.

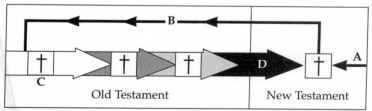

Non-Christian approach to the Old Testament

Old Testament | New Testament

Entry is made at any point (A). Since no New Testament presuppositions are involved, even discernment of the progressive nature of Old Testament theology is unlikely to lead to the New Testament as the goal of the Old.

Christian approach to the Old Testament

Old Testament | New Testament

Entry is made through the gospel (A) which sends us back to the Old Testament (B). With the prior knowledge that it is a book about Christ (C), we follow its progressive revelation until it leads us to its fulfillment in the gospel (D).

THE OLD TESTAMENT IS A PROGRESSIVELY REVEALED WORD

The gospel does not necessarily impress upon us the need to go back to deal with all the events of the Old Testament in chronological order. We may go back to some aspect of prophecy or, say, to the history of David. But in time we will see that the nature of the gospel as the end of a long line of particular events demands that we take seriously the total historical process in the Old Testament.

Once we enter into the study of the Old Testament it becomes clear that it is mounted on a historical framework that is not difficult to discern. Furthermore, there is plenty of evidence that the writers of the Old Testament saw a unity in that history. It tells a single, coherent story that centers upon a particular line of people. Thus, the account of each successive stage of Israel's history builds upon what has gone before.

Within the progression of the unified history of the Old Testament there is the progression of a unified theology. It is a progressive revelation of God and of his purposes for the salvation of his people. It will be our task in the main part of this study to examine the nature of that progressive revelation. The New Testament provides us with many pointers to this unified progression of revelation. Two key events, above all, are seen as the preparation for the coming of Jesus. These are the covenant promises to Abraham, Isaac and Jacob, and the reign of David. Three people, Abraham, David and Jesus, bind the saving purposes and acts of God into a single great work of salvation. The whole history of Israel is thus caught up into the redemptive revelation of God, which climaxes in Jesus Christ.

A few examples of this New Testament perspective on the Old Testament will suffice. The angel's promise to Mary concerning Jesus is:

The Lord God will give him the throne of his father David, and he will reign over the house of Jacob forever. (Lk 1:32-33)

Both Peter (Acts 2:30-31) and Paul (Acts 13:16-33; Gal 3:15-29) state that what is promised, either to Abraham or to David, is given its reality in Christ. The whole of the epistle to the Hebrews is a commentary on the relationship of Christ to the Old Testament, and this is reflected in the opening words:

In the past God spoke to our forefathers through the prophets at many times and in various ways, but in these last days he has spoken to us by his Son, whom he appointed heir of all things, and through whom he made the universe. **(Heb 1:1-2)**

Such statements prepare us for the study of the theology of the Old Testament as progressive, redemptive revelation. It is *revelation* because in it God makes himself known. It is *redemptive* because God reveals himself in the act of redeeming us. It is *progressive* because God makes himself and his purposes known by stages until the full light is revealed in Jesus Christ.

■ *The Old Testament*
progressively reveals the redemptive plans of God which are fulfilled by Jesus Christ.

STUDY GUIDE TO CHAPTER 5

1. What was Jesus' attitude to the authority of the Old Testament?

2. In what sense is the Old Testament a book about Jesus Christ?

3. What determines the Christian approach to the Old Testament, and how does it differ from non-Christian approaches?

4. What evidence is there in the New Testament for the progressive nature of Old Testament revelation? Consider this question in the light of such passages as

   a. Matthew 1:17
   b. Matthew 3:17—4:4, compare with Exodus 4:23; Hosea 11:1
   c. Luke 1:46-55
   d. John 3:14-15
   e. Acts 2:16-39
   f. Acts 7:2-56
   g. Acts 13:16-43.

FURTHER READING

1. J. I. Packer, *Fundamentalism and the Word of God* (London: Inter-Varsity Fellowship, 1958), chap. 3.
2. John Wenham, *Christ and the Bible* (Downers Grove, Ill.: InterVarsity Press, 1984), chap. 1.

6

THE BIBLE IS THE DIVINE-HUMAN WORD

God speaks through a word that is both divine and human. We see this in the Word of God, Jesus Christ, who is both God and man. We do not honor the divine nature of Christ by playing down his humanity, nor do we honor his humanity by ignoring his divinity. The fact that the Bible finds its meaning in the divine Word who becomes flesh, helps us to understand the nature of the Bible as a divine-human word. The word of God comes to mankind through the agency of human beings and in the midst of human history. This is overlooked in some methods of interpretation. These include the literalistic and the allegorical interpretations. The literalistic plays down the place of revelation as the interpreter of history, and the allegorical removes history as the stage for revelation. The Bible contains a structure of typology in which history is central to God's progressive revelation.

GOD ACTS AMONG US BY HIS WORD

Let us now review some of the key points that we have dealt with up to now. Before the fall, mankind perceived the truth about God from nature and conscience, but always needed the *supernatural* word, the word which came directly from God and not through nature. Without the supernatural word even sinless humanity could not interpret the universe correctly. *Natural* revelation always needed *supernatural* revelation. *Original sin* involved the suppression of the truth of God in nature and conscience, and also rebellion against every supernatural word from God. Ever since the original sin of Adam and Eve, all of mankind has been involved in sin and is characterized by sin.

The saving acts of God involve a new supernatural revelation from God given progressively throughout the whole history of redemption. This word is preserved for us in the divinely inspired Word of Scripture. The full significance of the redeeming word, which began with the first announcement of God's intention to deal with sin, is not revealed until the coming of Jesus Christ.

The relationship of Jesus Christ to the word of God in Scripture is that he sums it up, brings it to fulfillment and interprets it. Thus, the *Word of God* is Jesus Christ. Every word in Scripture points to Jesus and finds its meaning in him. Furthermore, John 1:1-3 and Colossians 1:16 tell us that Jesus Christ is the eternal Word of God by which the universe was created. These two passages indicate that his saving work in the world was not an afterthought because of sin, but was the eternal purpose of God. It was the plan of God before creation and from all eternity. Upon this plan God created all things. If we can imagine God drawing up the plans for the universe before he created it, and if we could examine these plans, we would not see Adam and Eve in the Garden of Eden, but Jesus Christ in the gospel.

The significance of this is worth repeating: Jesus Christ in his life, death and resurrection is the fixed point of reference for the understanding of the whole of reality. We must apply this fact to our doing of biblical theology. The gospel is the fixed point of reference for understanding the meaning of the whole range of biblical revelation. Thus, in order to do biblical theology we must start with a *dogmatic* basis, a *presupposition* or set of presuppositions that come to us from revelation.

We must constantly remind ourselves that presuppositions that come from revelation cannot be proved or authenticated by that which lies outside of revelation. By means of revelation God gives his interpretation of every fact in existence, and therefore it is above every other fact. The presupposition that Jesus Christ is *the* Word of God comes to us from the Bible alone. It can be relied upon because the Bible is God's inspired testimony to the living Word, Jesus Christ. It cannot be proven by empirical evidence because there is no greater truth that can substantiate it.

If Christ is the self-evident Word of God, why do so many people reject him? The answer lies in original sin, that original rejection of God's word by Adam in which the whole human race is involved. As Adam refused every supernatural word of God through which human existence and the world could be truly understood, so the children of Adam are born rebels who suppress the truth of God within them, and reject the supernatural world from without. Only God's grace in the saving work of Christ can restore the proper relationship between God and man, and thus cause us to accept the truth. Through the gospel God accepts us as his children. And through the work of the Holy Spirit, which the gospel wins for us, we are able to accept Christ as savior and know God as Father. The Spirit conquers our rebellious wills and lifts the self-imposed hatred of God from our hearts.

■ *God chose Jesus Christ*
the Word as the way he would speak and act among us.

JESUS IS THE DIVINE-HUMAN WORD OF GOD

Both the person and the work of Jesus are inseparably bound up in his being the Word of God. He is the Word *incarnate*, that is, come in human flesh. But this Word who takes upon himself a complete human nature (Jn 1:14), was God from the beginning (Jn 1:1). In becoming man, God did not drop some of his divine nature in order to accommodate humanity. Nor were certain human characteristics removed to let God "fit in." Jesus was fully God and fully man, yet he was one person, the *God-man*. In Jesus Christ God has communicated with us through a Word which is both divine and human. This, as we shall see, has important implications for the way that we do theology.

1. Jesus is God

He comes from the Father with whom he is one. To have seen him is to have seen the Father. God, who established every fact there is, and who alone can interpret all things, has become man. In Jesus we have the absolute truth of God. Everything revealed to us in Jesus is the truth, and he is our ultimate source of truth.

2. Jesus is man

He communicates with us through his humanity. He lived in human history as a first century Jew of Palestine. He spoke and acted and, so we must assume, he thought as a first century Jew. He was truly and fully human. He experienced the whole range of human emotions, suffering and temptations. The significant exception was that he was untouched by original sin, and he committed no actual sin. Thus in his manhood he was the truly beloved Son of God, and he lived every aspect of his life in a perfect relationship with God the Father.

It is not possible for us humans, even when regenerate, to know how Jesus could be *both* fully God *and* fully man. We have to be content to accept that he is, and not attempt any logical solutions. It is a mystery that is destroyed when we try to penetrate it by human logic or reason. The theologian accepts *that* Jesus is the God-man without understanding *how* it could be.

False solutions to the problem always reduce either the divinity of Christ or his humanity in order to accommodate the other. Thus, the reasoning goes, if he is man he cannot be God. He might be the best of all men, but not God. This was the solution of many Jews of Jesus' day. Others say that if he is God he cannot be man and his humanity was illusory. This was the solution of many of the Greeks. Some have proposed that Jesus was both God and man except that his human spirit was replaced by the divine Spirit. Others have suggested that for Jesus to be both God and man, it must mean that he was two persons.

These false solutions warn us that we always have to take account of both the divine and the human natures of Christ. We do not honor his divine nature by ignoring his human nature, and vice versa. Most importantly, we see that the relationships between God and man in the one person Jesus Christ opens up for us the way to know something of the relationship that we have with God through the redeeming work of Christ. Thus the proper relationship of God and man in no way reduces or compromises the character of each. God always remains the totally sovereign, creator and redeeming Lord, and man always remains the totally responsible creature in the image of God.

■ *Jesus Christ*
is revealed as a union of true God and true man in one person.

THE BIBLE IS THE DIVINE-HUMAN WORD OF GOD

The particular part of human history out of which the Bible came, and which is recorded in the Bible, includes the history of Jesus of Nazareth. Like any other historical character in the Bible he is part of the biblical history of redemption. But he is also a unique part of this history. As we have already seen, all the biblical history finds its goal and its meaning in him. We are justified in saying that the whole Bible, including the Old Testament, is God's testimony to Christ.

If, as we noted earlier, Jesus the Word was a divine-human Word, it should not surprise us to discover that the Bible is a divine-human Word. The prophetic word of the Old Testament found its fulfillment and significance in the divine-human Word incarnate. But the prophetic testimony itself was a testimony to the fact that the divine Word came through the human prophets, so that what the prophet of God said as an oracle of the Lord was what God himself said.

That the Bible is God's inspired testimony to the word of God as it came through the prophets and through Jesus Christ, means that the Bible is itself the Word of God. Yet it is a word given through human beings within their own history and culture. God did not suspend the humanity of the biblical authors any more than he suspended the humanity of Jesus. The Bible bears all the marks of its authors. Their language, thought forms, literary styles and forms, and their culture all shape the actual way the messages were given.

The incarnation of Christ was by the special operation of the Holy Spirit bringing about conception in the womb of the Virgin Mary. By this means, God broke the natural connection with sinful humanity and ensured that the humanity of Jesus was exactly the kind that was needed for the work of salvation: perfect. In the same way, God acted by his Spirit to inspire the biblical authors so that the humanity of the Bible would be exactly what was needed to convey the truth of God without error. When we speak about the infallibility of the Bible we mean that it conveys exactly what God intended it to. God does not allow human sinfulness to interfere with his communication of the truth to mankind.

In pointing to the parallels between the Word incarnate (become human) and the Word inscripturate (written in a book), we must be careful to note some important differences. Jesus, as the Word, is God and man. Therefore he has the same power and authority as God, and we worship him as God. The Bible, as the Word, is *not* God and cannot be worshiped as God. Its divine qualities are not inherent but are derived from two facts. First, it is inspired by the Holy Spirit, and second, it is the inspired record of the living Word who, at a point in time, became man.

■ *The Bible*
is a union of a truly divine word and a truly human word in one book.

JESUS IS GOD'S FINAL AND FULLEST REVELATION

The significance of Jesus was not self-evident to people who knew him. Flesh and blood, that is human understanding, could not reveal to Peter that Jesus was the Christ, the Son of the living God (Mt 16:15-17). Only

God could reveal that fact. This is an important point for us. No one is able to understand Christ without God's Word and the Holy Spirit. Even the disciples needed the outpouring of the Holy Spirit at Pentecost before they finally grasped the meaning of Christ's coming. In other words, historical facts don't interpret themselves. In secular history scholars may deduce many things about, say, the causes of the Second World War. But we can only know the ultimate significance of this catastrophic expression of human folly to the extent that it is revealed to us through the Word of God.

The mere facts of biblical history do not interpret themselves. They together make up the medium of God's *progressive revelation* of himself and his kingdom. At its simplest, progressive revelation means that God's revelation was not given all at once in the beginning, but was revealed by stages until the full light of truth was revealed in Jesus Christ. This revelation has at its center the promises of God and their fulfillment.

Let us suppose that God had revealed all the facts about Jesus (as we find them in the four Gospels) and their meaning to Abraham nearly two thousand years before the event. In that case God's revelation would have interpreted the history of Jesus before it occurred. It almost sounds from what Jesus says that it did happen like that:

Your father Abraham rejoiced at the thought of seeing my day; he saw it and was glad. (Jn 8:56)

But the evidence in the Bible does not allow this interpretation of the way revelation occurred. Abraham was actually promised certain things concerning his own descendants and the land of Canaan. There is no suggestion that Abraham was told anything specifically about Jesus. This is a false view of revelation.

Now let us suppose that God gave to Abraham the basic promises, and that he added further revelation at various stages through Old Testament history. Suppose that all the facts about Jesus and their meaning were in place by the time of the prophet Malachi. Again the history of Jesus would have been interpreted before the event. In this case the real significance of the promises to Abraham would be developed fully before we get to the actual events themselves. The events would then be nothing more than a literal fulfillment of the promises of the Old Testament. Not that such a literal fulfillment requires that all the facts be given beforehand. Again we find that this does not square with the way the Bible is, and we have another false view of revelation.

False view of revelation (1)

The whole truth about Christ is given to Abraham (A).
The rest of Old Testament history (B) merely links the promises with their
completely literal fulfillment (C). Christ is not himself revelation.
This is clearly false.

Contrary to these two models, we find that God in fact reserves his greatest revelation until the point of fulfillment. Jesus does not simply fulfill the promises. Rather, he is the final and the fullest revelation of what the promises are really about. This means that the form and the content of the fulfillment exceeds by far the form and content of the promises themselves. The very act of fulfilling the Old Testament promises is itself the most important revelation of all. An aspect of this final revelation is to make clear that it does in fact fulfill the expectations. This is not a self-evident fact. Revelation must show it to us. It was not self-evident that Jesus fulfilled the Old Testament promises. Those Jews who looked for a literal fulfillment of the Old Testament promises failed to recognize Jesus as the

False view of revelation (2)

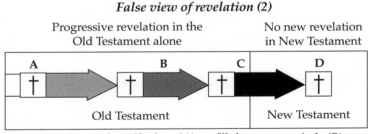

Promises made to Abraham (A) are filled out progressively (B).
By the end of the Old Testament period the full revelation of Christ has been given (C).
The New Testament simply relates the literal fulfillment of the Old (D).

fulfillment. They should have understood the Scriptures better than they did, but even that would not have been enough. It needed Jesus' own word about himself and the Holy Spirit's testimony through the apostles to show that all the Old Testament promises came to fulfillment in the resurrection of Jesus.

Biblical revelation

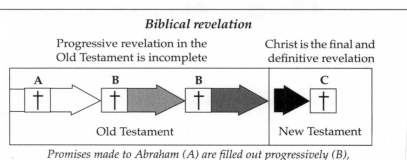

Progressive revelation in the   Christ is the final and
Old Testament is incomplete   definitive revelation

Old Testament   New Testament

Promises made to Abraham (A) are filled out progressively (B),
but without reaching completion in the Old Testament.
Christ comes as the final and fullest revelation of God (C),
fulfilling and interpreting all that has gone before.

In our first two models of revelation, the Old Testament takes priority over the New and interprets it. The gospel event is simply the occurrence in history of something that was long since revealed to the full. But according to the New Testament Jesus is the Word that explains all other words. He comes to achieve what was promised in the Old Testament and, in doing so, he shows that the promises were but shadows of the fulfillment. It is therefore not at all self-evident how any given promise will be fulfilled. We should not be surprised at this, for in the incarnation God accommodated his truth to a form that human beings could comprehend. Likewise, the nature of revelation as elemental promises, which are progressively built upon by further revelation, was an accommodation to the condition of mankind.

We must conclude that a method of interpretation that demands that the promises of the Old Testament be literally fulfilled, so that there is exact correspondence between what is promised and what eventually comes to pass, does not fit the evidence of the Bible. Of course, there are many details of fulfillment in the New Testament that exactly correspond to the promise. Such literal correspondence of a few details does not establish a principle of literal interpretation. Rather, it illustrates the different principle that God accommodates himself to human history when he reveals himself. If God chooses to reveal his purposes progressively, we can be sure that he has a reason and that it is for our good that he does so.

LITERALISM, ALLEGORY AND TYPOLOGY

Literalism involves the very serious error of not listening to what the New Testament says about fulfillment. It assumes that the fulfillment must correspond exactly to the form of the promise. In fact, literalism assumes that the meaning of history is self-evident. Such an assumption goes contrary to all that we have said about revelation and its necessity for the correct interpretation of any fact.

If literalism assumes that history is self-evident, then *allegory* assumes that history is worthless as history. Allegory results when a supposed hidden meaning is read out of something that on the surface is historical but which in fact has no value as history. In the case of the Bible, the history of the Old Testament was seen as worthless for the Christian. Under the influence of Greek culture some thinkers interpreted the gospel in terms of timeless ideals, or of the salvation of the soul apart from the body through a process of enlightenment. Once the gospel was thus cut free from the historical facts of Jesus of Nazareth it of course ceased to be the true gospel, and it obviously found no use for the historical facts of the Old Testament. The Old Testament could then be discarded altogether, or it could be allegorized. The allegorist was not interested in the historical facts at all, but only in the supposed hidden meaning behind them. Allegorical interpretation is entirely subjective in that it is a matter of personal preference as to whose interpretation is accepted as the true one. There is no objective word by which the interpretation can be tested.

If we rule out both literalism and allegory, is there any other way of expressing the relationship of the Old Testament to the New? Indeed there is. Progressive revelation establishes the principle of *typology*. While the underlying relationship remains the same, the form in which it is given undergoes a certain development or expansion until the fulfillment is reached. Thus, for example, Abraham was chosen as the father of the people of God. Promises were given to him regarding his natural descendants and the land they would inherit. The underlying relationship is expressed in the title "the people of God." Further revelation shows that Abraham's promised descendants are through Jacob (Israel), not Esau (Edom). As revelation progresses we learn that it is a restored remnant of Israel, a people made new through the Spirit of God, who are the people of God. Through these stages the *type* is progressively clarified. The fulfillment of all this is referred to as the *antitype*. The New Testament tells us that *the* descendant of Abraham to which all this points is Jesus Christ. The Church is also the antitype but only because it is *in Christ*.

Typology, then, takes account of the fact that God used a particular part of human history to reveal himself and his purposes to mankind. But it was a process, so that the historical types are incomplete revelations and depend on their antitype for their real meaning. Typology rejects the principle of literalism. The meaning of history, far from being self-evident, depends on revelation for its meaning. It also rejects the principle of allegorism. History, far from being meaningless, is controlled and interpreted by God in revelation. Typology assumes that all history is God's history, and that God has used a particular part of history along with his word to reveal himself to mankind. The New Testament recognizes the principle of typology in the fact that Christ fulfills the Old Testament promises in ways that differ from the actual terms of the promises. Typology is also established while literalism is rejected in the idea that the Old Testament revelation is only a shadow of the solid reality revealed in Christ (Col 2:17, Heb 10:1).

■ *Literalism*
says the historical promises lead to exactly corresponding historical fulfillments.

■ *Allegory*
says the historical promises and events are of significance only for the hidden meanings which lie beneath them.

■ *Typology*
says the historical promises are the first stages of progressively revealed truths. The historical fulfillments correspond to and develop the promises.

LITERAL OR LITERALISTIC

Our discussion of literal interpretation may cause some confusion among those familiar with the history of biblical interpretation. The Protestant Reformers of the sixteenth century saw themselves as moving away from the allegorical interpretations of the Middle Ages to recover the proper literal interpretation. What they meant by literal is very different from what is often meant in the debate today.

In the foregoing discussion I have used the terms literal and literalistic to refer to a method of interpreting the promises of the Old Testament. Thus, if God promised Abraham many descendants who would possess the land of Canaan, then that is exactly the way the ultimate fulfillment will be. If the prophets describe the day of salvation for Israel as a return of exiles to Palestine, a rebuilt temple and a restored Jerusalem, the fulfillment will be exactly that. Under these terms the promises still await fulfillment, and we have a problem of where Christ fits in since he is literally nowhere to be found in the promises.

The roots of evangelical interpretation lie in the Reformation, where the words *literal* or *natural* were used in another way. The literal or natural meaning of the text was what the text intended to convey to its original readers. It was thus a rejection of the allegorical interpretation that regarded such meaning as irrelevant. Most significantly, however, the reformers did not see the literal meaning as being exhausted until it found its fulfillment in Christ. Thus, they recognized that the literal meaning at the Old Testament level pointed to a future event with a fuller meaning. Unlike allegory, the connection between the two was a matter of revelation in the Bible itself. Also unlike allegory, the Old Testament revelation was the means of putting the people of its time in touch with the later reality of Christ. In their approach to the literal meaning of the Old Testament the Reformers established typology as the basis of evangelical interpretation.

STUDY GUIDE TO CHAPTER 6

1. It is time now for you to think about the way your own presuppositions are forming. Can you say why we have to depend on God's revelation in Scripture in order to know what is ultimately the truth?

2. How does Jesus as the divine-human Word help us to understand the Bible as divine-human Word?

3. What is wrong with assuming that the Bible must be understood in a literalistic way?

4. How does progressive revelation within history shape our view of the interpretation of the Bible?

FURTHER READING

1. Graeme Goldsworthy, *Gospel and Wisdom* (Exeter, U.K.: Paternoster, 1987), esp. chaps. 11 and 12.
2. F. F. Bruce, *This Is That* (Exeter, U.K.: Paternoster, 1968).
3. F. F. Bruce, *The Time Is Fulfilled* (Grand Rapids, Mich.: Eerdmans, 1978).

7

WE BEGIN AND END
WITH CHRIST

Biblical theology enables us to discover how any Bible text relates to ourselves. Be-
cause Christ is the fixed point of reference for theology, we are concerned with how the
text relates to Christ and how we relate to Christ. Both questions direct us to the way
Jesus understood the gospel. He saw it in terms of fulfillment of the Old Testament,
and of the coming of the kingdom of God which demands our submission. Such a gos-
pel points us to the dimensions of the Bible of which biblical theology continually
takes note. These are the literature or the words of the text, the history or biblical story
and the revelation that is conveyed through these dimensions. Biblical theology begins
with the word about Christ and seeks to understand how the New Testament's testi-
mony relates to all that God has revealed in the Old Testament. Christ gives us the
underlying pattern of biblical theology in that he reveals the central concern of the Bi-
ble in the relationship of God to his creation, and in particular to mankind.

CHRIST IS THE TRUTH

The matters discussed in chapters two and six point to the method that we
must adopt in doing biblical theology. Let us, for the moment, set aside all
thoughts of formal theological study that pressures us to be concerned
with courses of study, examinations and diplomas. Thus far I have tried to
give biblical answers to the question of why we should study biblical theology. These answers have little to do with gaining academic qualifica-
tions, but rather concern the more vital matter of how we read the Bible.
As Christians we should be interested in the proper interpretation of the
Bible so that we know and understand what God is saying to us all
through his Word. Without some understanding of the overall plan or
structure of the Bible it is difficult to correctly relate the various parts of the
Bible to ourselves.

In order to know how any given part of the Bible relates to us, we must
answer two prior questions: How does the text in question relate to Christ,
and how do we relate to Christ? Since Christ is *the truth*, God's final and

fullest word to mankind, all other words in the Bible are given their final meaning by him. The same Christ gives us our meaning and defines the significance of our existence in terms of our relationship to him.

Another way of stating this is that Jesus Christ is the one mediator between God and man (1 Tim 2:5). God's word to us in the Bible is mediated to us through Jesus Christ. There is no direct word from the Father to you or me. Every word of the Father comes to us through the person and work of Jesus. Even the words of the Old Testament are mediated through Christ in that we only know what God is saying to us through them when we see them fulfilled in Christ. Linked with this is the fact that the relationship of Jesus to the Father is the relationship to the Father that we share with him; we are joint heirs with Christ (Rom 8:17). All facts in the universe, including the facts of the Bible, must be interpreted in the light of God's revelation in Jesus Christ. Refer again to the diagram of Christian theism on page 49, and apply it now to the relation of every text in the Bible to us as Christians.

■ *Jesus Christ*
is the link between every part of the Bible and ourselves.

WE START WITH THE GOSPEL

The gospel is the power of God for salvation (Rom 1:16). By it we are brought from darkness into light. God rescues us from a condition in which our minds are darkened so that we do not know the truth, and he brings us to know the truth as it is found in Christ. By this means alone can we truly become theologians.

We can examine the Word of God for the content of Christ's gospel and for the clues to its relationship with all other pats of the Bible. We do this in response to the lordship of Christ, recognizing that he dictates to us the terms for understanding the Bible. What, then, lies at the heart of Jesus' teaching? We can hardly do better than to consider his gospel summary in Mark 1:15, "The time has come [is fulfilled]. . . . The kingdom of God is near. Repent and believe the good news!" It is important to see that Jesus did not come because the time was fulfilled, but rather he fulfilled the time by coming. Fulfillment is not a reference to history in general, but to the way Jesus fulfills all the expectations of the Old Testament at the time appointed by God.

As to the content of his message, Jesus tells us that its central theme is the coming of the kingdom of God. How near the kingdom is, and what it means for it to come is the subject of the gospel narratives and of the New Testament as a whole. The fact that Jesus announces the kingdom without explaining what he means by it suggests that he spoke of an already existing idea in the minds of the Jews. It is most likely that the Old Testament will help us understand what the idea was. But Jesus does point out the significance of the kingdom in saying that it demands repentance and faith. To repent is to turn away from our desire to be independent of God, which is, in effect, an allegiance to Satan's kingdom. Repentance is to turn to God in submission to his kingly rule. Such submission involves faith as confident reliance on the Word of the King himself. The Word speaks a message of God's love for rebellious sinners, which is shown in undeserved acts of redemption. God actually moves to restore to friendship with himself those who oppose and hate him.

The fact that God planned a kingdom of redeemed sinners points to another theme that is prominent for biblical theology, the covenant. I shall have much more to say about this subject. For the moment let us note that "covenant" is a biblical concept which refers primarily to God's commitment to his people, and that Jesus is presented as bringing about a renewal of the covenant of the Old Testament through the gospel event. We begin with Christ because we are redeemed under the new covenant. All other references to covenant in the Bible must be understood in relation to the new covenant in Christ.

■ *The gospel*
is the word about Jesus Christ and what he did for us in order to restore us to a right relationship with God.

THE FIRST INGREDIENT

Biblical theology deals with what God makes known to us in the Bible, and with the way he makes it known. There are three distinct but closely related ingredients to biblical theology, which we have already looked at. It is time now to set them up as the stepping-stones to a biblical theology. They are, in fact, the three major dimensions of the Bible itself: the literature, the historical record and the theology or revelation contained.

First, we consider the literature. We begin with the words of the Bible

about Christ, which come to us personally as the gospel. No matter how freely these words are paraphrased, restated or interpreted by the person who
tells them to us, we understand their meaning only as we understand the
way the Bible presents them. At the first level the problem of understanding
the Bible is the same as that of understanding any literature. How words are
used is a matter of prime importance. Jesus used words in a variety of ways,
and the biblical record as a whole uses words in an equally diverse manner.

I have mentioned that the incarnation means that God has revealed
himself through Jesus the Word who is both divine and human. This fact
requires us to take account of the humanity of Jesus as the "visible" form
of the Word. The incarnation also requires that we take careful account of
the humanity of the biblical record. Part of our grammatico-historical exegesis (see p. 34) is discerning how narrative, parable, hymn, legal precept
and apocalyptic vision, to name but a few, all use words in different ways
to communicate the truth of God.

These questions of the exegesis of the literature can never be separated
from concern for the other two dimensions of the Bible. The three go hand-in-
hand throughout the task of biblical theology. The words will constantly point
us to the historical events that provide the framework for biblical revelation.

■ *Understanding the Bible*
means understanding the words that the biblical authors used in the way they
intended them to be understood.

THE SECOND INGREDIENT

Not all the texts of the Bible describe directly the history of Israel and the
early church. Overall, however, the Bible is concerned with a particular
succession of historical events. While critical historians (using humanistic
presuppositions) may question whether biblical history tells it the way it
really was, there is no doubt that the Bible does tell it as a series of connected historical events which are of central significance to the biblical message. To begin with, we need an outline history that highlights the main
events in the biblical story.

Biblical history does not keep to all the rules that secular historians im-
pose, and this sometimes creates a tension between what the Bible says
and what modern historians will accept. Our assumptions about revela-

tion are important here. Obviously events such as creation and the fall are not open to historical investigation, but we accept them to be true on the basis of revelation from God. Some Christian historians feel that it is not acceptable and so find that they must be skeptical about those biblical events that are not attested by evidence from outside the Bible. What I said in chapter two is relevant here. Not only does the meaning of the historical events come to us by revelation from God, but also the facts themselves, especially when they lie beyond the normal means of historical investigation, can be revealed by God.

■ *Understanding the Bible*
means understanding the historical story within which the message of the Bible is unfolded.

THE THIRD INGREDIENT

Just as it is impossible to talk of the literature of the Bible without being involved in the history of the Bible, it is also impossible to talk about the literature or the history of the Bible without being involved in the revelation of the Bible. Because biblical history is inseparable from revelation it stretches beyond the limits of secular history in both directions. It sees history as meaningful, connected events in time emerging from a past eternity, and going beyond our time into a future where again it merges into eternity. Revelation can write a future history because the revealer is the Lord of history who is in complete control of events and is steering everything that exists to its final destiny.

Words, history and revelation are thus the basic dimensions of the Bible that can be clearly distinguished but not separated. Because the Bible as the Word of God derives its character from Jesus Christ the Word of God, we can see the same relationships in him. The words of Jesus and the inspired record of him are inseparable from the historic person and his deeds. All combine to be the revelation of God.

■ *Understanding the Bible*
means understanding the way words and history are used to reveal the truth about God and his redeeming activity.

CHRIST AS THE PATTERN OF BIBLICAL THEOLOGY

Because Christ sums up the whole of biblical revelation, what is revealed of him controls the way we do biblical theology. The historic event of Jesus of Nazareth is God's fullest self-disclosure to mankind. It brings to full clarity what has been present in the Old Testament as a shadow from the beginning. Although Christ is the fulfillment and the solid reality, he cannot be understood in isolation from the promises and shadows in the Old Testament. From our starting point with Christ we find ourselves moving backward and forward between the two Testaments. Our understanding of the gospel is enhanced by our understanding of its Old Testament roots, and at the same time the gospel shows us the true meaning of the Old Testament.

Such an interrelationship between the two Testaments would be difficult to represent in the actual writing of a biblical theology. Nevertheless, we must try to do so by highlighting Christ as both our starting point and the goal to which we move. Christ is the place we start because he shows us what the unfolding message of the Old Testament is really concerned with.

On the basis of the gospel we can say that a biblical theology will focus on certain key elements in the biblical message. The relationship of God to his creation in general, and to mankind in particular is one such element. The gospel shows what that relationship is intended to be. It shows that even though mankind rebelled against that relationship and spoiled it, God has revealed his way of restoring it.

■ *Jesus Christ*
shows us that biblical theology is about God bringing in his kingdom in which all relationships are restored to perfection.

CHOOSING A CENTRAL THEME

There is a great diversity in the Bible. The many authors come from a variety of backgrounds. They emphasize different aspects of what God is doing and how he is doing it. They use different ways of expressing the truth in words. Yet the clear assumption throughout Scripture is that the testimony is to a single work done by one God. On the basis of what Jesus and the apostles taught we accept that the diversity of expression in the Bible exists within an overall unity.

The problem for a biblical theology, especially if it is intended to be introductory as this one is, is what principle of unity can be focused on to show up the essential relationships of all parts of the Bible. Since the Bible does not consist of a lot of abstract ideas or philosophical thoughts, but rather emphasizes the acts of God within creation and in history, it is necessary for biblical theology to avoid the merely abstract and to concentrate on the actual events and their interpretation as given in the Bible.

In the next section of this book we will explore the historical progression of God's revelation with special emphasis upon the covenant relationship, and on how this fits into the rule of God over his creation in what comes to be referred to as the kingdom of God. We will not be so concerned with technical aspects of what covenant was, but with the notion of covenant as God's commitment to his creation in general and to humanity in particular, through creation and redemption. Because the covenant is first in evidence in God's commitment to his creation at the very beginning, and because the covenant of redemption is God's commitment to renew all things in a new creation, I have chosen the linked themes of the covenant and the new creation as a unifying element in the biblical message. Time and space do not permit us to explore in detail all the different themes that might be regarded as the basis of biblical unity. Most of them will appear in some way or another in our examination of biblical theology, but we need to focus on one in order to highlight the fact of unity.

■ *Biblical theology*

needs to emphasize some theme or themes which provide the basis for understanding the single, unified message of the Bible.

STUDY GUIDE TO CHAPTER 7

1. What are the reasons for regarding Jesus Christ as the starting point for doing biblical theology?

2. How would you describe the relationship between the literature, the history and the theology of the Bible?

3. In what way is Christ the pattern of biblical theology?

4. Biblical theology accepts both the unity and the development in the biblical message. Can you suggest a structure for a biblical theology using
   "the people of God" as the central theme?

FURTHER READING
1. *GK,* chaps. 3 and 4
2. *BT,* chap. 2.
3. Ronald Youngblood, *The Heart of the Old Testament* (Grand Rapids,
   Mich.: Baker, 1971).

BIBLICAL

THEOLOGY—

WHAT?

So far we have asked why and how we do biblical theology. Now we are in a position to ask what is the content of biblical theology. In this section we set out to describe some of the main themes of revelation which are progressively unfolded in the Bible until they are given their fullest expression in the person and work of Jesus Christ.

Outline of biblical history

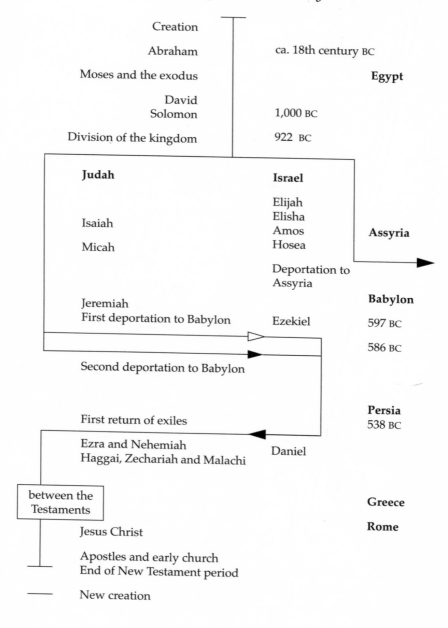

Creation

Abraham ca. 18th century BC

Moses and the exodus **Egypt**

David
Solomon 1,000 BC

Division of the kingdom 922 BC

Judah **Israel**

Elijah
Isaiah Elisha
Amos **Assyria**
Micah Hosea

Deportation to
Assyria

Jeremiah **Babylon**
First deportation to Babylon Ezekiel 597 BC

586 BC

Second deportation to Babylon

Persia
First return of exiles 538 BC

Ezra and Nehemiah
Haggai, Zechariah and Malachi Daniel

between the
Testaments **Greece**

Rome
Jesus Christ

Apostles and early church
End of New Testament period

New creation

8

I AM THE FIRST
AND THE LAST

I am the first and the last. I am the Living One; I was dead, and behold I am alive for ever and ever! (Rev 1:17-18)

THE GOSPEL OF JESUS CHRIST

The main message of the Bible about Jesus Christ can easily become mixed with all sorts of things that are related to it. We see this in the way people define or preach the gospel. But it is important to keep the gospel itself clearly distinct from our response to it or from the results of it in our lives and in the world. If our proper response to the gospel message is faith, then we should not make faith part of the gospel itself. It would be absurd to call people to have faith in faith! While the new birth bears a close relationship to faith in Christ, it is a mistake to speak of the new birth as if it were itself the gospel. Faith in the new birth as such will not save us.

It is, therefore, important to understand both what the gospel is, so that we include what must be believed, and what the gospel is not, so that we don't require people to believe more than is necessary for salvation. The Bible contains a number of gospel expressions, one of the clearest being in Romans 1:1-4. From this we learn four main things about the gospel.

1. The gospel of God . . .
2. the gospel he promised beforehand through his prophets . . .
3. regarding his Son, who . . . was a descendant of David . . .
4. declared with power to be the Son of God, by his resurrection . . .

First, it is God's gospel. He is the author of it and the one who puts it into effect. It achieves what he wants it to, and in the way he determines. It deals with the problems that he perceives and defines. It does not primarily deal with our needs as we perceive them—how can I live a better life, overcome my hang-ups, make sense of my existence—although it may include these. The gospel is God's way of dealing with his "problem" of how he, a holy and just God, can justify and accept the sinner. Only God's wisdom is great enough to devise a plan that will achieve this.

Second, it is the gospel of the Old Testament. An important part of biblical theology is to try to understand how the promises given in the Old Testament are actually fulfilled in the New. In other words, the Christian's use of the Old Testament is guided by the way we see its message relating to Christ and, through him, to us. Because Jesus is our final authority, we are vitally interested in how he and the apostles preached the gospel using the Old Testament as their Scriptures.

Third, there is the defined subject matter of the gospel. It is about the Son in a way that it is not about the Father, or the Holy Spirit, or the believer. The Son is clearly identified. He is not only God the Son, the second person of the eternal Trinity. He is Jesus of Nazareth who is descended from David the King of Israel. This sets the limits of the gospel to the Jesus of history and his birth into a significant family, his life, death, resurrection and ascension. To be preaching the gospel we must be speaking about these things and their meaning for our salvation.

Fourth, there is the central fact of the gospel, which is the resurrection of Jesus from the dead. Paul says that the resurrection identified Jesus as the Son of God. Resurrection is not clearly seen in the Old Testament for reasons we shall note later. But there is some mention of the Son of God as the title of the people of God. We shall ask how the resurrection shows that Jesus is this Son of God.

TRUTH THAT IS VITAL BUT NOT GOSPEL

Related to the gospel event are other important aspects of God's work which are not themselves the gospel. If we believe the gospel we will probably also believe these, but they are not the focus of our trust the way that the saving work of Jesus is. We do not preach them as the heart of our message to unbelievers.

First, there is the distinct work of God the Father. The Bible tells us that God is not divided; he is one. Thus Father, Son and Holy Spirit are involved in every aspect of God's work. But the three-ness of the one God means that each person has distinct roles even if the other two persons are involved. The Father, it would appear, is distinctly the person who elects, creates and sends the Son into the world. To preach the Father's work, even if it is "God so loved the world" out of John 3:16, is not to preach the gospel unless we get to the facts about the Son's person and work.

Second, there is the distinct work of the Holy Spirit. He gives faith and new birth, he testifies to our hearts about Christ, he indwells the people of God and sanctifies them. All of these are good and necessary works of God and they do not exist without the gospel. We must, however, distinguish them from the gospel. They are the results or fruits of the gospel work of Jesus.

Third, we note that what you or I do in response to the gospel is not itself the gospel. You cannot say that repentance and faith are the gospel. They are what the Holy Spirit enables us to do about the gospel. If you tell unbelievers that they should trust Christ, believe the good news, or confess their sin, these things are undoubtedly true, but they are not the gospel. We must tell them what it is about Christ that they should trust, what the good news is so that they can believe it and why sins should be confessed.

The New Testament emphasizes the historic person of Christ and what he did to make it possible for us, through faith, to become the friends of God. The emphasis is also on him as the one who sums up and brings to their fitting climax all the promises and expectations raised in the Old Testament. There is a priority of order here that we must take into account if we are to understand the Bible correctly. It is the gospel event that brings about faith in the people of God, and the gospel that will motivate, direct, pattern and empower the life of the Christian community. So we start from the gospel and move to an understanding of Christian living, and of the final goal toward which we are moving.

Again, we start from the gospel and move back into the Old Testament to see what lies behind the person and work of Christ. The Old Testament is not completely superseded by the gospel, for that would make it irrelevant to us. It helps us understand the gospel by showing us the origins and meanings of the various ideas and special words used to describe Christ and his works in the New Testament. Yet we also recognize that Christ is God's fullest and final word to mankind. As such, he reveals to us the final meaning of the Old Testament. But more of that as we go on.

THE FOUR GOSPELS AS WITNESSES TO THE GOSPEL

The four Gospels are distinct literary forms so named because their main content is the gospel. How have their authors presented the gospel? I

will give special attention to the two-volume work by Luke consisting of
his Gospel and the Acts. But first let us note the introductions of the other
three Gospels. Each writer has a distinctive approach, but they all have
one thing in common: they make an immediate link between their message and that of the Old Testament. Matthew establishes the historic family link from Jesus to Abraham, and thus relates the history of Israel to
the gospel. Mark sees the gospel of Jesus Christ as having its basis in an
Old Testament prophetic message. John recalls the opening words of
Genesis and so points to Jesus of Nazareth as the Creator who has now
come in the flesh.

When Matthew begins with the family tree of Jesus, moving through
three groups of fourteen generations, he is not merely giving a record of
human descent. The three groups go from Abraham to David, from David
to the exile, and from the exile to Christ. The theological significance of
these milestones in Israel's history stands behind the interpretation of
Christ in Matthew's Gospel. Abraham and David are the key recipients of
the promises of God, while the exile shows the failure of Israel to receive
the blessings of these promises. Jesus Christ is set forth in the Gospel as the
one through whom the promises are brought to fulfillment.

*A record of the genealogy of Jesus Christ the son of David, the son of
Abraham. (Mt 1:1)*

*The beginning of the gospel about Jesus Christ, the Son of God.
It is written in Isaiah the prophet. (Mk 1:1-2)*

*In the beginning was the Word, and the Word was with God, and the
Word was God. . . . Through him all things were made. . . . The Word became flesh and made his dwelling among us. (Jn 1:1, 3, 14)*

Mark begins with a couple of prophecies from the later part of Israel's
history. They are concerned with the announcement of the final acts of
God for the salvation of his people. Mark links these prophecies to John
the Baptist who prepares the way for Jesus, and thus introduces his Gospel as an account of what Jesus did to fulfil the expectations of the Old
Testament.

John's recalling of the creation has not so much the beginning of the universe in mind, but the fact that God created by his word. The word of creation is the word by which he reveals himself and by which he redeems his people. One of John's key themes is life. Mankind received life from God at creation, but lost it through disobedience in the fall. John develops many of the themes of the Old Testament in order to show that life is restored to those who believe in Jesus Christ (Jn 20:31).

THE WITNESS OF LUKE-ACTS

Luke begins his Gospel with an address to a certain Theophilus. The introduction to the Acts, also addressed to Theophilus, shows that it is intended to be sequel to the Gospel which Luke describes as an account of what Jesus *began* to do and teach. Since the Gospel takes us up to the ascension of Jesus into heaven, the implication seems to be that Acts is about what Jesus *continued* to do through the Holy Spirit.

Old Testament theme	Luke
Elijah the prophet will return to prepare the way for the Savior. (Mal 4:5-6)	John the Baptist fulfills the Elijah role. (Lk 1:17)
God promised to David that his descendants will always possess the throne. (2 Sam 7:12-14)	Jesus is that descendant and fulfills the role of David's line. (Lk 1:27-32)
God promised to Abraham that his descendants would be the people of God. (Gen 17:1-8)	Mary understands the birth of Jesus as a fulfillment of the promises to Abraham. (Lk 1:54-55)
God's covenant promises to Abraham and David. (Gen 17; 2 Sam 7)	Zechariah understands the birth of John the Baptist in the light of the covenant promises. (Lk 1:70-75)
The salvation of Israel will have its effects for the nations. (Is 42:6; 52:10)	Simeon sees Jesus as bringer of this salvation. (Lk 2:29-32)
The people of God referred to as the son of God. (Ex 4:22)	Jesus is called son of God at his baptism. (Lk 3:22-28)
Adam and Israel fail when tempted. (Gen 3; Deut 8)	Jesus overcomes the temptation of Satan. (Lk 4:1-12)
The messiah promised by the prophet. (Is 61)	Jesus fulfills the promise. (Lk 4:16-21)

Our present interest in this two-part work is directed to its emphasis on the Old Testament and its relationship to the person and work of Jesus. In the first four chapters of Luke we find that a number of Old Testament themes are recalled, including those in the diagram on page 85.

This sense of Old Testament fulfillment is strongest in the post-resurrection discourses of Jesus. The two disciples on the road to Emmaus thought that the death of Jesus meant the end of all their hopes. Jesus rebukes them because they should have understood better the gospel from the Old Testament. The death of the Christ (Messiah) is definitely part of the message of the prophets.

"How foolish you are, and how slow of heart to believe all that the prophets have spoken! Did not the Christ have to suffer these things and then enter his glory?" (Lk 24:25-26)

This led to what were to be two of the most important pieces of instruction that Jesus ever gave.

And beginning with Moses and all the Prophets, he explained to them what was said in all the Scriptures concerning himself. (Lk 24:27)

He said to them, "This is what I told you while I was still with you: Everything must be fulfilled that is written about me in the Law of Moses, the Prophets and the Psalms." Then he opened their minds so they could understand the Scriptures. (Lk 24:44-45)

We can only suppose that Luke does not go into detail here about Jesus' own method of interpreting the Old Testament because it will receive ample demonstration in the sermons of the apostles recorded in Acts.

Acts contains the same heavy emphasis on the relationship of the gospel to the message of the Old Testament. On a number of occasions Luke records, and presumably summarizes, a gospel address or sermon. We find them in Acts 2:14-39; 3:13-26; 4:10-12; 5:30-32; 10:36-43; 13:17-41. To them we could add Paul's address to the Athenians in Acts 17:22-31. These all show some common elements that indicate the content of the gospel as preached by the apostles. The fulfillment of the Old Testament is one of these elements, which is constantly referred to. If, as is generally thought,

Luke was a non-Jew writing for other non-Jews, it is more remarkable that he does not regard the Old Testament roots of the gospel as of interest to Jews only. Rather he constantly refers to the apostolic gospel as that which is preached from the Old Testament and which is inexplicable without the Old Testament. The first recorded sermons of both Peter and Paul are given in some detail, and the Old Testament content can be easily seen.

Gospel	Peter (Acts 2)	Paul (Acts 13)
1. The Old Testament is fulfilled	verses 16-21, 25-31, 34-36	verses 16-23, 32-39
2. in the person and work of Jesus of Nazareth	verse 22	verses 23-26
3. who died	verse 23	verses 27-29
4. and rose again	verses 24, 32	verses 30-31, 34-37
5. and is now exalted	verses 33, 36	verse 34
6. Through him is forgiveness of sins	verse 38	verses 38-39
7. Therefore . . .	verses 38-40	verses 40-41

Enough has been said to indicate the perspective of the New Testament on the person of Christ. It would be quite impossible to proclaim Jesus Christ as the Savior without constant reference to the foundations which have been laid in the history of God's saving work in the Old Testament. Alpha (A) and Omega (Ω) are the first and last letters of the Greek alphabet. When Jesus is spoken of as the A and the Ω, the first and the last, the beginning and the end (Rev 22:13), it means of course that he is God (see Rev 1:8, 17-18). But it also points us to the reality we have been examining in this chapter: Jesus is our starting point for all true knowledge, and therefore for theology. He is the goal toward which we move. We see this in our Christian existence, for we begin life as God's children when we are united to Christ by faith in his saving work, and our destiny is to be finally made like his image.

Now that we have seen some of the Old Testament themes that are picked up in the New Testament, we are compelled to examine the whole

Old Testament foundation of the gospel. Indeed there is a real sense in which the gospel cannot be the gospel without the Old Testament. As we move back to the beginning of the biblical story and follow it through until we arrive again at the gospel, we will do so with the Christian perspective that the progression of events will only find its true meaning in Christ. This can never be stated too often. The Old Testament is a story without an ending. Judaism and Islam have both provided their endings to the story that we as Christians cannot accept as valid. Jesus Christ is the goal of the Old Testament and provides its true meaning. Any understanding of, and commentary on, the Old Testament that does not show up this fact is at best incomplete and at worst un-Christian.

Some Old Testament themes applied by the New Testament to Christ		
Creator	Son of Abraham	New Covenant
Word	Son of David	Salvation
Wisdom	Prophet	Servant of God
Son of God	Priest	Anointed One
Adam	King	Redemption
Israel	Light of nations	Shepherd

STUDY GUIDE TO CHAPTER 8

1. What elements of the gospel are mentioned in 1 Corinthians 15:1-11 and 2 Timothy 2:8?

2. Using the sermon outlines in Acts 3:13-26; 4:10-12; 5:30-32; 10:36-43, make a chart of their contents similar to that on p. 85.

3. What else besides the gospel would an evangelistic sermon contain, and why?

4. Is the greater emphasis in the New Testament on understanding Christ by the Old Testament, or on understanding the Old Testament by Christ? Set out reasons for your answer.

FURTHER READING

1. *IBD* article on "Gospels."
2. J. C. Chapman, *Know and Tell the Gospel* (London: Hodder & Stoughton, 1985).
3. Michael Green, *Evangelism in the Early Church* (London: Hodder & Stoughton, 1970), esp. chap. 3.
4. Donald Robinson, *Faith's Framework* (Exeter, U.K.: Paternoster, 1985).

9

CREATION BY WORD

In the beginning was the Word, and the Word was with God, and the Word was God. He was with God in the beginning. Through him all things were made; without him nothing was made that has been made. (Jn 1:1-3)

For by him all things were created . . . all things were created by him and for him. (Col 1:16)

OUTLINE OF BIBLICAL HISTORY, GENESIS 1—2
In the beginning God created everything that exists. He made Adam and Eve and placed them in the garden of Eden. God spoke to them and gave them certain tasks in the world. For food he allowed them the fruit of all the trees in the garden except one. He warned them that they would die if they ate the fruit of that one tree.

GOD CREATES BY HIS WORD

The gospel of Jesus Christ reveals God to us. This gospel has meaning only if the God who devised it is the ruling Lord and Creator of the universe. Through the gospel we learn the purpose of creation and the meaning of the universe. The accounts of creation in Genesis 1 and 2 tell us about the beginning of all things, and they also tell us about relationships between things. How things were meant to relate is closely tied to their purpose. These relationships, which were later confused by sin, are at the heart of the gospel by which God is restoring all things to their proper relationships.

The biblical accounts of creation are tantalizing for modern-minded people because they refuse to address the questions we want answered. How can I know there is a God? Where did God come from? What was before the beginning, and can we even contemplate a beginning? How can God create out of nothing? What is the meaning of eternity? And so on. We must be content with trying to understand what the Bible is saying to us. Our chief source is Genesis 1 and 2, although many other passages in the Bible address the subject of creation.

What does the Bible mean when it says that God created by his word? The New Testament makes several references to this: John 1:3; Colossians 1:16; Hebrews 11:3; 2 Peter 3:5-7. These texts are important for our understanding of the Old Testament teaching. But it is still important for us to examine the Old Testament texts in their original Israelite contexts. We do not know who first possessed the revelation of God about creation. There is much argument about when Genesis 1—2 was written in the form that we now have it. Even if these texts are, as most conservative estimates put them, from Moses, then they still enter the stream of Israelite thought a long way down the track of biblical history. I mention this not to stir up a lot of doubts about the trustworthiness of these accounts but on the contrary, to point to the consciousness in Israel of the absolute sovereignty of God and his word. *Sovereignty* means exercising kingly power. We use the word in relation to God meaning that there is absolutely nothing that he does not control. Creation is a demonstration of this sovereignty.

God had no beginning, but the universe did. Therefore it was made from nothing, a fact that is often expressed by the Latin words *ex nihilo* (from nothing). The greatness of God is shown by his needing only to say, "Let there be . . ." for things to be brought into existence. Nothing compelled him to create for there was no one or nothing to compel him. Nor was he compelled by something within himself such as loneliness. His sovereignty in creation means his absolute freedom. Absolute sovereignty and absolute freedom are qualities beyond our comprehension because we can never experience them. Nevertheless, we have to accept them as facts concerning God and learn to recognize them in his works and words.

Creation by God's word also has the effect of showing that God has chosen to relate to all things by his word. This truth cannot be over-emphasized. The supremacy of the word of God in the world goes back to creation. All creatures must bow to his word. The rule of God over creation through his word points to the real distinction between God and the creation. Some modern ideas lean heavily on eastern religions that teach that there is no real distinction between God and creation. God is thought of as everything and everything as God. But the Bible teaches that God is distinct from and beyond everything that has been made and that exists in the universe. The word used to describe this is *transcendence*. The recent fad based on Hinduism known as transcendental meditation is in fact a denial that there is a transcendent being or God.

■ *God the Lord*
chooses to relate to his creation by means of his word.

THE WORD AND ESTABLISHED ORDER

Why does Genesis 1 describe creation having taken place in six days? Different answers have been given to that question, ranging from "because that's the way it literally happened," to "because such an artificial arrangement is an aid to memorizing the details." It is true that the Hebrew word for day *(yom)* is used throughout the Old Testament for the normal day as we know it. But it is also true that it is used for longer unspecified periods of time. This is not the place to enter into that discussion, particularly as it touches on the creation-evolution debate.

Two comments, however, can be made. First, the passage is unique and thus presents some difficulties in interpretation. The possibilities are far more numerous than a simple choice between strictly literalistic history (usually taken to mean creation in six periods of twenty-four hours), and non-historical myth (usually taken to mean no relation to historical fact). It is clear that the New Testament texts quoted above (Jn 1:3; Heb 11:3; 2 Pet 3:5-7) understand creation as a historical event.

Second, when we face such ambiguities, that is, when more than one possible way exists of understanding something in the Bible, the gospel must instruct us since it is God's final and fullest word to man. It is clear from the gospel that God created all things for a purpose, and that he exercises his rule over creation by his word. It is not at all clear from the gospel that the creation took place in six twenty-four hour periods. Nor is it clear from the gospel that it did not happen in that way. The question is not whether the Bible tells the truth, but how it tells it.

Out of both accounts of creation (Gen 1 and Gen 2) we may draw a number of truths which are essential to the biblical message. Creation is not only a question of beginnings, but of purpose and relationships. The two accounts provide different perspectives on the one reality, which is a creation in which there is perfect harmony. By harmony we mean that there is no conflict in the creation between its various parts. The biblical accounts constantly challenge our tendency to assume that the meanings of certain qualities such as harmony, goodness and the like, are self-evident. The Genesis accounts tell that there is a structure to the creation which is described first in terms of the main elements of the universe and their relationships (Gen 1), and second in terms of human beings and their relationships (Gen 2). In the first account there is a progressive affirmation by God of the goodness of creation (Gen 1:10, 12, 18, 21, 25). Finally God declares the entire creation to be "very good" (Gen 1:31). There is no suggestion of a self-evident standard of goodness and harmony outside of God to which he conformed his creation. God, who is the source of both, must define them by setting forth an arrangement that is the expression of his goodness and harmony.

Thus, the good order of the universe is good because God declares it to be so. Order means that there is a proper function for everything and a proper relationship that it bears to everything else. Order also means rank. The Creator is Lord over all and exercises that lordship by his word. Next to God is humanity, which is given a secondary lordship over the rest of creation. Thus, goodness and harmony are expressions that can be defined only by God as he established relationships between himself and everything he made.

Later, when Israel came to understand goodness in the light of God's revelation of his saving grace, the creation narratives would remind her that God is the only source of goodness and the one by whom it is defined. This revelation would also be a witness to the fact that the disruptions in relationships, which are so evident in biblical history, were not original to the order of things and do not characterize the God who created all things good.

God not only creates the universe but he governs it. This *providence*, or the continuing government of the universe by the Creator, becomes a prominent feature of the biblical understanding of the ultimate purpose of God which nothing, not even sin, is allowed to frustrate. By setting up the relationships of all things in creation and designating their functions, God upholds the order. Sun, moon and stars will regulate day and night and the seasons of the year (Gen 1:14-19). Plants and animals will propagate according to their species (Gen 1:11-13, 24-25). Human existence somehow images God and is characterized by dominion over the rest of creation (Gen 1:26-30). Human life is defined by its God-given freedom and by bounds and sanctions. Only a God who is constantly involved in ruling the universe can warn against rejection of his rule by saying, "In the day that you eat of it you shall die" (Gen 2:15-17).

■ *By his word*
God established all things in ordered relationships.

■ *By his word*
God continues to uphold order in the universe.

GOD LOVES HIS CREATION

The creation accounts do not argue for the existence of God or try to explain how he can be eternally there. Being the only one who is eternally there means that only he can tell us that he is. That is why his Word cannot be tested or proven; it must be self-evident as his Word. In the same way, the creation is self-evidently his creation. The Word of God and the creation establish in the only possible way that God exists. Now, you might suppose from this that when a non-Christian asks, "How can I know that God exists?" all you need to say is, "His Word and his creation prove it." It is an accurate reply, but it will not convince a non-Christian, for reasons we must leave until the next chapter.

The self-evident Creator, then, has made all things and established them in a fixed order of relationships that he declared to be very good. How can we understand the meaning of these words: "and behold it was very good"? They are words written within and to Israel which belong to a world that goes on existing and hearing of the love of God *after* sin enters the world. Within this wider context, the free act of creation and God's approval indicated by the words "very good," point to a loving and immensely strong commitment on God's part towards his creation. In the immediate context of Genesis 1 the words do not necessarily imply God's loving commitment and intention of permanence, but they are consistent with these facts as they emerge later in the biblical records. All that the Bible says about God's commitment to his creation and to his people proceeds from the opening announcement: "In the beginning God created the heavens and the earth."

It does not take much imagination to realize that the God who creates is also the God who rules. The *kingdom of God* is a name that is not used in the

Bible until much later, but the idea of it immediately comes to mind as we think of creation. This free act of God and his continuing rule over all creation, his sovereignty, establish the vital fact of biblical theology which I referred to earlier in this chapter: God is distinct from his creation. We must never think of ourselves or of nature as part of God. Nor is God a part of "nature" or its processes. Therefore, he is not bound to those observed regularities in the order of things that we refer to as the laws of nature. It is this distinction between the Creator and the creation, over which he has complete control, that underlies miracles.

How may we describe the kingdom of God as it has been revealed up to this point in Scripture? God's rule involves the relationships that he has set up between himself and everything in creation. In other words, God makes the rules for all existence. Both accounts of creation show mankind as the center of God's attention and the recipient of a unique relationship with him. Thus the focus of the kingdom of God is on the relationship between God and his people. Man is subject to God, while the rest of creation is subject to man and exists for his benefit. The kingdom means God ruling over his people in the material universe. This basic understanding of the kingdom is never changed in Scripture.

■ *The goodness of creation:*
In the universe he has made for them, God rules over his people in continual and loving self-commitment to the whole creation. This is the kingdom of God.

MAN MADE IN GOD'S IMAGE

There are only three references in the Old Testament to man being created in the image of God: Genesis 1:26, 27; 9:6. None of these really tell us what it means. The first links the image (Hebrew: *tselem*) to likeness (Hebrew: *demuth*), and then to man's dominion over creation. The second links it to creation of man as male and female. In neither case can we say that there is any intention to define what it means to be made in God's image. The third reference gives creation in the image of God as the reason for making murder a capital offense.

If there are so few references to creation in the image of God we might think that it is not a very significant idea. But it would be safer to conclude that what is meant by the image of God is spoken of in other ways in Scripture. The Bible presents man as having a special dignity before God. The image of God is one way of referring to this. We can certainly say that the image points to the uniqueness of human beings, which consists at least in a special relationship to God. Being in the likeness of God (Gen 1:26) is another way of saying being in God's image, and does not refer to a quality which is distinct from the image. Dominion is not the definition of the image, but is probably a consequence of it. If human sexuality (Gen 1:27) is related to the image, it must be at a level not shared by the other creatures which also have a physical sexuality.

The image of God in man, then, shows that it belongs to the dignity of man to be next to God in the order of things (Ps 8:5). Although God commits himself to the whole of his creation for its good order and preservation, humanity is the special focus of this care. Creation is there for our benefit. Humanity is the representative of the whole creation so that God deals with creation on the basis of how he deals with humans. Only man is addressed as one who knows God and who is created to live purposefully for God. When man falls because of sin the creation is made to fall with him. In order to restore the whole of creation, God works through his Son who becomes a man to restore man. The whole creation waits eagerly for the redeemed people of God to be finally revealed as God's perfected children, because at that point the creation will be released from its own bondage (Rom 8:19-23). This overview of man as the object of God's covenant love and redemption confirms the central significance given to man in Genesis 1—2.

■ *The image of God in man:*
Mankind is created in a unique relationship to God. Man also is addressed personally by God as the highest creation and the focus of his purposes.

MAN A CREATURE WHO IS RULED

Modern man thinks of himself as being in charge. He sets his own pace, makes his own rules and thanks no one but himself for progress and life's benefits. The biblical doctrine of creation challenges all of this. Everything we are and have is God's gift. The uniqueness of the human race lies not in our having developed more or survived better, but in being created in God's image. The human race is the creature of God and this fact cannot be changed by denying or ignoring it. As creatures of God we are totally dependent upon him for everything. We are dependent not only on the continual rule or providence of God in nature for the production of food and other goods, but also for every moment of our existence. We draw the next breath, our hearts beat the next beat, we are conscious of the next moment of our existence only because God goes on sustaining the very substance of creation. There are no laws of nature that are self-sustaining. If God were to withdraw for a split second his powerful word, the universe would cease to exist in that same split second. That is why man does not live by bread alone, but by every word that comes from the mouth of God (Deut 8:3; see also Ps 104:24-30). So Christ, as the creative Word of God, sustains "all things by his powerful word" (Heb 1:3), and "in him all things hold together" (Col 1:17).

But what is man? We go on asking that question as the psalmist did in Psalm 8. People answer it in a variety of ways. The atheistic evolutionist sees man as the most complex development of life form due to a combination of time plus chance. The theistic or Christian evolutionist sees man as the result of time plus the continual intervention of God in the evolutionary process. Others concentrate on the description of some aspect of man such as his physical structure, his psychological processes or his social relationships.

The creation accounts teach us that no attempt to define human beings is adequate unless it at least includes the recognition of our creation in the image of God. Even though we hesitate to define what it means, the fact of the image of God tells us that humanity does not truly exist apart from a special relationship with God. All attempts to say what it means to be human must fail when they leave God out of the reckoning. Furthermore, it belongs to the God-man relationship that man is told what his functions are (Gen 1:26-28). Our human sexuality is to be understood in terms of this relationship, as is the dominion that we exercise over creation. The human search for knowledge and technology, and indeed our whole cultural development, are tasks assigned to us by God.

Man is uniquely responsible to God. Responsibility means being answerable to someone for what we do. We have weakened the meaning of the word by making it refer to a quality that people have in varying degrees. But the person who we might describe as irresponsible and the one we regard as responsible are equally answerable to God. We are made responsible to God whether we like it or not, and we have no choice in the matter.

At the heart of human responsibility lies freedom. The meaning of freedom is defined in the creation narratives. In Genesis 1:28 it is implied that we are created to make real choices between real options, even though this freedom is bound by the prescription to be fruitful and rule the earth. Without the freedom to make real choices it would be impossible to rule. In recognition of this, most English versions of the Bible translate Genesis 2:16 as permission to "freely eat" of all the trees in the garden. There is no "freely" in the Hebrew text which, in fact, uses the same construction here that is used in verse 17, "you will surely die." In the context we see that Adam and Eve have the freedom to choose what to eat from all the trees, but they have no freedom as to the consequences if they eat of the one forbidden tree.

Thus, with freedom and responsibility comes a test of obedience in the prohibition placed on eating from the tree of the knowledge of good and evil. Nothing in the text suggests that the fruit of this tree (which is never referred to as an apple tree!) has some magical quality which will produce the knowledge of good and evil in anyone who eats it. This would be completely out of character for biblical literature. It is more likely that God designates the tree as off limits as the means of showing the difference between good and evil. The choice for Adam and Eve was not between ignorance and the knowledge of good and evil, but between remaining good and becoming evil themselves. The nature of the test was such that whatever choice they made they would know both good and evil. They were moral beings who would know right and wrong through their personal response to God. God is not a force or some other impersonal power. No matter how hard it is for us to conceive of God as person without at the same time reducing him to a superhuman being, the Bible consistently refers to him in personal terms. He is the source of our personhood.

■ *The rule of God*
and the image of God in mankind mean that we are uniquely answerable to God for all that we do.

THE PATTERN OF THE KINGDOM

The generation, or creation, of the heavens and the earth, of the whole universe and everything in it, centers on the people of God in the place where they are put to live under the loving guidance and rule of God. Adam and Eve living before God in the Garden of Eden provide us with the pattern of the kingdom of God. All the essential relationships that structure the universe are set out in these creation accounts. In this twentieth century, characterized as it is by enormous strides made through science and technology, we cannot look to new principles as if these biblical ones are out of date. Science can enable us to view more of the details of only some of the relationships established in creation.

When Adam named the animals he began the process of observation, classification and description which is the heart of scientific knowledge. But he could never deduce his own relationship to God or even to the world purely by observation. Rather it was the word of God that came to Adam to tell him how he related to God and to the world. It is the word of God which informs man that he is to be a scientist and loving caretaker of the world rather than a magician and power-motivated exploiter of the world. Creation means that true science or knowledge needs God's revelation in his word to give it direction, and to prevent it from entering the realm of superstition and magic. Creation reminds us that modern theories which suggest that life, personhood, love and moral value are all the result of chance, have long since abandoned the realm of real science.

The pattern of the kingdom of God is this: God establishes a perfect creation that he loves and over which he rules. The highest honor is given to mankind as the only part of creation made in God's image. The kingdom means that everything in creation relates perfectly, that is, as God intends it should, to everything else and to God himself.

■ *The kingdom of God at creation*
was everything in existence: God, mankind, and the rest of creation, all relating perfectly as God intended.

CREATION (GENERATION) OF THE KINGDOM OF GOD

SUMMARY   Creation results in the kingdom as God, mankind and the rest of creation all relating perfectly.

KINGDOM	GOD	MANKIND	WORLD
CREATION	GOD	ADAM AND EVE	EDEN

MAIN THEMES   Sovereignty of God

Creation *ex nihilo* (out of nothing) by the word of God

Order and goodness of creation

Image of God in man

Responsibility of man before God

SOME KEY WORDS   Creation/generation

Sovereignty

Image

Kingdom

THE PATH AHEAD   Adam—Last Adam, 1 Corinthians 15:45

Creation—New creation, 2 Corinthians 5:17

Heavens and earth—New heavens and earth, Isaiah 65:17; 2 Peter 3:13; Revelation 21:1

Note: The diagram above represents the kingdom as God, the people of God, and the rest of creation, all relating as God intends. At the end of each subsequent chapter this diagram will be added to according to the revelation of the kingdom at each stage in salvation history. Thus we will observe the progression from creation to new creation in Christ. The diagram represents the ideal which is revealed, though because of sin the historical experience never matches this ideal until we reach the person of Christ.

STUDY GUIDE TO CHAPTER 9

1. Read Genesis 1—2. List the things mentioned which seem to you to be most important in the teaching of these chapters.

2. God created by his word. He spoke to man before man spoke to him or understood himself. How does this help us to understand the authority of God's Word for us today?

3. List some of the reasons why Christians should not neglect the biblical teaching that God is the Creator of all things.

FURTHER READING

1. *BT*, chap. 3.
2. James Houston, *I Believe in the Creator* (London: Hodder & Stoughton, 1979).
3. E. J. Young, *In the Beginning* (Edinburgh: Banner of Truth, 1976).
4. Alan Hayward, *Creation and Evolution* (London: Triangle, 1985).
5. Dietrich Bonhoeffer, *Creation and Fall* (London: SCM Press, 1959), chaps. 1-2.
6. Howard J. Van Till, *The Fourth Day* (Grand Rapids, Mich.: Eerdmans, 1986).

10

THE FALL

The devil said to him, "If you are the Son of God, tell this stone to become bread." Jesus answered, "It is written: 'Man does not live on bread alone.'" (Lk 4:3-4)

But we have one who has been tempted in every way, just as we are—yet was without sin. (Heb 4:15)

OUTLINE OF BIBLICAL HISTORY, GENESIS 3
The snake persuaded Eve to disobey God and to eat the forbidden fruit. She gave some to Adam and he ate also. Then God spoke to them in judgment, and sent them out of the garden into a world that came under the same judgment.

TEMPTATION

Genesis 3 also leaves us with many unanswered questions. Why a snake as the tempter of mankind? Where did evil begin? In the book of Revelation the snake is equated with the devil (Rev 12:9; 20:2), but this does not tell us the origin of evil, and it is doubtful that the Bible ever gives us a clue to the problem. It is sometimes suggested that Isaiah 14:12-15 is about Satan's rebellion against God in the heavenly places before his assault on Eden, but the passage is actually describing an ancient king of Babylon (verse 4). Nowhere are we told why Satan became evil or why the snake should represent him in the Garden of Eden. However, the Bible does not allow a *dualism* of good and evil in which the forces of good have been eternally in conflict with the forces of evil.

The conversation between the snake and the woman brilliantly portrays the process by which the human race became rebellious against the authority of the Creator. Opinions differ greatly as to the exact nature of this account. Some regard it as absolutely literal history, others see it as a symbolic account of something that actually happened in history, still others see it as a kind of myth or allegory of the ever-present problem of evil in our human condition. The temptation story, like the creation accounts, is an unusual piece of literature and unique in the Bible. How we should handle and understand this passage is by no means clear when we treat it on its own. That is why the gospel and the overall message of the Bible must guide us when we deal with it. There are certain elements of New Testament teaching which see the person and work of Jesus Christ as answering the temptation and fall of mankind as recorded in Genesis 3. In those terms the gospel makes sense only if there was a real temptation and fall which radically altered the course of human nature and the history of mankind thereafter. We must assert that there really was one man, Adam, through whom sin and death entered the world, as Paul says in Romans 5:12.

Let's return, then, to the snake and the woman. The crafty creature begins by raising a religious question, "Did God really say . . . ?" The possibility of discussing God and the truth of his word had not occurred to the woman up to this point. The humans existed in God's creation and depended on God's word for the true interpretation of reality. In chapter three I have considered this question as it relates to how we can know the truth, so I will not repeat the discussion here. However, it is important to recognize that if God is the creator of everything, he is also the source of all truth. There is no truth apart from his truth, which he communicates to us by his Word. God is the final and absolute authority and, since he has chosen to communicate by his Word, his Word has absolute and final authority. The religious question has great potential for evil because it casts doubt on the authority of God's Word.

So the snake raises the first question: "Did God really say 'You must not eat from any tree in the garden'?" The snake knew, and Eve knew, that God had not said that at all. Only the fruit of one tree was forbidden. Eve corrects the statement but in so doing permits the word of God to become for her a matter of questioning. Doubt was being cast on the credentials of the word. The assumption was being formed that the word not only could be analyzed and evaluated, but probably needed to be. But on what basis could Eve evaluate God's word? Any standard for testing the truth of God's word would have to be the word of an even greater authority than God, which is impossible.

The next statement of the snake actually contradicts the word of God: "You will not surely die." The challenge to the authority of God is now direct. God did not tell the truth when he said, "When you eat of it you will surely die" (Gen 2:17). It was, charges the snake, a deliberate lie: "For God

knows that when you eat of it your eyes will be opened, and you will be like
God, knowing good and evil" (Gen 3:5). Thus God is accused of being motivated by selfishness. This means that he is neither loving nor trustworthy.

■ *The temptation:*
Satan's suggestion that God's word could not be relied upon as the absolute au-
thority and source of truth for mankind.

FALL

The cunning of the snake is seen again in that he presents his lies in the
context of truth. Eating the forbidden fruit did indeed mean that the humans came to know good and evil (Gen 3:22). But the process by which
they achieved that involved a rebellion against truth and its source. Instead of knowing good and evil by rejecting evil and remaining good, they
choose rather to reject good and become evil. The most important effect of
this is that God is no longer regarded as the self-evident Creator and Lord.
His Word is no longer accepted as self-evident truth, but is reduced to the
status of the word of the creature. Both God and his Word are seen as lesser
authorities that must constantly be tested by higher authorities. Again the
cunning of the snake: he does not suggest that the humans transfer their
allegiance from God to himself, but only that they themselves should consider and evaluate God's claim to truth. The final effect was the same as if
they had installed Satan as Lord, but it is achieved without the humans re-
alizing it. They rebel against God not by consciously making Satan their
new final authority, but by taking that function to themselves. The truth of
any proposition would from this point onward be tested by what was in
humans themselves. In this sense they became as God.

So the woman does the unthinkable. She decides that God can't be trust-
ed. She takes some of the forbidden fruit and eats it, and then gives some to
the man who likewise eats it. By what process we cannot know, but this act
of disobedience results in their eyes being opened to their own nakedness.

Their first reaction is to cover their nakedness (Gen 3:7). But why?
Worldly wise people today express their rebellion against God by exhibit-
ing their nakedness and flaunting their sexuality. Fornication and adultery
were not problems for Adam and Eve since they were legitimate sexual
partners. Yet the sense of shame is portrayed as the first effect of sin against

God. The shame is again seen as Adam expresses his nakedness as a cause for fear before God (Gen 3:10). Is this the first stirring of conscience, the conflict between the harmony of God's image and the discord of sin? Is it that rebellion against the Creator means a denial of creatureliness in which sexuality is the reminder that we cannot create but only procreate? Just as the presence of God in the garden displays the very thing they denied, their limited existence and being, so sexuality reminds them of their interdependence and challenges their assumptions of independence and Godlikeness. Clumsily they try to cover up, but they will learn that conscience cannot be so easily dulled. Nor is the all-seeing eye of God deceived.

The fall was a giant leap upward that went horribly wrong because it simply could not succeed. Dissatisfied with their humanness, the couple reached for godhood. In lusting after a throne that was not theirs they lost the privileges they already had. They degraded themselves by trying to become what they could never be. The result was not the "humanness" to which mankind has always appealed in order to excuse its lesser sins. It was rather a condition that is less than human because it no longer consists primarily in a relationship with God that is characterized by love and trust.

■ *The fall:*
The rebellion of the whole human race against God through the historic act of our first parents. Their disobedience was a failed attempt to become as God.

JUDGMENT

When confronted by God the man blames the woman and she in turn blames the snake (Gen 3:12-13). Both thereby blame God. Adam accuses the woman whom God gave to him as a companion and for whom God is thus responsible. Eve blames the snake who is one of God's creatures and for whom God is also responsible. But it is the humans who are responsible for what they have done. Their first and most damaging crime is to reject the authority of God's Word.

Genesis 3:14-24 is about God's judgment upon the disobedience of mankind. The nature of the narrative is not without difficulties as to the meaning of some of the details. What, for example, is the significance of the cursing of the snake? God does not question the snake perhaps, as one commentator suggests, because as an animal it can have no responsibility for sin, while Satan has no hope of pardon. The snake is cursed, but it cannot be suggested that the temptation in Eden was the original sin of Satan that brought God's judgment upon him. It is possible that the snake's lowly, legless, dust-crawling form symbolizes the curse upon creation. The text says he is cursed "above all" creatures, that is, he is cursed more than the others. All creatures somehow come under the curse, but the snake as Satan's agent will express it more vividly.

Genesis 3:15 is sometimes referred to as the *protevangelium*, the first hint of the gospel. This is because the enmity between the snake's offspring and the woman's offspring foreshadows the conflict between Christ and Satan. The New Testament gives only the briefest support for this in the reference to God crushing Satan under the feet of Christians (Rom 16:20). It is possible that God's Son being born of a woman also recalls this prediction (Gal 4:4). The word of curse on the snake implies grace to the human race and a recovery from the fall.

The judgment on the woman (Gen 3:16) introduces pain as a reality of the fallen world. It is not simply that physical pain becomes our lot, but there is also a disruption of the most intimate human relationship; that of a man and a woman in marriage. Passion and power will characterize the instincts of fallen man, and the pleasure of sexual relationships will be accompanied by pain and sorrow.

God's judgment on the man is the most comprehensive (Gen 3:17-24). In creation he (and Eve) had been given dominion over the earth and all other creatures. Now this dominion is challenged on every hand by the earth itself. The rebel against legitimate rule receives some of his own medicine and experiences rebellion against his own legitimate rule. The curse on the ground is in fact a curse on Adam. The king of the earth has now no obedient servant in the soil. The freedom to eat of all the trees in the garden is replaced by the struggle to get the earth to yield the necessary daily bread. Weeds flourish where food-yielding plants grow with difficulty. The end of man is to nourish the earth by returning to the dust from whence he came.

Finally, there is the loss of paradise. The picture of the fall and judgment is completed as the human race is removed from the place in which life is truly life. Hereafter what humans call life is existence in the midst of death. The narrative does not resort to a distinction between physical and spiritual death. If God says, "When you eat of it you will surely die," then what is described here is death. To live is to live in fellowship with God. When that fellowship is broken by rebellion, the sentence of death is executed. Yet it is not immediate destruction. The human race, though dead, continues, multiplies and goes on in some way bearing the image of God. The grace of God allows the dead race to exist so that some greater purpose might be fulfilled in it. Meanwhile, each individual of the race of Adam looks forward to the inevitable and final experience of death. This continuance of the race rather than immediate obliteration foreshadows the amazing fact that in the goodness of God humanity is here to stay.

■ *The judgment:*
The original sin of mankind brings the sentence of death. Fellowship with God is broken, dominion is challenged, and humans face an inevitable demise. Yet alongside of judgment the grace of God operates for the good of the human race.

HUMAN CONFLICT

The narrative does not tell us how Adam and Eve perceived their fallen condition. Outside Eden we have only two statements attributed to Eve which are expressions of faith (Gen 4:1, 25). Genesis 4 illustrates human sinfulness and what its logical outcome is in human relationships. Cain refuses God's verdict in which his offering is rejected and his brother's accepted. He responds with anger directed at Abel and kills him. Human conflict is thus shown to be the consequence of broken fellowship with God. There is anger at the grace of God when it is shown to another. The acceptance of Abel's offering is not explained and any attempt we make to do so is liable to obscure the *sovereignty of grace*: God has mercy on whom he pleases to have mercy. The fact that Abel made his offering "by faith" (Heb 11:4) does not remove the reality of grace.

The grace shown to Abel is representative of the kindness of God that will be shown to men and women down the ages. It provokes Cain to anger and thus demonstrates its effect of bringing about an actual distinction between those who receive it and those who don't. This distinction is an essential and continuing part of revelation throughout the biblical story. Yet the sovereignty of grace should not be misread as a cruel fatalism. The first murderer receives a judgment that is similar to the judgment on Adam (Gen 4:11-12). The earth will resist him and he is banished from his

familiar territory. There is also mercy, for God places a mark on him to pro-
tect him from the vengeance of men (Gen 4:15) even though he has forfeit-
ed all claim to such protection. There is a grace that operates for the
unrepentant in order to preserve the human race.

Cain's descendants are marked by a further retreat from God. Cain
builds a city in an attempt, it would seem, to find safety from those who
would kill him. Cities come to figure prominently in the Bible as the expression of human wickedness. Babel, Sodom and Gomorrah, the cities of
Egypt and Canaan, and finally Babylon and Rome all represent concentra-
tions of human godlessness. It is not human society in itself that is wrong,
but the use of it to escape the implications of God's claim to rule. There is
a city of God, Jerusalem or Zion, but it becomes the city in which the Son
of God is condemned to death. Only the heavenly Jerusalem, whose builder and maker is God, brings human society into perfect relationship with
the rule of God.

Cain's descendants are noted for the domestication of animals, for art
and music, and for violence (Gen 4:17-24). In this is the evidence of God's
goodness or common grace continuing in a world of godless people, and
alongside increasing displays of wickedness. Society, domestication of animals and the arts are not inherently evil but each has a great potential for
evil as some of our modern social and environmental problems show. By
the grace of God human society continues, but within it are the seeds of
self-destruction in the breakdown of human relationships. This grace is
the gift of the preservation of the race for a time, but it is not grace that acts
to redeem and to restore a people to friendship with God.

■ *Human relationships*
break down as a direct result of the break in the relationship between God and
mankind. All human conflict reflects our conflict with God.

THE WICKEDNESS OF MANKIND

Genesis 6 depicts a climax in human wickedness. The sons of God began
to marry the daughters of men, and this brings a response of judgment
from God (Gen 6:1-4). This short section is difficult both to translate (compare verse 3 in RSV and NIV) and to interpret (Who are the sons of God and
the daughters of men?). The 120 years granted to men could mean a reduc-

tion in the hitherto enormous lifespan—Methuselah's 969 years or La-
mech's 777 years—or it could refer to the time left before the destruction
of society in the flood.

Things really look bad for humanity when God is said to be grieved
by the fact that he had ever made people on the earth (Gen 6:5-7). This
suggests that whatever was involved in the intermarriage of the sons of
God and the daughters of men, it was the last straw for God in the increasing wickedness in the world. The following judgment in the form of
the great flood is also difficult. I am not referring here to the historical
problems that are often argued, such as how widespread the flood was
and what geological records it left. But rather what is the theological significance of the flood? Death is already a reality as a judgment upon sin.
God clearly is not using the flood to show that he is withdrawing his
grace, for Noah finds grace before God both for the preservation of the
race and for the salvation of a people for God. Nor does the flood solve
the problem of human wickedness, as the subsequent history of the human race will show.

When death and destruction at the hand of God are recorded in the Bible they cause many people to react with a sense of moral outrage. Such
judgments must be seen for what they are, for the Bible consistently represents them as the expressions of God's righteousness. Judgements are always deserved by those who suffer them. God's judgment in the flood was
an expression of his righteousness within which the grace of God is seen
working to rescue an undeserving but chosen group of people. The flood
did not purge the earth of wickedness and we cannot suppose that such
was its purpose. It was one of many judgments which occur in human history foreshadowing the final fate of rebellious mankind, and in the light of
which the nature of salvation can be understood. Throughout the Bible salvation and judgment are inseparable and complementary aspects of the
action of God in bringing in his kingdom.

■ *God's judgment*
*continued to be shown after the first sentence of death and ejection from Eden.
Judgments in biblical history foreshadow final judgment, and show the situation from which God saves us.*

FALL (DEGENERATION) OF CREATION

SUMMARY   Mankind's rebellion against God results in
                       the fall of the whole created order from its
                       place in the kingdom of God.

KINGDOM	GOD	MANKIND	WORLD
CREATION	GOD	ADAM AND EVE	EDEN
FALL			

MAIN THEMES   Temptation

                       Disobedience

                       Mankind becomes self-centered
                          instead of God-centered

                       Judgment and death

                       Dislocation of all relationships in creation

                       Grace of God

SOME KEY WORDS   Fall

                       Judgment

                       Death

                       Grace

THE PATH AHEAD   Temptation of Adam—temptation of Israel—
                          temptation of Christ, Luke 4:1-12

                       Snake—Satan, Revelation 12:9

                       Eden lost—Eden regained, Deuteronomy 8:7-9;

                       Ezekiel 47:1-12; Revelation 22:1-6

                       Judgment—Final judgment, Matthew 7:15-23;
                          Revelation 20:11-15

THE KINGDOM AND THE FALL

God's ultimate purpose for his kingdom means that he will not withdraw his love from the fallen universe. However, the sin of mankind has resulted in the confusion of all relationships between God and the creation, and within the creation. God is still sovereign, and even human rebellion can never thwart his purpose. But this sovereign rule of God in a fallen universe needs to be distinguished from the kingdom of God. The kingdom is God's rule over his people in a realm in which all relationships are perfect. The fallen universe is the very opposite of the kingdom. Only through salvation will the kingdom be restored, for salvation is God bringing all things back to their right relationships. It is the task of biblical theology to describe the way the Bible reveals this restoration as taking place.

■ *The rebellion of mankind*
caused all relationships of the kingdom of God to be dislocated. God, mankind and the rest of creation no longer relate in the perfect way that God intended.

STUDY GUIDE TO CHAPTER 10

1. Read Genesis 3 and note the stages by which the snake entices the humans to become rebels against God.

2. In what ways is our humanness lost in the fall?

3. How did the fall affect the harmony of relationships that existed from creation?

4. How does the grace of God show itself alongside of his judgment?

FURTHER READING

1. *BT*, chap. 3.
2. Dietrich Bonhoeffer, *Creation and Fall* (London: SCM Press 1959), chaps. 3-4.
3. E. J. Young, *Genesis 3* (London: Banner of Truth, 1966).
4. O. Palmer Robertson, *The Christ of the Covenants* (Phillipsburg, N.J.: Presbyterian & Reformed, 1980).

11

FIRST REVELATION
OF REDEMPTION

As it was in the days of Noah, so it will be at the coming of the Son of Man. (Mt 24:37)

By his faith he [Noah] condemned the world and became heir of the righteousness that comes by faith. (Heb 11:7)

OUTLINE OF BIBLICAL HISTORY, GENESIS 4—11
Outside Eden, Cain and Abel were born to Adam and Eve. Cain murdered Abel and Eve bore another son, Seth. Eventually the human race became so wicked that God determined to destroy every living thing with a flood. Noah and his family were saved by building a great boat at God's command. The human race began again with Noah and his three sons with their families. Sometime after the flood a still unified human race attempted a godless act to assert its power in the building of a high tower. God thwarted these plans by scattering the people and confusing their language.

GOD'S COMMITMENT

The background to God's work of rescuing sinners is his commitment to his creation. There is no hint in Scripture that God created the universe on a trial basis, or with a view to scrapping it after a period of time. When God saw that everything was very good (Gen 1:31), he approved of all he had made and set his love upon it. The strength of God's commitment becomes clearer as the narrative progresses. Mankind's rebellion brings judgment but not instant destruction. God preserves order in the universe and in human society, and at the same time begins to reveal his purposes to overcome the effects of human sin.

In Eden there were two trees referred to as being in the middle of the garden: the tree of life and the tree of the knowledge of good and evil. The humans were prohibited only from eating the fruit of the tree of the knowledge of good and evil. We must assume that the tree of life was

open to them, and that it symbolizes the gift of eternal life. Had they refused the tempter, their obedience to God would have been symbolized
by partaking of the tree of life. Once they learn good and evil through
disobedience, they cannot be permitted to enjoy the fruit of the tree of
life and are sent out of the garden. Yet the tree remains and, though not
a prominent theme in the Bible, it will recur as a symbol of eternal life
for those who are redeemed (Rev 2:7). God judges sinners by denying
them eternal life. But this also shows the mercy of God in that the kingdom of God will require all rebellion to be eradicated. The very act of
judgment is a sign of God's commitment to humankind that, although
we are not yet told how, there will be a race of people who live for ever
as friends of God.

After the death of Abel at the hands of Cain, Adam and Eve have another son, named Seth (Gen 4:24). Eve recognizes that God has given them another son in the place of Abel. He is not simply a replacement because they
are numerically down one son. Rather Seth stands in the place of righteous
Abel as a witness to the goodness of God at work in the human race. He is
the head of a new line of people through which the blessings of God will
come to the world. At that time people begin to call on the name of the
Lord (Gen 4:26). Both Cain and Abel, the first generation of outside-Eden
people, sacrifice to God, and this shows that judgment has not removed
from them the sense of the reality of God and the need to relate to him. The
Sethites now begin to worship God by calling on his name. To call on
God's name means to express trust and confidence in the God who has revealed his character. In the time of the prophets it means to believe God for
salvation (Joel 2:32).

This godly, though still sinful, line of Seth's descendants is described in
Genesis 5 as the legitimate descendants of Adam. It seems that the writer
of this account has chosen and arranged his material in order to impress
upon us the theological significance of the line. There is a direct link from
Adam through Seth to Noah, and this whole line contrasts with the godless line of Cain in Genesis 4.

■ *God's commitment to creation*
is seen in the preservation of mankind, and the establishment of a line of people
which is the object of God's special redeeming love.

NOAH AND THE COVENANT

Two important words are used for the first time in the Noah narrative (Gen 6—9). These are *grace* and *covenant*. While mankind, because of its wickedness, provokes God's anger, Noah finds grace in God's eyes (Gen 6:8). This man is righteous and blameless, and he walks with God. In other words, he lives by faith in the word of God however it should come to him. When it comes with a specific command to build the ark, Noah obeys even though there is no reason open to him why such an enormous boat should be needed. When the reason does appear, he and his family are saved from the devastation of the flood. Grace is not clearly explained here. The Hebrew phrase "Noah found grace in the eyes of the Lord" means nothing more than "God liked him." Here the significance of the phrase lies in what God does for the man whom he likes. He rescues him. Noah's righteousness is simply stated alongside God's grace without any comment about whether it is the cause or effect of God's attitude toward him. Later it will become much clearer that God's grace is the cause of sinful people becoming righteous. Grace then is an attitude of God for the good of those who do not deserve the good.

In telling Noah how to escape the flood God says, "I will establish my covenant with you, and you will enter the ark" (Gen 6:18). This is the first reference to *covenant*, a word that will become a key biblical word used to express the relationship between God and his people. In ordinary life, covenant is a word that can be used to refer to an agreement between persons, which is a binding commitment of all concerned. But we can only grasp the meaning of God's covenant by seeing how it operates and with what effect.

The first reference to covenant, then, involves God's commitment to save Noah and his family from destruction. This salvation does not mean eternal life in itself, but we must say that it certainly points in that direction. Eternal life as it is spoken of in the New Testament is way over the horizon from the Old Testament person's view. The movement from the Old Testament expressions of salvation, which are tied to historical events in this life, towards the full New Testament understanding of eternal life is something our survey of biblical theology will uncover. We are justified in referring to the first covenant statement as a covenant of salvation, even though the fuller meaning of salvation has yet to be revealed.

Noah and his family show their trust in God's word by obeying. They exist in a unique relationship to God along with all the animals on their little floating world. When they disembark into a new world God promises that even though mankind, including Noah, is still inclined to evil, God will never again destroy the world in a flood (Gen 8:21). God calls on Noah to fill the earth and exercise dominion just as he had commanded Adam (Gen 9:1-3). Then comes the second reference to the covenant (Gen 9:8-17), which is God's commitment never to repeat the flood.

In both these covenant statements God makes the first move and establishes a relationship that works for the good of the creation. He calls it "my covenant" each time and, although the details are different, we must say they are different expressions of the one covenant. Furthermore, it is now apparent that the covenant is an expression of the relationship that always existed because of the creation of all things by God. God is refusing to allow human rebellion to divert him from his purpose to create a people to be *his* people in a perfect universe.

■ *God's commitment to creation*
is shown in the covenant with Noah. The restoration of the human race is foreshadowed in the rescue of Noah and his family. This leads to the promise that the earth will also be preserved.

THE DIVISION OF MANKIND

Noah and his family leave the security of the ark and become a new beginning of the human race (Gen 9:19). The narrative relates how Noah lies one day in a drunken stupor, and how his sons react. The result is a new division between people stemming from the blessings and curses that Noah pronounces on his sons. Ham's son Canaan is cursed, and Shem is blessed, while Japheth is to share the blessings of Shem (Gen 9:20-27). There are some difficulties in this passage. The plain meaning of the text is that Noah and his family alone survived the flood, and all the nations of the earth descended from them. The genealogies (family trees) in Genesis 10 are based on the prophetic word of Noah about the three sons. But why is the youngest son of Ham singled out to be cursed for his father's sin? What relationship do these words have to the future of the nations mentioned? At least we can say that the blessing of Shem points to the special place that he and his descendants have in the purpose of God. This purpose is in line with the covenant with Noah.

It is difficult to trace all the actual nations mentioned in the genealogies. The placing of Shem's line last is suggestive of the special significance it has in the purpose of God. This is borne out later in the more detailed genealogy from

Shem to Abram (Gen 11:10-32). Natural descent within a chosen line mingles with the sovereign grace of God, which can and does transcend all natural boundaries throughout the history of redemption. The significance of these divisions will become clearer as that history is unfolded. Irrespective of how these national identities function (Genesis 10 is noncommittal about them), the subsequent mingling of sovereign grace with national election involves three types of people: the chosen covenant people as a nation, others from nonelect nations who surprisingly are included in the national covenant blessings, and those nations which remain outside the covenant. How the gospel qualifies these divisions is something that we shall see later on.

Between the tables of the nations and the detailed genealogy from Shem to Abram we find another difficult passage: the account of the tower of Babel. This is a flashback to a period before the division of the nations and their languages, but how it is supposed to fit historically with the post-flood events recorded in Genesis 9:18-28 is not clear. The narrative (Gen 11:1-9) indicates that the human race had plans for unity and power based on self-interest. Unity in itself is not a bad thing, in fact it is a mark of the people of God when they conform to God's purpose. But unity under God is one thing, and unity as proud independence from God is another. At Babel we see a collective expression of the original attempt of Adam and Eve to displace God from his rightful place as Lord of the universe. In a right relationship to God people need only God's approval to be fulfilled. Sinners are not content to be known by God's name and reach for their own reputation, for fame and renown.

So that this rebellion against God might not exhibit undivided strength, God confounds the unity that the people wish to maintain for their evil ends. We are not told how this is achieved, but theologically it is seen as another statement of God's judgment on the whole human race. Despite the desire for world unity there is an inevitable breakdown of society into smaller units all seeking their own advantage. Sin has a fragmenting effect on human life. This confusion of languages and division of the nations will characterize sinful humanity until the redemptive power of God unites in Christ a people drawn from all nations, tribes and languages (Rev 7:9).

■ *God's covenant*
distinguishes between those who are chosen as the objects of blessing, those who will somehow share this blessing, and those who are under judgment.

THE TWO LINES OF THE HUMAN RACE

As we survey Genesis 4—11 we can see certain key elements that stand out. One of these is the division of mankind into at least two main groups that have quite different relationships to God through his covenant. The covenant continues as God's refusal to allow sin to destroy his purpose to make for himself a people in perfect relationship to himself. This commitment existed before the rebellion of Adam and Eve, and its expression as a covenant of redemption shows that God is ever faithful to his undertakings, even when they are directed toward a people that refuse this love. God's grace is his unceasing loving commitment to a race that has acted in a way that not only does not deserve such love, but actually deserves the very opposite.

Mankind without God is represented in the line of Cain. I say represented, because we have to assume that even the descendants of Seth, except Noah, are numbered amongst the ungodly at the time of the flood. These genealogies are based on natural descent to begin with, but their real nature is to show the discrimination between two types of people, those under grace and those under the curse. On these terms, then, Cain's godless line ends at the flood. But sin is not so easily disposed of. The godly line of Seth, which leads to Noah, survives with one man's family only to divide again so that another godless race emerges in Canaan. Shem's line continues the line of Seth and leads to Terah the father of Abram. Shem is the Hebrew word for *name*, and the godless race seeks for its *shem* by its own efforts (Gen 11:4) only to be frustrated by the judgment of God. This contrasts with the godly line of Shem which shows that we can achieve a name only as the objects of God's saving grace. The only renown that counts is to be known as the people of God who are called by his name.

These first chapters of the Bible establish the fact that God's plans for the rescue of mankind involve an ongoing distinction between those rescued by grace and those lost as a judgment on their sin. The final destiny of people under judgment in the Old Testament is not always clear, but there is nevertheless a constant discrimination that points us towards the New Testament doctrine of election to eternal life. Thus Abel, not Cain, finds favor. Noah and his family are saved while the rest of the human race perishes. Japheth shares the blessings of Shem and Canaan is cursed. Finally, out of the mass of humanity under judgment, one man is singled out, Abram, who is the chosen head of a family through which the redemptive plan of God will be effected.

FIRST PROMISES OF REGENERATION

SUMMARY   Immediately after the fall God begins his work of restoring the whole created order to its right relationship to himself. He acts on the basis of his covenant commitment to creation, and reveals his kingdom by the election of certain people through whom he will work out his purposes.

KINGDOM	GOD	MANKIND	WORLD
CREATION	GOD	ADAM AND EVE	EDEN
FALL			
FLOOD	GOD	NOAH	ARK

MAIN THEMES   God's covenant commitment to his people despite their rebellion

Election on the basis of grace

Division of human race into elect and nonelect

SOME KEY WORDS   Covenant

Election

Life

THE PATH AHEAD   Noah—Christian baptism, 1 Peter 3:20-21

Election of Abram—Election of Israel—

Election of Christ—Election of those who are in Christ, Ephesians 1:3-10

This discrimination between the chosen and the unchosen is without any basis in the people concerned. This is not so obvious in the early stages of biblical revelation, and some will be inclined to suggest that Abel, Seth, Noah, Shem and Abram had certain virtues of faith or good works which are the reason they were chosen. Such an approach undermines the meaning of grace as it is made clear in its wider biblical use, and it is explicitly denied in many parts of Scripture. This choice or *election* by God is seen to be absolutely unconditional. The reason God chooses one and not another lies in God alone, for no rebel against the sovereign Lord God deserves to be chosen or can ever do anything that would move God to choose him.

■ *God's covenant*
is shown to have its outworking in a plan of redemption. This involves the election of representative individuals through whom the plan of God will be effected. Election is based on nothing in those who are elect.

STUDY GUIDE TO CHAPTER 11

1. Prepare an outline or diagram of Genesis 4—11 showing the theological (covenant) history of mankind from Adam to Abram.

2. What are the main things about the covenant that emerge in Genesis 1—11? Is it realistic to speak of God's covenant made with creation at the very beginning?

3. In what way does the story of Noah and the flood illustrate that grace and election are not conditioned by anything in those who are their objects?

4. What are the main lessons from the story of the tower of Babel?

FURTHER READING

1. *BT*, chaps. 4-6.
2. William J. Dumbrell, *Covenant and Creation* (Exeter, U.K.: Paternoster, 1984), chap. 1.
3. Derek Kidner, *Genesis*, TOTC (Downers Grove, Ill.: InterVarsity Press, 1967).
4. O. Palmer Robertson, *The Christ of the Covenants* (Phillipsburg, N.J.: Presbyterian & Reformed, 1980), chaps. 5-7.

12

ABRAHAM OUR FATHER

"Your father Abraham rejoiced at the thought of seeing my day; he saw it and was glad." (Jn 8:56)

"Before Abraham was born, I am!" (Jn 8:58)

If you belong to Christ, then you are Abraham's seed, and heirs according to the promise. (Gal 3:29)

OUTLINE OF BIBLICAL HISTORY, GENESIS 12—50
Sometime in the early second millennium B.C. God called Abraham out of Mesopotamia to Canaan. He promised to give this land to Abraham's descendants and to bless them as his people. Abraham went, and many years later he had a son, Isaac. Isaac in turn had two sons, Esau and Jacob. The promises of God were established with Jacob and his descendants. He had twelve sons, and in time they all went to live in Egypt because of famine in Canaan.

ABRAHAM

The first eleven chapters of Genesis compress the history of mankind from creation to the early second millennium B.C. into a brief overview that is written from a theological perspective. The rest of Genesis, thirty-nine chapters in all, deals with only four generations of one family: Abraham, Isaac, Jacob and Joseph. Their history is also written with the theological significance in view, but the greater detail is demanded by the unique significance of the family within the plan of God for the human race. All of world history is related to the promises that God makes to Abraham. The final meaning of history will be found in the person of Jesus of Nazareth, a descendant of Abraham.

At the age of seventy-five Abram (as he was then named) left Haran in northern Mesopotamia and, in obedience to God, traveled to Canaan with his nephew Lot and their respective households. The central theme that runs through the narrative is the covenant promise to Abram and the way that it is given. The promise is repeatedly made against a background of events that seem to threaten it and make its fulfillment impossible. By this means Abraham learns that he must live by faith in the promises of God even when it seems that the promises have been destroyed by circumstances. At a critical point, God changes the name of the patriarch from Abram (exalted father) to Abraham (father of a multitude), thus signifying a prominent aspect of the covenant: Abraham will be the father of many nations. At the same time (Gen 17:1-14) God indicates that the covenant is signed with the sign of circumcision. This mark in the flesh of every Hebrew male child is to signify the special relationship that the covenant establishes between God and his people.

The contrast between Abraham and the people of Babel is immediately obvious. Babel expresses the desire for a great name without God, and this is shown to be futile. Following this account we have the genealogy of Shem ("name") leading to Abraham. God promises to make his name great (Gen 12:2), and we see that the only name that matters comes at the blessing of God. The covenant is presented to Abraham in the form of a fourfold promise that will remain at the heart of biblical theology:

1. God will give Abraham many descendants.
2. They will possess the Promised Land.
3. God will be their God.
4. Through them all the nations of the world will be blessed.

The importance of the threats to fulfillment lies in the fact that the promises point to an ultimate fulfillment that can be achieved only by the supernatural work of God. It is not something within the control of man, nor is it simply a matter of natural events.

Thus, at the time of his call out of Haran, Abraham is promised possession of Canaan by a nation of his descendants who will know the blessing of God and be the channel of blessing to the whole world (Gen 12:1-3). In apparent opposition to these promises are the facts that the promised land is possessed by the Canaanites, Abraham and Sarah are old, and Sarah, through the foolishness of Abraham, is almost taken as a wife by the king of Egypt. When Abraham and Lot settle in Canaan they soon find the need to split up to prevent overcrowding by their flocks and herds. Lot chooses the fertile Jordan valley for himself leaving Abraham to go elsewhere. God again reassures Abraham that he and his descendants will possess the land (Gen 13:14-18).

For twenty-five years after God first made these promises Abraham remains childless. At critical times during that period God reminds Abraham of his promises to sustain him in the face of the seemingly impossible odds against their coming true (Gen 15:4-6, 13-21; 17:1-21; 18:16-19).

Some important biblical themes are intertwined with the history of Abraham and the covenant. The first is *grace*. As with Noah there is nothing special about Abraham that deserves the goodness of God in calling him into these blessings. All we know of him is that he lives among pagan peoples and responds with obedience and faith to the call of God. We know nothing of Abraham's faith and knowledge of God before this. There is no hint that God was responding to Abraham's goodness. On the contrary, the narrative is brutally honest in its "warts and all" portrayal of the patriarch. He is not above lying about his wife on two separate occasions in order, so he thought, to preserve his life (Gen 12:11-20; 20:1-18). In so putting his marriage with Sarah at risk he shows lack of faith in God's promises and actually works to undermine the promise that Sarah would be the mother of the promised descendants. It is clear from the narrative that we cannot see God's goodness to Abraham as deserved. Rather, the biblical picture of God's free and sovereign grace is developed.

The second theme, which goes together with grace, is *election*. Whenever God acts for the good of the people he is acting against what they deserve as rebellious sinners, and that action is grace. Election means that God chooses some and not others as objects of his grace. It is no use asking why we find a godly line and a godless line in the early chapters of Genesis, or why Noah and not someone else finds grace, or why Abraham and not some other person is chosen as the father of a blessed race. We are told later that election works for God's glory (Rom 9:19-24), for it demonstrates divine sovereignty. Election is a principle that is developed throughout the biblical history, and we should be careful not to misunderstand it or try to reshape it by human logic into a more acceptable doctrine. We cannot solve this mystery by resorting to easy solutions such as suggesting that God foresees the faith of those whom he subsequently, and on that basis, elects. Nor may we erect false, if apparently logical, objections to the doctrine such as saying that election based on God's free grace reduces us to robots or puppets on a string with no wills or power to make choices.

The third theme is *faith* as the means of restoration to God. Abraham's faith is certainly not perfect, not always strong, and sometimes borders on disbelief (Gen 15:2-3). Yet at the crucial times he takes God at his Word and believes his promises. The key is not the strength or perfection of Abraham's faith, but the strength and perfection of the God he trusts. Abraham learns that God is utterly reliable and faithful to his word. And since Abraham deserves nothing of what he is promised, it must be seen as a pure and unmerited gift. That is why he is accounted as righteous before God by simply believing (Gen 15:6).

As the biblical history unfolds the meaning of grace, election and faith also unfold. Progressive revelation requires that we must always allow God's later and fuller words to interpret the meaning of the earlier and less explicit words. All the key themes in the theological history of Genesis will be developed throughout the Old Testament and find fulfillment in the gospel event. Again I must stress that while earlier expressions help us understand the later, it is the later fulfillment which must interpret the real significance of the earlier expressions. This means, of course, that the earlier expressions point to things beyond themselves that are greater than the meaning that would have been perceived by those receiving these earlier expressions.

■ *The covenant with Abraham*
includes God's promises that his descendants will become a great nation, will possess the promised land, and will be God's people. Through them all nations will be blessed. The covenant expresses the grace of God in election, and its blessings are received by faith.

ISAAC

The history of Isaac begins when Abraham is one hundred years old (Gen 21:5). This emphasizes the fact that the birth of the child is due to the promise of God, which is incapable of being fulfilled by purely natural means. Isaac is a gift of grace, and his birth to extremely aged parents signifies the supernatural element in the birth of the covenant people. Against all natural odds God is shown to be absolutely faithful to his promises. Abraham attempts to get around the difficulty of being old and childless by producing children through the servant woman Hagar and other women. But Isaac is God's chosen and Abraham cannot change that. The most significant challenge to Abraham's trust in the God of the covenant comes with the demand that he offer the boy as a sacrifice. If Isaac dies how can the promises be fulfilled through him? In fact he does not die and God provides a substitute sacrifice in the form of a ram caught in a bush. The offering of sacrifices goes right back to Cain and Abel, and the first mention of an altar is when Abraham arrives in Canaan (Gen 12:7). Little is said by way of explaining the meaning of sacrifices in terms of restoring fellowship with God. The narrative of the offering of Isaac implies the principle of the substitute, and this principle will be made clearer as revelation progresses.

The lengthy account of the servant of Abraham going to get a wife for Isaac from among kinsfolk in Mesopotamia is clearly seen as necessary under the terms of the covenant (Gen 24:1-7). Isaac has to learn that the promises to his father now rest on him. After the death of Abraham, there is another famine in the land. Isaac is warned not to leave the Promised Land and is again assured that his descendants will possess it (Gen 26:1-6). There are Philistines in that part of the land and Isaac uses the same faithless trick that Abraham had done by denying that Rebekah is his wife (Gen 26:7-16). The narrative tells us very few of the details of Isaac's life and we must infer from this that his principal significance is seen in the repetition of the covenant promises to him, and in the fact that he is living proof of the faithfulness of God to his promises made to Abraham

---

■ *Isaac*

is shown to be the descendant of Abraham through whom the promises of God will be effected. His birth shows the faithfulness of God to those promises.

JACOB

Isaac's wife Rebekah is infertile until Isaac reaches sixty years of age (Gen 25:21). Thus the birth of their twins must be reckoned as a supernatural birth just as Isaac's was. Before their birth the two struggle in the womb, and God tells Rebekah that they will be fathers of two nations, and the older shall serve the younger. Esau is the first to be born, but it is soon clear that the other, Jacob, is the one chosen by God. Again the covenant of grace works against natural choice. It is true that Esau despises his birthright as the older twin, but it is also true that Jacob is not a very nice person at all. Genesis 27 describes at length the cunning of Jacob in deceiving his now feeble and nearly blind father. He tricks Isaac into giving to him the blessing that belongs to the firstborn.

If there is any doubt that God will confirm this arrangement it is soon dispelled. Isaac invokes upon Jacob the blessing of the covenant to Abraham (Gen 28:3) and sends him off to find a wife from among the kinsfolk in Mesopotamia. On the way out of the Promised Land God speaks to Jacob in a dream and affirms that all the promises of Abraham belong to him (Gen 28:13-15). Jacob calls the place Bethel—"house of God." He then goes to Padan Aram in Mesopotamia and meets his cousin Rachel. He wishes to marry her, and works for her father for seven years. Laban then gives his older daughter Leah, instead of Rachel, to Jacob, who then must work another seven years for Rachel. This trial appears as another of the challenges to the fulfillment of the covenant promises, although it might seem a just retribution on the man who tricked his brother out of his birthright. But God is with Jacob, and Jacob finally leaves Laban's employ with his wives and children and returns to Canaan. It is quite clear that Jacob's election is grace and not what he deserves.

Upon returning to Canaan Jacob prepares for the worst, as he fears the anger of his brother Esau. He is armed only with the promises of God (Gen 32:9-12). It is not Esau he meets first but an unnamed man who for some reason starts to wrestle with Jacob (Gen 32:22-32). Jacob perceives that this is no ordinary man but a messenger of God. A certain mystery surrounds this event. The man appears to impede Jacob's return to the land of promise, and yet when he would call off the struggle Jacob refuses to let him go. He recognizes the divine origin, perhaps even the divine nature, of his opponent. With only the promises of God to sustain him he demands a blessing before he will let the man go. The blessing is given and with it a change of name from Jacob to Israel, signifying that he has struggled with God. We can only suppose that this was some kind of conversion experience for Jacob.

From now on Jacob is a changed man. He is no longer the cunning deceiver, but the godly patriarch. As if to confirm this, he is well received by Esau. Later he moves to Bethel (where God first appeared to him in a dream), and there his name Israel is linked with the covenant promises. Thus God is known as the God of Abraham, Isaac and Jacob (Gen 35:9-15).

Up to this point the principle of election has been seen to work to distinguish certain families within a larger family. Abraham is chosen as the father of the covenant people, but not Lot. Lot's descendants, through an incestuous union with his two daughters, are Moab and Ben-ammi. The resulting nations of the Moabites and the Ammonites are thus kinsfolk of Israel and afforded protection from the Israelites when they later move to establish possession of the Promised Land (Deut 2:9, 19). Of Abraham's descendants the covenant belongs to Isaac the son of Sarah, not to Ishmael the son of Hagar. Of Isaac's descendants, Jacob and not Esau is the recipient of the covenant blessings. Esau is Edom, and his descendants are also protected from Israel (Deut 2:4-5). In different ways these non-elect brethren, and especially Edom, come into occasional conflict with Israel.

Once we reach Jacob and his family, the election process remains firmly with his descendants. Israel is the elect nation, but subsequent revelation will show that this outward election proceeds side by side with an inner election to eternal life. Not all Israel are Israel, the apostle Paul will later conclude (Rom 9:6). God's dealings with the nation as a nation will have to be distinguished from his dealings with individuals for their eternal salvation. These two aspects of election will also be distinguished from the election of certain representative individuals upon whom God focuses his purposes in a special way.

■ *The covenant principles*
continue to be demonstrated in Jacob. Through the election of grace he becomes the descendant of Abraham through Isaac to whom the promises of God are made.

JOSEPH AND THE SONS OF JACOB

The great truths introduced with Abraham are reaffirmed and developed with each generation. The process continues with Joseph (Gen 37—50). He is the eleventh of the sons of Jacob and the first born to Rachel. When he is seventeen his brothers sell him, because of envy, to Ishmaelite traders. These in turn sell him to an official in Egypt. He is jailed on false charges but released some time later after he interprets the Pharaoh's dreams. At the age of thirty he is given a high administrative office in Egypt. When his brothers come to Egypt to buy grain on account of a severe famine in Canaan, Joseph eventually makes himself known to them and they are all reconciled. Finally, the brothers are persuaded to bring Jacob and their households to settle in Egypt.

At the end of the narrative we are told in Joseph's words the significance of the episode: "You intended to harm me, but God intended it for good to accomplish what is now being done, the saving of many lives" (Gen 50:20). We may well wonder why God didn't save their lives by providing rain and good harvests in Canaan. According to everything we have learned about the covenant, Egypt is not the right place for the people of God to be. They were not meant to be servants of an alien king in a foreign land. We shall learn the reason for this from the narrative as it unfolds.

One final point from Genesis. After the reunion of Joseph with his family we reach the time of Jacob's death. Before he dies he does two significant things. He accepts the two sons of Joseph, Ephraim and Manasseh, as his own (Gen 48:5). This makes them heads of the half-tribes, which are ever after numbered among the tribes of Israel. Jacob makes it clear that this adoption is integral to the fulfillment of the covenant (Gen 48:3-6). Jacob also blesses the two boys but crosses his hands so that his right hand of blessing is upon the head of Ephraim the younger (Gen 48:8-14). Then he gathers his twelve sons and makes prophetic blessings on each. Of these the one above all to watch is Judah, for in his blessing Jacob says, "The scepter will not depart from Judah, nor the ruler's staff from between his feet" (Gen 49:10). Out of Judah (the Jews) would come David and his royal line leading eventually to Jesus of Nazareth.

This ruling function of the tribe of Judah will receive much emphasis in later revelation. As we shall see in chapter 17, the royal line of David receives the promises of God which focus all God's plans for his people onto the king, as representative of the people of God. For this reason we shall need to distinguish the Jews from Israel as a whole. It is in the light of this distinction that we can understand what Jesus meant when he told the Samaritan woman that "salvation is from the Jews" (Jn 4:22). Jacob's prophecy concerning Judah also explains the history of the divided kingdom (after the death of Solomon), in which the southern kingdom of Judah is ruled continuously by the dynasty of David from about 925 to 586 B.C., while the northern kingdom of Israel has some thirteen dynasties over a period of two centuries (925 to 722 B.C.).

■ *The sojourn in Egypt*
of Joseph and then of the whole family of Jacob appears to contradict the covenant promises of God. Yet God is seen to bless his people in Egypt, and the covenant promises are passed on to the sons of Jacob.

FURTHER PROMISES OF REGENERATION

SUMMARY God's covenant commitment is given its next main expression in the promises made to Abraham. Election and grace are demonstrated in the way the promises are given and sustained in the face of what seem to be impossible obstacles. The promises are that Abraham's descendants through Isaac and Jacob will possess the land, be God's special people, and be the instrument of blessing for all nations.

KINGDOM	GOD	MANKIND	WORLD
CREATION:	GOD	ADAM AND EVE	EDEN
FALL			
FLOOD	GOD	NOAH	ARK
ABRAHAM	GOD	ABRAHAM'S DESCENDANTS	CANAAN

MAIN THEMES Covenant with Abraham, Isaac and Jacob

Promised Land

Abraham's descendants as people of God

Blessing to the nations

SOME KEY WORDS Promise

Faith

THE PATH AHEAD Promise to Abraham—Fulfilled in Christ, Galatians 3

Abraham's faith—Justification by faith, Romans 4

STUDY GUIDE TO CHAPTER 12

1. Beginning with Genesis 12:1-3, list the covenant promises made to Abraham and the occasions on which they were made.

2. What are some of the main lessons that Paul sees in God's dealings with Abraham (see Gal 3 and Rom 4)?

3. How is grace illustrated in the history of Jacob and Esau?

4. In what way does the experience of Joseph in Egypt confirm the covenant, and in what way does it seem to contradict the covenant?

FURTHER READING

1. *BT*, chap. 7.
2. William J. Dumbrell, *Covenant and Creation* (Exeter, U.K.: Paternoster, 1984), chap. 2.
3. T. E. McComisky, *The Covenants of Promise* (Grand Rapids, Mich.: Baker, 1985).
4. O. Palmer Robertson, *The Christ of the Covenants* (Phillipsburg, N.J.: Presbyterian & Reformed, 1980), chaps. 8-9.

13

EXODUS: PATTERN OF REDEMPTION

So he [Joseph] got up, took the child [Jesus] and his mother during the night and left for Egypt, where he stayed until the death of Herod. And so was fulfilled what the Lord had said through the prophet: "Out of Egypt I called my son." (Mt 2:14-15)

Christ, our Passover lamb, has been sacrificed. (1 Cor 5:7)

OUTLINE OF BIBLICAL HISTORY, EXODUS 1—15
In time the descendants of Jacob living in Egypt multiplied to become a very large number of people. The Egyptians no longer regarded them with friendliness and made them slaves. God appointed Moses to be the one who would lead Israel out of Egypt to the Promised Land of Canaan. When the moment came for Moses to demand the freedom of his people the Pharaoh refused to let them go. Through Moses God worked ten miracle-plagues which brought hardship, destruction and death to the Egyptians. Finally Pharaoh let Israel go, but then pursued them and trapped them at the Red Sea (or Sea of Reeds). Then God opened a way in the sea for Israel to cross on dry land, but closed the water over the Egyptian army, destroying it.

CAPTIVITY

Up to this point some very clear theological themes have emerged, and some interesting questions have been raised which demand answers. Why did the land seem so constantly out of the reach of those to whom it was promised while they yet lived in it? And why did the purpose of God include the complete removal of the people from their land so that they became dwellers in Egypt? The first question is partly answered by the fact that faith in the promises of God is an important perspective that is introduced in the early stages of the revelation of the kingdom of God. Both questions are answered by the historical reality of Israel's stay in Egypt and by the biblical interpretation of that event.

The semi-nomadic wanderings of Abraham and his descendants in Canaan did not serve God's purposes of revelation fully enough. Throughout the Old Testament, possession of the land is presented as a shadow of the future reality of living as God's people in his kingdom. But it provided no vivid pattern of the necessary route by which any child of God enters the kingdom. For this some graphic and unmistakable experience of redemption from an alien power was necessary. Remember that all mankind has been outside Eden since the rebellion of Adam and Eve. Any revelation of the kingdom of God within the historical framework of the chosen people must take account of the fact that even the elect are sinners needing redemption. Already this truth has been expressed in Noah's deliverance from the watery judgment of the whole world. The exodus from Egypt repeats this picture with greater detail and clarity, so that the condition of sinners and the nature of God's work to deal with this condition remain as the pattern of redemption until the coming of Christ.

At the beginning of Exodus we find the descendants of Israel in Egypt having multiplied to become a great crowd of people. The land is now governed by a king who has no regard for the services rendered by Joseph. Rather he sees the Israelites as an internal threat to the security of the nation, and makes them slaves of the state (Ex 1). Once again the reality of the promises of God seems to recede out of reach. Certainly Abraham's descendants are now many, but they are in the wrong place and under the wrong rule. To all outward appearances Israel's God is powerless to keep faith with his chosen, and unable to prevent foreign gods from exercising rule over his people.

The theological meaning of the captivity in Egypt lies in its opposition to the covenant. The pharaoh is a semi-divine being and his rule is understood by the Egyptians as a reflection of the power of the Egyptian gods. But the enemy is not only outside the Israelites, for within them is their own spiritual condition. There is no indication at this stage that the captivity was due to Israel's sin. When Abraham was told that his people would be oppressed there was no suggestion that it would be a judgment on their sin (Gen 15:13-16). Only upon later reflection does the question of Israel serving foreign gods arise (Josh 24:14; Ezek 23:19-21). At this point the condition of Israel is identified primarily as political and social slavery.

■ *The captivity in Egypt*
expresses the ultimate challenge to the covenant promises. The people of the covenant are shown to be subjects of alien powers in a land not their own.

THE COVENANT IN ACTION

The already serious situation of Israel becomes worse when Pharaoh orders that all newborn boys should be drowned in the Nile. When the mother of Moses hides him in a waterproofed basket in the reeds of the river, he is discovered by the royal princess and rescued. He is given to his own mother to be nursed and then adopted by the princess. Thus Moses is saved from death and given both a Hebrew and an Egyptian upbringing in preparation for his ministry. The theological significance of Moses' deliverance lies not in a general providential care for little children, but in the overruling of the powers opposed to God's kingdom so that they cannot hurt the one chosen to mediate God's plan of salvation.

The next state of Moses' preparation is in Midian where, as an adult, he takes refuge after killing an Egyptian. Back in Egypt the Israelites are crying out for help. God hears them and remembers his covenant with their forefathers (Ex 2:23-25). This does not imply that he could ever forget his promises, but rather that he is about to act on the basis of those promises. The theology of Exodus is primarily the theology of the covenant in action.

Moses' ministry is to be the human instrument through which God will act to redeem his people. It is vital that we understand the place given to certain key figures, such as Moses, in Old Testament revelation. Their significance for us is not primarily in the way they stand as examples of godliness and faith, but rather in the role they play in revealing and foreshadowing the nature of the work of Christ. Moses is the divinely appointed man to who God reveals his purposes and will for his people.

God reveals himself to Moses at Mount Sinai (Horeb) out of the burning bush (Ex 3:1—4:17). He identifies himself as the God of the patriarchs (Ex 3:6), which means that he is the one who promised that Israel would be his free people in their own land. He announces that he is about to fulfill that promise by releasing the Israelites from Egypt (Ex 3:7-9). Then he commissions Moses to confront Pharaoh and to lead the Israelites out of Egypt. Nevertheless, it will be God's power that secures their freedom through signs and wonders.

Moses is concerned that the Israelites will not believe him when he returns to Egypt and claims to be God's chosen (Ex 3:13; 4:1). He is reassured on two grounds. First, he will identify the God who has spoken to him as "I AM" and as the God of their fathers (Ex 3:14-16). Second, Moses is given

some miraculous signs, which he will be able to repeat to persuade the Israelites of his mission (Ex 4:1-9). These two themes of the *name of God* and
the signs *and wonders* are closely woven into the redemptive event by
which Israel is freed. Another important and related theme is that of the
identity of Israel as the people of God. For the first time Israel is named as
the *son of God,* a name not often used, but nevertheless of great importance
(Ex 4:22-23). To be the covenant people of God also means that they are
known by his name (Deut 28:10). Centuries later, when the nation is held
in a second captivity, God promises redemption to "everyone who is
called by my name" (Is 43:7).

Moses returns to Egypt and convinces his brother Aaron and all the
people of his God-given task (Ex 4:27-31). But when his first demands to
Pharaoh are met by the imposition of even harder conditions on the captives, the people are restless (Ex 5:21). Then God gives Moses one of the
great covenant statements of the Bible (Ex 6:1-8). In experiencing the inevitable release from slavery the people will know God in a new way as
the God who keeps his covenant. This will be indicated by the name *the
LORD* or *YHWH.*[1] This name, often pronounced as Jehovah or Yahweh, is
probably linked with the Hebrew verb "to be" which gives the identity
"I AM" in Exodus 3:14. At some stage in their history the Israelites ceased
to pronounce the holy name YHWH and substituted the name *Adonai* (my
Lord), which is why most English translations put LORD for YHWH. The
important thing is that this is the personal name of God, and it is linked
to his character as the God who makes the gracious commitment of himself to his people; and who is revealing what it means for him to be faithful to that commitment.

■ *The covenant in action*
*means that God acts to fulfill his promises of which the captivity in Egypt is a
denial. Israel is God's son and will know him by his name YHWH, which identifies him as the God who is faithful to his covenant.*

SIGNS AND WONDERS

In the Bible signs may or may not be miraculous. But when the word
sign is linked with wonder we are dealing with miraculous events that
cluster in two main places. The first is in the account of the release of

Israel from Egypt (Ex 7:3), or in later references to the exodus (Deut 4:34; Neh 9:10; Jer 32:20-21). The second is in the ministry of Jesus and his apostles. This fact alone suggests that *signs and wonders* is a technical term for miracles which accompany, and even constitute, the redemptive event.

The ten plagues that God performs through Moses are signs and wonders that have saving significance for the Israelites, and at the same time are judgments on Egypt. Through this means God reveals himself to Israel and to the Egyptians as YHWH (Ex 6:6-7; 7:5). The saving-judging quality of the plagues includes a demonstration that the gods of Egypt are powerless. Although each plague in turn inflicts great discomfort and hardship on the Egyptians, Pharaoh persistently refuses to allow the Israelites to leave. There is an apparent problem in that God is said to harden Pharaoh's heart (Ex 4:21; 7:3; 9:12; 10:1), and at the same time Pharaoh hardens his own heart (Ex 8:15; 9:34). Notice how the writer in one breath, as it were, speaks in three ways of the hardening: Pharaoh hardened his heart; the heart of Pharaoh was hardened; the Lord said, "I have hardened his heart" (Ex 9:34—10:1). One might well wonder who did harden his heart. There is no doubt that Pharaoh's hardening of his own heart is deliberate, and he is judged for this. On the other hand, God is still sovereign in the matter as the apostle Paul later recognizes when he discusses it in the framework of God's election (Rom 9:14-18). This biblical perspective which asserts that human responsibility and divine sovereignty are somehow intertwined without either being in any way compromised, is something that we must come to terms with even though it is beyond our powers of understanding.

■ *Signs and wonders*
are miraculous events which accompany the saving acts of God. They act as judgments on Pharaoh because his heart is hardened against God's word. At the same time they work for the salvation of Israel.

THE PASSOVER

After nine successive plagues, Pharaoh still holds out against Moses' demands. When God had previously named Israel as his firstborn son, he threatened the death of Pharaoh's firstborn son if he would not free Israel (Ex 4:22-23). None of the earlier plagues had actually touched the Israelites who were living separately from the bulk of the Egyptians. Now they and the whole Egyptian nation are drawn into the final stroke, for every firstborn in Egypt will die (Ex 11:4-5).

Israel's involvement in the tenth plague is an important part of God's revelation of the kingdom (Ex 12:1-13). Unless they believe God and follow his directions all the firstborn of Israel will also die. In this is the revelation of some of the key elements of redemption. On a specified day a yearling male lamb without defect is to be taken for each Israelite household. Four days later the lamb is to be killed and some of the blood placed on the doorposts of each house. The flesh is to be roasted, then eaten with herbs and unleavened bread. Each person is to be dressed and ready for a journey. On that night, God says, "I will execute judgment on the gods of Egypt." Where the blood is seen on the house the Lord will pass over it and no death will plague those within.

God also instructs Moses to establish the feast of the Passover as a memorial forever (Ex 12:14-20). This shows how important the Passover is in patterning the redemptive work of God, although there is virtually no theological reason given for the particular form it takes. We can safely infer that the lamb's blood somehow covered the believing and therefore obedient Israelites so that they suffered no judgment. The covenant principle works by households, so that the faith of the head of the household has saving significance for the whole household. Other aspects of the Passover symbolism become clearer as the saving event moves towards its completion in the history of Israel.

■ *The Passover*
shows that redemption involves not only the release from slavery, but also the shedding of blood as a means of escape from judgment.

REDEMPTION

The ten plagues cause hardship enough for the Egyptians, but God is not finished with them yet. The actual crossing of the sea that he will accomplish for the Israelites spells disaster for the armies of Pharaoh. Once again there is a hardening of Pharaoh's heart so that God's power might be demonstrated (Ex 14:4, 8). The sea will also serve to impress upon Israel that the exodus from Egypt is no ordinary trek from one place to another. Thus, instead of leading the people by way of the well-worn roads out of Egypt, God brings them into an apparently blind alley against the Sea of Reeds where the Egyptian army has them trapped (Ex 13:17-18; 14:1-4).

Into this hopeless situation the word of God through Moses sounds the good news of salvation: "Do not be afraid. Stand firm and you will see the deliverance the LORD will bring you today. . . . The LORD will fight for you; you need only to be still" (Ex 14:13-14). And so it happens. The waters are driven back and the Israelites walk to freedom while the waters close again over their pursuers.

As we reflect on the elements of redemption revealed in the exodus event, we are able to see why God led Joseph and his brothers to Egypt. Possession of the Promised Land and the freedom to be the people of God is not a matter of simply walking over the border into the kingdom of God, and much less is it something we are born into. The Israelites, even as the chosen people, are by nature aliens and strangers to God's kingdom because they are Adam's children outside of Eden. God chose to reveal his redemptive purpose in the context of Israel's history. Thus the captivity in Egypt and the exodus demonstrate the captivity of the human race to the powers of evil, and the necessary powerful work of God himself to rescue his people from that awful slavery. When God the warrior fights for his people against the enemy, victory is certain (Ex 14:14; 15:1-3).

We can now summarize the dimensions of redemption that are revealed in the history of the exodus. Israel's slavery is a contradiction of the covenant promises made to the fathers of the nation: Abraham, Isaac and Jacob. On the basis of these promises God announces that he will show his faithfulness by bringing Israel out of its captivity (Ex 2:23-25; 6:1-6). In so doing he is revealing his character as the God who is absolutely true to his covenant commitment. The name "The LORD" will ever after speak of this covenant faithfulness (Ex 3:13-15; 6:2-5). Redemption is God's act of judgment upon his enemies whereby he retrieves his lost people and makes them his in the place he prepares for them (Ex 6:6-8). It is thus a supernatural act of salvation worked by God for a people powerless to help themselves (Ex 3:19-20; 7:3-5; 10:1-2; 14:13-14). Interwoven with these events is a sacrificial offering, the slaying of the Passover lamb, which delivers Israel from judgment so they can go free.

The end of the exodus is freedom, faith and celebration. Of course faith was active all through the events of Exodus 1—14. But in a special way, when the people are free, they see what God has done for them, and they fear the Lord and believe in him (Ex 14:31). Reverent awe of God and trust in him are evoked by the redemptive event itself. Then they celebrate! In the song of Moses and the people we see the spontaneous act of worship which becomes a kind of model for worship ever after (Ex 15:1-18). God reveals himself by his deeds, and through his word about those deeds. Worship must therefore center on retelling what God has done. The song of Moses is not a vindictive gloating over the Egyptians, but rather an account of what God has done to show his covenant faithfulness (Hebrew: *hesed*, Ex 15:13).[2] The other act of worship has already been prescribed for them in the celebration of the Passover meal and the feast of unleavened bread. In this holy meal they will not repeat the redemption of the exodus every year, but celebrate the one completed act of God on their behalf.

Redemption as a release from slavery or from a position of misfortune now becomes one of the most significant themes in the Bible. In this regard the book of Ruth provides an illustration as Boaz acts with kindness to perform the duty of a close relative to redeem Ruth's land (Ruth 4:1-11). The latter part of the book of Isaiah refers frequently to God as the redeemer of Israel in the light of the impending release of God's people from their captivity in Babylon. We shall see also the repetition of the idea of the exodus as the pattern of redemption. There is this first exodus from Egypt, a second involving the return of the captives from Babylon in the sixth century B.C. and then the true exodus in which Jesus takes his people out of the captivity to sin and death.

The exodus is the end of captivity, but it is only the beginning of freedom. God has yet much work to do in order to show his people what it means to live freely as his people.

■ *Redemption*

is God's act of releasing his people from an alien power, and of bringing them to freedom so that they can live as his people according to the covenant promises.

REGENERATION OF A NATION

SUMMARY   God's covenant promises appear to have no substance when the chosen people find themselves in slavery to a foreign power. But God's faithfulness is shown in the redemptive act by which he saves Israel from their captivity. Signs and wonders demonstrate that entry into God's kingdom is only possible through a supernatural work of God himself.

KINGDOM	GOD	MANKIND	WORLD
CREATION	GOD	ADAM AND EVE	EDEN
FALL			
FLOOD	GOD	NOAH	ARK
ABRAHAM	GOD	ABRAHAM'S DESCENDANTS	CANAAN
MOSES	THE LORD	ISRAEL	CANAAN

MAIN THEMES   Captivity
Covenant faithfulness of God
Name of God
Signs and wonders
Supernatural redemption

SOME KEY WORDS   Covenant
Passover
Redemption
Salvation

THE PATH AHEAD   Exodus from Egypt—Second exodus from
Babylonian captivity—Exodus of Christ
Passover—Christ our passover, 1 Corinthians 5:7
Israel is son of God, Exodus 4:22-23; Hosea
11:1—Jesus is (Israel) Son of God, Luke 3:22-
38; 4:3

STUDY GUIDE TO CHAPTER 13

1. What are the unique features of the life and ministry of Moses in Exodus 1—15?

2. What is the significance of the captivity in Egypt in the light of the covenant?

3. What are the key elements revealed in the release of Israel from Egypt which show the meaning of redemption?

4. What is the significance of God's name "The LORD," and how can his people worship him?

FURTHER READING

1. *BT*, chap. 8.
2. Alan Cole, *Exodus*, TOTC (Downers Grove, Ill.: InterVarsity Press, 1973).
3. *GK*, chap. 7.

NOTES

1. The fact that the patriarchal narratives in Genesis often refer to God as Lord could mean either that the writer is identifying the God of Abraham as the God who revealed the name YHWH to Moses, or that the name was known before the event in Exodus 6 but the redemptive significance of the name was not revealed until that event.

2. The Hebrew word *hesed* is translated in a variety of ways. In Exodus 15:13 it appears as "steadfast love" (RSV) and "unfailing love" (NIV). It is a word that takes on a technical meaning when referring to God, and means his unfailing, loving commitment to the covenant. It is the key word in the refrain to each verse of Psalm 136, but the reference to the covenant is not clear in the English versions.

14

NEW LIFE: GIFT AND TASK

"Do not think that I have come to abolish the Law or the Prophets; I have not come to abolish them but to fulfill them." (Mt 5:17)

So the law was put in charge to lead us to Christ that we might be justified by faith. Now that faith has come, we are no longer under the supervision of the law. (Gal 3:24-25)

OUTLINE OF BIBLICAL HISTORY, EXODUS 16—40, LEVITICUS
After their release from Egypt, Moses led the Israelites to Mount Sinai. God then gave them his law which they were commanded to keep. At one point Moses held a covenant renewal ceremony in which the covenant arrangement was sealed in blood. However, while Moses was away on the mountain, the people persuaded Aaron to fashion a golden calf. Thus they showed their inclination to forsake the covenant and to engage in idolatry. God also commanded the building of the tabernacle and gave all the rules of sacrificial worship by which Israel might approach him.

THE NEW LIFE

Escape from Egypt means new life, a rebirth of the nation of Israel. The journey from the Sea of Reeds to Sinai takes the people through inhospitable country where they immediately learn the faithfulness of God to provide for their needs, even though they begin to murmur their discontent (Ex 16; 17). They also find deliverance from the armies of hostile Amalek. In these short episodes the quality of the redeemed life that exists even now for Christians, and will exist until the return of Christ, is revealed. Redemption, though real, is in an important sense incomplete. The new life is characterized by the saying of Paul, "We live by faith, not by sight" (2 Cor 5:7). The Egyptian experience has revealed to Israel the necessity of redemption for entry into the promised kingdom of God. But, as Abraham did before them, Israel discovers that there is an element of not yet having what is promised: Thus they must look to the future in hope, and live by faith in the promises of God.

Israel stands before God at Mount Sinai. There the first word of God to Moses, who acts as God's mediator, concerns the covenant. Virtually the whole theology of redemption and the new life is summed up in Exodus 19:4-6: God has judged the enemies of his people and of his kingdom (v. 4a). He has redeemed his people and reconciled them to himself (v. 4b). If they show that their redemption is not merely outward but a thing of the heart, if they obey God's word, they shall be his special possession out of all the peoples under his sovereign rule (v. 5). As a people they shall then exist in a unique relationship to God while representing him to the whole world as priests (v. 6). This priestly function in a world that belongs to God gives further meaning to the original covenant promise that all the nations of the earth would be blessed through Abraham's descendants (Gen 12:3). It is the function of a priest to approach God on behalf of others and to approach people on behalf of God. By means of its own chosen representatives, the Levitical priests, Israel would learn how it as a nation could approach God through a priestly ministry. Then it would learn that the blessings of the covenant would one day overflow through them into the whole world.

Israel is called God's son. Rarely is the term used in the Old Testament, but the relationship shines through these events. Only later will the full import of this be apparent as the perfect Son of God comes to fulfill in his own life all God's purposes for Israel. But even though the people imperfectly grasp the significance of the redemption from Egypt, they perceive that it calls for their response. Aware that the covenant faithfulness of God has done a great thing for them, and before they even know the details of God's word which they must obey, the people respond with their own affirmation of obedience (Ex 19:8). It may seem somewhat premature and rash, and yet it is the only response they can make under the circumstances. There is no such thing as a conditional acceptance of God's grace.

■ *The new life*

through redemption involves a relationship with God that is structured by the law. Israel as the people of God is called to be a nation of priests that will somehow be the agent of God's blessing to all nations.

FREEDOM TO LIVE FOR GOD

In trying to make sense of the Old Testament, many Christians bog down in the details of the law. Space permits only a brief analysis of the nature and meaning of the law. At this stage we are concerned with the function of the law in ancient Israel. The relationship of the law to the gospel will be considered when we come to the New Testament. However, we must not overlook the relationship of law to grace in the Old Testament.

The first word at Sinai was a word about grace (redemption) and cove-nant to which an obedient response was demanded (Ex 19:4-6). The same pattern of the priority of grace is expressed in the giving of the Ten Com-mandments. "I am YHWH (Yahweh) your God, who brought you out of Egypt," is quite explicit (Ex 20:2). He is their God, and he *has saved* them. On this basis the law is given. Clearly, all the conditional statements notwith-standing, the law is given to those who have already experienced the grace of God in salvation, and it is not the basis upon which they will be saved.

The task of obedience is given because the relationship of sonship has already been established as an undeserved gift. This fact is reinforced in the form of the Ten Commandments (or *decalogue*). It has been recognized for some time that the decalogue follows the form of a covenant treaty which was well known in the ancient, near eastern world. The stipulations or requirements of this type of treaty were imposed by a conquering king upon a subdued people because they had already been made his subjects. The privileges of this relationship would be maintained by obedience to the stipulations. The implication is that God deliberately gives the law in this form because it is appropriate to the nature of the relationship. The gift of God is such that it can be received only for what it is. Salvation or re-demption means being restored to a position of sonship and fellowship with God. To claim to have received the gift of friendship with God while persisting in a life marked by alienation and enmity is clearly nonsense.

The first of the ten words of the decalogue is really inclusive of every-thing that follows. "You shall have no other gods before me" is a claim to ex-clusive, sovereign power. But sinful and ignorant human beings cannot know what this means in every area of life. The Israelites were dependent on God's revelation for a proper understanding of the appropriate respons-es to the command. Beginning with the decalogue, the law details the impli-cations of God's exclusive claim over his people through the covenant. God, of course, has exclusive claim over the whole creation, but the covenant relationship was his gift to the chosen people alone. The demands of the law are not arbitrary or capricious. They stem from and reflect the character of God and his purpose for mankind in creation and redemption. They point to the nature of the reconstruction of the perfect relationship that God built into creation but which was disrupted by human sin. Some of the laws often referred to as moral reflect these relationships more directly than others. Other laws address the situation of Israel as it is in its historical experience. Still others appear to have a certain arbitrariness about them as they relate certain aspects of experience to the ritual life of the nation.

As the first of the commandments is a word that includes the other nine, so the ten words include the principles which govern all the laws of God. We can see this principle in the way Jesus selected two commandments as those upon which everything in the law and the prophets is based (Mt 22:34-40). Love for God (Deut 6:5) and love for one's neighbor (Lev 19:18) are implications of the first of the commandments. But what does it mean to love God and love one's neighbor? It is appropriate at the point in the progressive revelation of the kingdom of God, to which the Sinai events belong, that the response of the redeemed to the grace of God should be detailed in the way it is. All the implications of loving God, or of having no other gods before him, spread out like ripples in a pond for all aspects of the Israelites' lives.

If the covenant means that Israel should respond appropriately to God's acts toward them, then what is seen to be appropriate depends at least in part on how clearly or fully this saving action of God is revealed. Redemption from slavery in Egypt foreshadows the saving work of Christ. It contains the structure of the gospel but does not reveal the fullness of it. Because the revelation in the exodus is incomplete it requires a more detailed exposition of what it means to live as redeemed people. In their spiritual infancy the Israelites need to be tutored much more directly in holy living (see Gal 3:23-25). Only in this way will they learn what manner of liberty they have in being set free from their slavery to Egypt.

■ *The law*
is given to the chosen and already redeemed people of God so that they might know what their new relationship to God means for the way they live. The law of Sinai is the expression of the character of God as it relates to the revelation of his kingdom at that time.

FREEDOM TO APPROACH GOD

The covenant is characterized by the willingness of God to be God to an un-deserving people. Something of this relationship as it was intended to be can be seen in the fellowship of Adam and Eve with God in the Garden of Eden. But now sinful humanity is being restored from its God-denying con-dition. How can people who are still sinful approach a holy God? The bib-lical answer is through a go-between, a mediator. Moses is the mediator of God's saving acts in the exodus, and also of the word of God that interprets the redeemed existence brought about by the saving acts of God in the ex-odus. Now a mediating priesthood is needed along with the means of giv-ing expression to where they are at the present in the process of restoration.

The means God gives is the tabernacle. The word tabernacle simply means a tent, but we retain the word because it comes to signify a special tent. In Exodus 25—30 God gives Moses the details of the tabernacle and of the priestly functions associated with it. In Exodus 35—40 we have a de-scription of the construction of the tabernacle. Then in Leviticus the vari-ous sacrifices to be performed at the tabernacle are given. No detail in the construction of the tent and its contents is left to the imagination of the people, for they are completely dependent upon the revelation of God for knowledge of their relationship to him.

The layout and form of the tabernacle is important as it provides a graphic expression of the spiritual state of Israel as the covenant and re-deemed people who are yet sinful. A courtyard with a high fence around the tent indicates the separation that sin causes between sinners and a holy God. The courtyard fence has an entrance at one end facing the door of the tent. Inside the entrance lies the altar of sacrifice. Somehow the shedding of blood gains entrance for the penitent worshiper, but only by proxy. The Israelite priest represents the people and can move into the tent on their behalf, but only after offering a sacrifice and cleansing himself in the bath for ritual washing which is before the tent. Inside the tent are a lampstand, a table and an altar for burning incense. The far end of the tent is parti-tioned with a curtain, and behind this, in a cubic room, is the ark of the covenant. Everything about this structure speaks of three great truths: God wills to dwell among his people and to meet with them; sin separates peo-ple from God; and God provides a way of reconciliation through sacrifice and the mediatorial office of the priest.

There is no explicit statement of a theology of atonement attaching to the sacrifices instituted at Sinai. However, in some aspects at least, the implicit meaning is clear. To begin with, the Israelites are told that the faithful application of the sacrificial system is acceptable in God's sight and somehow works the pardon of sin. The five main sacrificial offerings referred to in Leviticus 1—6 combine to express the totality of reconciliation and restoration of fellowship with God. Starting with the offenders' guilt before a holy God, the different aspects of these sacrifices point to the sacrifice of an acceptable victim who takes the place of the offerer, the covering or atonement of sins, restitution to people who have been wronged, obedience and dedication to God, and fellowship (in a meal) with him. The ritual of the Day of Atonement *(yom kippur)* in Leviticus 16 is especially eloquent of the substitutionary sacrifice as the means of acceptance with God.

■ *The tabernacle and sacrifices*
serve to portray and to effect the relationship of the redeemed sinner to a holy God. God dwells among his people, but can only be approached through a mediator who offers an acceptable sacrifice for sin.

HOLY TO THE LORD

Of all the words used in the Bible to express the character of God, *holy* is one of the most prominent. The origins of the word (Hebrew: *qadosh*) are obscure, but the essential meaning stands out particularly in relation to the law in Exodus and Leviticus. If we say, "God is holy," for many this implies that we are saying something about God on the basis of an already known concept. Thus holy means good or pure, and so God is good or pure. But the method used in the law to prescribe holiness in the people of God indicates the opposite approach. The whole complexity of laws relating to holiness is meant to bring home to Israel that God reveals his holiness in his saving acts, and calls upon them to be conformed to that standard.

The holiness theology in Leviticus expresses the covenant status of Israel that was established in the redemption from Egypt. What may appear to us to be rather arbitrary and irrelevant laws of clean and unclean foods (Lev 11) are commanded on the basis of the covenant, which is the chief revelation of the character of God.

I am the LORD your God; consecrate yourselves and be holy, because I am holy. Do not make yourselves unclean by any creature that moves about on the ground. I am the LORD who brought you up out of Egypt to be your God; therefore be holy, because I am holy. (Lev 11:44-45. See also Lev 19:34-36; 22:31-33; 23:43; 25:38, 42, 55; 26:12-13, 45)

The covenant as the possession of the elect nation means that the character of God revealed in his word and acts must be the mark of his people (Lev 19:2, 34-37). The law, which was so easily misused and made to be the grounds of exclusiveness and self-righteousness, was in fact that which highlighted the nature of the new creation which was being formed around the faithful while they remained within the old, fallen and sinful confused world.

The theology of Leviticus and of the law in general is summarized in Leviticus 26. God has saved Israel because he is faithful to his covenant promises made to Abraham, Isaac and Jacob, that he would be their God and they his people. By bringing them out of Egypt he has openly declared that they belong to him, and in his law he reveals how they should live as his people. Thus their real desire to live according to the word of God is the indication that they are the redeemed. As such they will know the blessings of the new Eden (Lev 26:1-13). Apostasy will lead to disqualification from the blessings, and the curses will become a reality (Lev 26:14-39). The covenant encompasses a third possibility beyond those of acceptable obedience and willful disobedience. If Israel, having rejected God's ways and fallen under the curses of the covenant, should repent and turn back to the Lord, they shall again know the blessings of the covenant (Lev 26:40-45). However, the results of their disobedience will still be with them and they will suffer the results. The apparent contradiction of covenant blessings alongside the continuing effects of sin is not clearly resolved here. This will, in fact, be the experience of Israel in its later history, and the prophets will point to the resolution of the paradox in the gospel.

We may now summarize some of the main features of the law in relation to the covenant of redemption. God's promises to Israel, first expressed as the covenant with Abraham, are irrevocable. God cannot go back on his word. The redemption from Egypt is a key element in the outworking of the covenant promises. "I will walk among you and be your God, and you will be my people" (Lev 26:12) becomes a standard and frequently repeated summary of the covenant. The law functions to inform Israel how this new relationship to God should be expressed in their lives. If they forget this and live as the Gentiles do, they will receive not the

THE MEANING OF REGENERATION

SUMMARY
Regeneration is more than a movement from one land to another. It also involves coming under the rule of God and being conformed to his character. Israel, living as God's people in the Promised Land, is to be characterized as a people whose God dwells with them and enables them to approach him through the ministry of the tabernacle.

KINGDOM	GOD	MANKIND	WORLD
CREATION:	GOD	ADAM AND EVE	EDEN
FALL			
FLOOD	GOD	NOAH	ARK
ABRAHAM	GOD	ABRAHAM'S DESCENDANTS	CANAAN
MOSES	THE LORD	ISRAEL	CANAAN

MAIN THEMES
The law of Sinai
Freedom through redemption
Priesthood and mediation
Holy to the Lord

SOME KEY WORDS
Sonship
Law and grace
Substitutionary sacrifice
Holy

THE PATH AHEAD
The law written on stone—The law written on their hearts, Jeremiah 31:31-34—Christ fulfilling the law, Matthew 5:17—Not under law but under grace, Romans 6:14
Tabernacle—Temple—Christ, the new temple

blessings but the curses. Yet experience will show that even with the best of intentions they will always go on falling short of the glory of God. The law will constantly remind them of their inability to achieve God's standard of holiness and to love him with all their heart, soul and strength (Deut 6:5). It is precisely then that the law also instructs them to avail themselves of the laws of sacrifice as they repent and cast themselves on God's mercy. Thus they learn that they cannot keep the law only by recognizing their inability to keep it, and by receiving forgiveness of sins and their acceptance with God as a gift.

■ *The laws of holiness*
stress the differences between God and sinful people. The redeemed are called to share in God's holiness by being separate and different from the rest of humanity.

STUDY GUIDE TO CHAPTER 14

1. Read Exodus 19:4-6. What are the main features of the description of Israel given here? What parallels do you see between these and our position under the gospel?

2. Why is it wrong to say that Israel was saved by obedience to the law? Where does the law fit into the scheme of salvation by grace alone?

3. Draw a rough diagram of the tabernacle on the basis of the description given in Exodus 25—30. Identify the key aspects of its design which portray the nature of salvation.

4. Summarize the content of Leviticus 26. How does this passage help us understand the place of the law in the purposes of God, and the meaning of holiness?

FURTHER READING

1. William J. Dumbrell, *Covenant and Creation* (Exeter, U.K.: Paternoster, 1984), chap. 3.
2. *IBD* articles on "Covenant," "Law," "Tabernacle."
3. O. P. Robertson, *The Christ of the Covenants* (Phillipsburg, N.J.: Presbyterian & Reformed, 1980), chap. 10.
4. R. K. Harrison, *Leviticus*, TOTC (Downers Grove, Ill.: InterVarsity Press, 1980).

15

THE TEMPTATION IN THE WILDERNESS

The tempter came to him and said, "If you are the Son of God, tell these stones to become bread."

Jesus answered, "It is written: 'Man does not live on bread alone, but on every word that comes from the mouth of God.'" (Mt 4:3-4)

Just as Moses lifted up the snake in the desert, so the Son of Man must be lifted up, that everyone who believes in him may have eternal life. (Jn 3:14-15)

OUTLINE OF BIBLICAL HISTORY, NUMBERS, DEUTERONOMY
After giving the law to the Israelites at Sinai, God directed them to go in and take possession of the Promised Land. Fearing the inhabitants of Canaan, they refused to do so, thus showing their lack of confidence in the promises of God. The whole adult generation that had come out of Egypt, with the exception of Joshua and Caleb, was condemned to wander and die in the desert. Israel was forbidden to dispossess its kinsfolk, the nations of Edom, Moab and Ammon, but was given victory over other nations that opposed it. Finally, forty years after leaving Egypt, Israel arrived in the Moabite territory on the east side of the Jordan. Here Moses prepared the people for their possession of Canaan, and commissioned Joshua as their new leader.

ISRAEL UNDER GOD'S NAME

A new nation has been born as the people of God, and the promises made to the patriarchs appear now to be gaining substance. Israel's experiences of redemption from Egypt and of the presence and word of the ruling Lord at Sinai, point in one direction only: possession of a new Eden, the Promised Land of Canaan. Nothing summarizes the position of Israel and the nature of God so well as the famous blessing that God told Aaron to pronounce over the people:

> The LORD bless you
>   and keep you;

the LORD make his face shine upon you
   and be gracious to you;
the LORD turn his face toward you
   and give you peace.
(Num 6:24-26)

These words have a very specific meaning. They speak of the restoration to a right relationship with God, of God's continual provision of every need and of healing the fallen creation. So the name of God rests upon Israel (Num 6:27). They will bear his name among the nations of the world but, as the third commandment reminds them, they must not bear this name in vain by bringing it into disrepute.

The book of Numbers places special emphasis on the importance of the tabernacle in the organization and governance of the nation. Moses continues his unique ministry, which combines the functions of prophet and priest. God goes on speaking to him from above the mercy seat in the tabernacle, revealing further details of the way the nation is to be regulated. Once the tabernacle was built, a cloud by day and a fire by night rested on it to signify the presence of the Lord. The sense that God actually lives among his people is enhanced by the guidance of Israel by the cloud. Whenever it is taken up from the tabernacle the people move on until the cloud stops at the place they are at rest. This is a pilgrim people whose God goes with them. God is the warrior who fights for his cause, which is to bring blessing to Israel. Thus, when the movement of the cloud signals the time for departure Moses says:

Rise up, O LORD!
May your enemies be scattered;
may your foes flee before you.

Then as the ark comes to rest he says:

Return, O LORD,
to the countless thousands of Israel. (Num 10:35-36)

■ *The name of God*
rests on Israel signifying the new relationships of the kingdom of God.

ISRAEL THE COVENANT BREAKER
Nothing is more remarkable than the grace of God, and nothing illustrates

that grace more than God's perseverance and goodness to a continually rebellious people. Even while Moses was away on Mount Sinai, the people
grumbled and were openly rebellious (Ex 32). The making of the golden
calf was probably not a deliberate attempt to replace YHWH with another
deity, but it was a refusal to accept the revelation of God. Even if, as some
think, the calf was not intended to be an image of God but rather a pedestal
for him, it still implied an idea of God which was the product of sinful
imagination. It was therefore idolatry. Only the intercession of Moses for
the people prevented their destruction. Because of their faithfulness during this time the Levites were appointed as guardians of the tabernacle.

Now the people are on the move and rebellion becomes an all too frequent occurrence. Even Aaron and Miriam question the unique prophetic
role of Moses (Num 12:1-2). God rebukes them and affirms that with no
other prophet does he speak "face to face." Again the intercession of Moses
leads to an expression of grace in the midst of judgment (Num 12:3-15).

Of all the rebellions of Israel, their refusal to enter the Promised Land
must have tested the Lord's patience the most. A party of twelve scouts
spy out the land of Canaan and return to report. Ten of them are fearful because of the strength of the opposition they have seen, and their report
puts fear into all the people. The other two, Joshua and Caleb, urge the
people to go in and claim the promises of God (Num 13:30; 14:6-9). They
are overruled as the Israelites clamor for a return to Egypt. The Lord's response is chilling: "How long will they refuse to believe in me, in spite of
all the miraculous signs I have performed among them?" (Num 14:11).
Again it is Moses' prayer for them that prevents destruction (Num 14:13-20).
Nevertheless there is judgment. The generation that experienced the miraculous signs in Egypt and the exodus will not enter the Promised Land
but wander forty years in the wilderness and die there. Only Joshua and
Caleb are to accompany the new generation into the land (Num 14:21-35).

Other rebellions are recorded, and it becomes clear that Israel is incapable of keeping the covenant. The positive side of this gloomy fact is
that faithlessness and failure never prevail against the faithfulness of
God. Every time the grace and covenant faithfulness of God are highlighted we are made to look to the future when the problem of human sin
will be truly overcome in one surprisingly unimposing redeeming act.
That event is foreshadowed in the wilderness in unparalleled fashion
when a plague of deadly snakes is sent as judgment on the people's

grumbling. Moses cries to God for mercy and is commanded to set a bronze snake on a pole in the midst of the camp. Anyone who is bitten has only to look at the bronze snake to be saved from death (Num 21:4-9; Jn 3:14-15). There is no obvious logic to this measure other than a response of faith to a word of promise.

In these events of the wilderness wandering, we see an emerging pattern of Israel's rejection of paradise. God's people living in covenant relationship to their Lord in the land he gives them is the substance of the promises. But they reject the land flowing with milk and honey because they are afraid and they do not believe that God really is giving them the land. Now they shall remain in the wilderness until they die. Their children must now decide whether or not to receive the gift.

■ *Israel's rebelliousness*
shows that the covenant relationship is yet imperfect. But Israel's faithlessness is met by God's faithfulness.

PREPARING THE NEW GENERATION

Forty years after the exodus the new adult generation stands in the plains of Moab on the east side of the Jordan. The book of Deuteronomy records Moses' words to the nation as it prepares to enter the Promised Land. It is generally recognized that Deuteronomy is written in the form of a treaty covenant and represents a renewal of the covenant to the new generation about to move under a new leader, Joshua. The first section outlines the history of Israel during the period covered by the book of Numbers. It emphasizes the covenant love of God as he performs mighty deeds to fulfill his promises to Israel. It also recounts the faithlessness and rebellion of the people in the wilderness (Deut 1—3).

Now there is opportunity for a new beginning. The Lord assures Joshua that he is a God who fights for his people. But, as ever, the covenant has a conditional side to it. Deuteronomy repeats the stipulations of the covenant that are to be obeyed (Deut 4—26). These stipulations express the relationship of covenant faithfulness, which is summarized in the words: "Hear, O Israel: The LORD our God, the LORD is one. Love the LORD your God with all your heart and with all your soul and with all your strength" (Deut 6:4-5).

These regulations for holy living are covered by sanctions, that is, by what happens if you obey and what happens if you don't. These blessings and curses are scattered throughout the book but a comprehensive collection of them is found in Deuteronomy 28. Thus the book emphasizes the goodness of God in his choice of Israel and the covenant blessings that he gives to his people. It also points repeatedly to Israel's responsibility to live consistently with its being the holy people of God. Should the nation refuse those responsibilities, it will in turn be denied the blessings. Such rebellion not only deserves the withdrawal of the blessings but also invites the curses.

Nowhere have we found more eloquent expressions of the kingdom of God and of the purpose of the new creation than in Deuteronomy. Here God speaks of his absolute sovereignty in the election of Israel, a choice that can be explained only by the mystery of God's love. He chooses because he loves and he loves because he loves (Deut 7:6-11)! The goal of this election is that Israel should be his people in the good land, the new Eden (Deut 8:7-10). They will be tempted to think that God drives their enemies out before them because they themselves are righteous and deserve to possess the land. Then they must remember that the good they receive they do not deserve, but the evil that any nation receives is richly deserved (Deut 9:1-24).

It would be a mistake to think that Deuteronomy uses the promise of the kingdom and the threat of destruction as the only motivations for covenant faithfulness. This would be to reduce salvation to a reward for good works. The sense of history in the book is consistent with what went before in the Sinai covenant. Above all, it is because of God's redemptive love in the exodus event that Israel is called to be obedient (Deut 4:20, 37-40; 5:15; 10:20-22). Nor may obedience be a merely formal or outward thing such as the bare sign of circumcision, for the response to God must be from the heart (Deut 10:12-16).

Deuteronomy also provides valuable insights into the family as the basic unit of the covenant society. The knowledge of election, of the covenant and its demands, and of redemption is to be passed on within the family from generation to generation (Deut 6:6-9). The only explanation for the laws and regulations that can be given to a curious child is the historical act of redemption by which they were freed from slavery in Egypt (Deut 6:20-25). They are called to live as those who have been saved by grace.

PROMISES OF A REGENERATED WORLD

SUMMARY

A regenerated nation without a regenerated land would be like Adam and Eve without Eden. The promise of possession of the land is the promise of a land that is renewed in a way that points to the removal of all the ill effects of the fall. Such a land is part of the kingdom that can be received only by faith.

KINGDOM	GOD	MANKIND	WORLD
CREATION	GOD	ADAM AND EVE	EDEN
FALL			
FLOOD	GOD	NOAH	ARK
ABRAHAM	GOD	ABRAHAM'S DESCENDANTS	CANAAN
MOSES	THE LORD	ISRAEL	CANAAN

MAIN THEMES

Name of God

God dwelling with his people

Promised Land

Israel's disobedience

SOME KEY WORDS

Blessing and curse

Faith

Idolatry

THE PATH AHEAD

Israel's failure to enter—A warning to Christians, 1 Corinthians 10:1-13

Sabbath rest for the people of God, Hebrews 4:1-13

Moses finishes his last great discourse as the prophet of God by pronouncing a blessing on each of the tribes of Israel. He then dies in the land of Moab (Deut 33—34). Joshua stands ready to lead his people into the kingdom God has prepared for them.

■ *The new generation*
stands under the renewed covenant with all the assurances that God will give his chosen the Promised Land.

STUDY GUIDE TO CHAPTER 15

1. In what sense could the land of Canaan be seen as a new Eden? Look up Exodus 3:16-17; 15:17-18; Deuteronomy 8:7-10.

2. In what sense was Israel "saved" by the release from Egypt? What are some of the events that show the nation to be "unsaved"?

3. How do the events in the wilderness show the way God deals with Israel's unfaithfulness while he himself remains faithful to his promises?

4. How does Paul apply the Israelite situation to Christians in 1 Corinthians 10:1-13?

FURTHER READING

1. G. J. Wenham, *Numbers,* TOTC (Downers Grove, Ill.: InterVarsity Press, 1981).
2. J. A. Thompson, *Deuteronomy,* TOTC (Downers Grove, Ill.: InterVarsity Press, 1974).
3. *IBD* article on "Deuteronomy, Book of."

16

INTO THE GOOD LAND

There remains, then, a Sabbath-rest for the people of God. (Heb 4:9)

"I tell you the truth, today you will be with me in paradise." (Lk 23:43)

OUTLINE OF BIBLICAL HISTORY, JOSHUA, JUDGES, RUTH
Under Joshua's leadership the Israelites crossed the Jordan and began the task of driving out the inhabitants of Canaan. After the conquest the land was divided between the tribes, each being allotted its own region. Only the tribe of Levi was without an inheritance of land because of its special priestly relationship to God. There remained pockets of Canaanites in the land and, from time to time, these threatened Israel's hold on their new possession. From the one-man leaderships of Moses and Joshua the nation moved into a period of relative instability during which judges exercised some measure of control over the affairs of the people.

■ *An explanation*
It will have become obvious to you that I have steadily increased the amount of biblical material covered by each chapter. The reason is simple. Most of the main themes that concern us as biblical theologians are introduced in the early stages of the Bible. Genesis and Exodus are therefore considered in greater detail than most of the subsequent books. You might wonder why the biblical writers did not adopt the same attitude. Suffice it to say that they were writing for the needs of their own times and not purely for our benefit. We do not ignore the material of the later books, but it can be dealt with in less detail once the foundations are laid.

THE PROMISES

Forty years in the wilderness is a long time! Perhaps it is long enough for the people of the new generation to forget the awful failure of their parents to claim the promises of God. But now, buoyed up by their victories over the kings of the Transjordan, they make ready to face the enemy. Joshua, their leader, hears again the promises of God: he is giving them the land;

no one will be able to stop them because God is causing them to inherit the land (Josh 1:1-9). The condition laid upon their achievement of this goal is obedience to God's word. No doubt obedience is required of all the people, but here it is laid especially upon Joshua as the leader. He is to meditate on God's law and be careful to do it. Faith and courage go together with obedience, for God is with his people (Josh 1:9).

This obedience to the covenant that is required of the leader of Israel has been foreshadowed in Deuteronomy 17:14-20. When the people settle in the land and eventually decide to have a king, the one they choose must be a leader who lives by the law. The king or leader represents the people and his personal holiness affects the life of the nation. Viewing this from the theological angle, we see that God's rule over his people in the place that he gives them is mediated through a human ruler who must reflect the character of God to the people. This theme, which develops into even greater prominence in the Old Testament, is important for understanding the kingdom of God in the New Testament. The promises of God are fulfilled by a human, kingly figure who is worthy to lead God's people into the Promised Land.

■ *The fulfillment*
of God's promises is to be achieved by God working through chosen human beings.

THE FULFILLMENT

The theological thrust of the book of Joshua can be grasped from a reading of the first and the last two chapters. As promised, Israel enters the land where the Lord gives them rest in the form of unchallenged possession (Josh 23:1-13). The only reason they possess the land is that the Lord has fought for them. Although there is still some territory to be acquired (Josh 23:4-5), the promises are deemed as fulfilled. "You know with all your heart and soul that not one of all the good promises the Lord your God gave you has failed. Every promise has been fulfilled; not one has failed" (Josh 23:14; see also 21:43-45).

The bulk of the book of Joshua describes the way to fulfillment. As the way out of Egypt was marked by the miracle of God removing the sea that lay in the way, so the way into Canaan involves a similar miracle. This time the Jordan River is stopped so that the people are able to cross on foot (Josh 3:1-17). This is a sign that God is with them and that he will drive out the inhabitants of the land (Josh 3:10). In the course of the crossing, God commands Joshua to take twelve stones out of the river and set up a monument at the place where they first camp in the Promised Land. Once again the opportunity is there to answer the child's curious "Why?" with an explanation of the Lord's saving acts when he made a way through the Red Sea and the Jordan (Josh 4:21-24; compare Deut 6:20-25). Notice how consistently the gospel, in its Old Testament form, of the saving acts of God is presented as the one way to make sense of the Israelite's existence.

The account of the capture of Jericho illustrates the outworking of this theology. Before the battle an angelic commander of the Lord's armies appears to Joshua. He commands a strategy for the overthrow of the city that involves armed men marching around the city with the ark of the covenant. The implication is that the battle is the Lord's and that his power will subdue Jericho. Yet the miracle of destruction is not without human involvement (Josh 5:13—6:7). Mediation of God's acts through certain chosen people is a constant biblical theme.

In the process of conquest, certain parts of the land were put under a ban so that Israel might know that the earth is the Lord's. Jericho is one such place devoted to the Lord, which means that it is to be totally destroyed. Any Israelite who takes anything that is devoted to God will himself fall under the ban (Josh 6:17-21). Against this background we understand the sin of Achan who looted some of the devoted things in Jericho. The immediate effect is a disastrous defeat of the Israelites at the hands of the men of Ai (Josh 7:1-5). When Achan is revealed as the offender, he and his whole household are destroyed (Josh 7:6-26). Here we see the principle of corporateness that operates in Scripture. The one represents the many because of the corporate solidarity or oneness of the group. Thus the whole human race sinned in Adam. Because Noah found grace in the eyes of the Lord, his whole family was saved. In Abraham the whole nation was chosen. Through the ministrations of one priest all the people are reconciled to God. And so it will develop until the ideas of representation and substitution become fixed in the concept of salvation. Now the one leader, Joshua (whose name means "Jehovah is salvation"), mediates the saving and judging acts of God.

■ *The power of God*
subdues the opposition to the fulfillment of his promises.

ALL NATIONS WILL BE BLESSED

Now let us remember the last element of the promise to Abraham in Genesis 12:3—all nations will be blessed through his descendants. The one nation, a priestly nation, will mediate God's blessings to all the nations of the world. The foundation of Christian mission lies in that promise. Does that mean that Israel had a mission similar to the missionary task of the church? To put the question like that is to risk reading into the Old Testament a New Testament understanding of mission. It is better if we ask how Israel was to bring a blessing to all nations. Already at least part of the answer is beginning to emerge. Certain Gentiles are brought in by various means to share with Israel the promises of God.

This must not be misunderstood as contradicting the very strict notions of Israel's holiness and separateness from the nations which is expressed in the ban on mixed marriages. For what then shall we say of Moses' marriage to a Midianite (Ex 2:21) and to a Cushite (Num 12:1)? We must understand that marriage to foreigners was acceptable if the foreigner was a proselyte, a convert to the faith of Israel. The case of Rahab is slightly different (Josh 2:8-14; 6:17, 25). She entered Israel, not by marriage, but by an active confession in Israel's God. She was convinced that God was giving Canaan to the Israelites, so she and her whole household are saved and delivered from the ban on Jericho.

In this theological context comes the book of Ruth, which is placed after Judges because of its historical context. (In the Hebrew Bible it is found in the last of the three sections of the canon.) It tells of a Moabite woman's devotion to God. This woman finds acceptance in Israel, is redeemed by a kinsman, and becomes an ancestor of King David. But, whatever way these proselytes come in, it is *into* Israel that they come. There is no other revealed way of salvation than to become an Israelite, yet the Israelites do not find themselves compelled to go out and to persuade foreigners to become proselytes.

■ *Gentiles*
begin to share in the covenant blessings from the beginning of God's saving acts.

THE PATTERN OF SALVATION

If the book of Joshua highlights the successful possession of the land, the book of Judges concentrates on the blemishes on this achievement. In many places the Israelites retain their conquered foes for forced labor (Judg 1:27-36). The Lord rebukes them for making covenants with the Canaanites and reminds them that these foreigners will become a snare to them (Judg 2:2-3).

The theme of the book is set out in Judges 2:11-23. Once the Israelites are in general possession of the land the pattern of events becomes a repetitious cycle. The people rebel against the Lord and indulge in religious syncretism (the mixing of pagan ideas with their own) and even apostasy. Obviously the religion of Canaan is very attractive to them (Judg 2:11-13). Consequently, God punishes them by allowing foreigners to invade and oppress them. Then, as they cry out under their affliction, God sends judges to save them from their enemies (Judg 2:14-23).

In different ways the judges, whose deeds are recorded in this book, are used by God to save the people from the results of their folly. Of some it is recorded that the Spirit of the Lord comes upon them (Judg 3:10; 6:34; 11:29; 13:25; 14:19; 15:14, 19) thus, they are able to do great deeds or exercise great strength in defeating the enemies of Israel. When the situation is stable for a time, they judge Israel, which probably means that they exercise some kind of leadership and ruling office.

Thus, this crucial period in Israel's history reinforces the salvation pattern established in the exodus. Although the Israelites dwell physically in the Promised Land their disobedience prevents their enjoyment of the promised blessings. They repeatedly enter into a kind of captivity and, unlike the Egyptian captivity, the reason for it is obviously their sinful rejection of the Lord. But then the Lord's covenant faithfulness and love lead to their salvation through some saving act of God in which a chosen representative person figures. The giving of the Spirit to the judges indicates that what the Israelites cannot do for themselves, God does for them through a chosen, Spirit-empowered human being.

■ *The pattern of salvation*
is repeated many times in Israel's history, reinforcing the revelation of God in the exodus.

KINGSHIP IN THE KINGDOM
How does God rule in his kingdom? In Eden he ruled by speaking to

Adam and Eve and by giving them rule over the rest of creation. God was ruling when he called Abraham. He was ruling when he spoke to Moses out of the burning bush and when he gave him the law on Mount Sinai. Already we see that God's choice is to rule his kingdom, even before the fall, through human beings. Moses, the prophet and priest, also mediated God's kingship through the law and in his personal leadership. Joshua's leadership upheld the law of Moses and asserted itself against the nations which opposed the coming of God's kingdom. The destruction of the Canaanites must be understood as the invasion of the kingdom of God into an alien and rebellious world. The saving acts of God on behalf of his chosen people are thus acts of judgment on godless nations (Deut 9).

In the same way that the chosen people as a whole is a much blemished race, which is better able to break the covenant than to keep it, so also the kingly figures are flawed. Even Moses is denied entry into the land because of an angry outburst in the wilderness (Num 20:10-13). The judges are not an altogether attractive lot. Ehud appears to be a sly character, Gideon argues with God about whether he really has the go-ahead for his task (Judg 6:36-40) and Samson appears as somewhat of a blockhead and a womanizer. In the period after the judges the kingdom of Israel is ruled by Saul, David and Solomon, all of whom have stains on their characters.

We need to distinguish between the pattern of events and their perfection. The events of saving history in the Old Testament prefigure and demonstrate the pattern of the one true and perfect saving act yet to come. They do it well enough to point the people of that time to the way of salvation by grace through faith. God is not playing games with Israel for the sake of us who come afterward. His promises are true for them, and the way of salvation is made plain. Yet the failures of the saving figures, the prophets, the priests and the kings, as well as the overall failure of Israel, all point to the fact that the real saving event still lies in the future.

This redemptive function of the imperfect people and events of the Old Testament illustrates the idea of typology that I discussed on page 68. Typology sees the historical events in the Old Testament as providing the focus of faith in the promises of God which point beyond these events to the reality which is to come in Christ. Thus, we not only distinguish between the pattern and the perfection (which is lacking), but also between the inadequacy of the Old Testament type to save and its function of pointing forward to the only true basis of salvation in Jesus Christ. The epistle to

FORETASTE OF A REGENERATED WORLD

SUMMARY The land of Canaan was a good land ready to be possessed and enjoyed by the people of God. Their entry into the land was attended by signs of the regenerating power of God. But even as they took possession, their disobedience and failure threatened their status as the redeemed people of God enjoying the blessings of the covenant.

KINGDOM	GOD	MANKIND	WORLD
CREATION	GOD	ADAM AND EVE	EDEN
FALL			
FLOOD	GOD	NOAH	ARK
ABRAHAM	GOD	ABRAHAM'S DESCENDANTS	CANAAN
MOSES	THE LORD	ISRAEL	CANAAN

MAIN THEMES Promise of possession
The Lord's holy war
Conquest

SOME KEY WORDS Mediation
Kingship
Proselyte

THE PATH AHEAD Israel enters the promised land—The return of the exiles, Ezekiel 36:8-12—Sabbath rest for the people of God, Hebrews 4:1-13 the Hebrews shows us that a principal point of unity between the two Testaments is the pattern of redemption, while the real distinction lies in the fact that only the saving work of Jesus suffices to save anyone.

■ *Human kingship*
begins to emerge as the means God uses to rule over his people.

STUDY GUIDE TO CHAPTER 16

1. List the people of biblical history up to this point who mediate God's word and deeds. In what way does each stand as "one on behalf of the many"?

2. How do the events of the exodus and the entry into Canaan pattern salvation? How do they fail to give the full significance of salvation?

3. What place would you give creation and covenant in a biblical theology of Christian mission?

4. Summarize the significance of the book of Judges for biblical theology.

FURTHER READING

1. A. E. Cundall, *Judges*, TOTC (Downers Grove, Ill.: InterVarsity Press, 1968).
2. *IBD* articles on "Judges, Book of," "Mediator."

17

GOD'S RULE
IN GOD'S LAND

You will be with child and give birth to a son, and you are to give him the name Jesus. He will be great and will be called the Son of the Most High. The Lord God will give him the throne of his father David. (Lk 1:31-32)

Destroy this temple, and I will raise it again in three days. (Jn 2:19)

OUTLINE OF BIBLICAL HISTORY, 1 AND 2 SAMUEL, 1 KINGS 1—10, 1 CHRONICLES, 2 CHRONICLES 1—9
Samuel became judge and prophet in all Israel at a time when the Philistines threatened the freedom of the nation. An earlier movement for kingship was revived and the demand put to a reluctant Samuel. The first king, Saul, had a promising start to his reign but eventually showed himself unsuitable as the ruler of the covenant people. While Saul still reigned, David was anointed to succeed him. Because of Saul's jealousy, David became an outcast. However, when Saul died in battle, David returned and became king (about 1000 B.C.). Due to his successes Israel became a powerful and stable nation. He established a central sanctuary at Jerusalem and created a professional bureaucracy and a permanent army. David's son, Solomon, succeeded him (about 961 B.C.) and the prosperity of Israel continued. The building of the temple at Jerusalem was one of Solomon's more notable achievements.

SAUL

When Israel's possession of the Promised Land is threatened, the people naturally look for help, but not necessarily for the right kind of help. After Gideon's successes against the marauding Midianites, the Israelites make a bid to have him establish a dynasty of kings. Gideon rejects this on the grounds that the Lord alone is King (Judg 8:22-23). After the death of Gideon, one of his sons, Abimelech, succeeds in being made ruler for a while, probably over only a relatively small region (Judg 9). The judges continue to rule. The book of Judges concludes with a reference to instability and chaos in the land as due to the lack of a king (Judg 21:25).

During the time of the prophet and judge Samuel, some disastrous encounters with the Philistines lead to a revival of the kingship movement.
There is some apparent ambivalence in Judges and 1 Samuel about the de-
sirability of a kingship. Gideon rejected it, and now Samuel does also. It is
sometimes suggested that 1 Samuel contains two strands, one drawn from
a pro-king document and the other from an anti-king document. I find it
difficult to believe that the author of 1 Samuel, as we now have it, was so
inept that he couldn't sort out and avoid contradictory ideas. The ambivalence is not in the writing but in the real historical situation.

We need to remember that the idea of kingship was established long before this. Jacob prophesied of the kingship of Judah, with no suggestion
that this would not be God's will (Gen 49:8-10). Written into the statutes
and ordinances of Deuteronomy is the provision for a king (Deut 17:14-20).
Strict guidelines are given which clearly distinguish between the usual
type of pagan despotic ruler and the king whose rule reflects the covenant
relationship with the living God. Israel's kings must fear the Lord, keep his
law and not lift up their heart above their brethren. In other words, kingship for Israel is defined by the covenant. Unfortunately the people don't
always see it that way. Rather than taking the covenant as the model of
kingship, they undoubtedly desire the benefits that appear to come from
the autocratic rule of the Canaanite and Philistine kings.

Thus, the request for a king, which Samuel at first refuses, is born of the
desire to imitate the pagan nations. This was indeed a rejection of the covenant model and, therefore, a rejection of God's rule (1 Sam 8:4-8). We may
assume that God tells Samuel to comply with the request because it was
always his will to rule Israel through a king. The people are to learn the
hard way what the reality of covenant rule is. So Samuel warns them that
the kind of king they ask for will not turn out to be what they want (1 Sam
8:10-18). They are not interested in the covenant so much as in safety, security and strength. They forget that God has committed himself in the
covenant to give them those things in a way that no pagan ruler could.

When Saul is chosen publicly by the drawing of lots, there is no suggestion that he will be a failure. In fact, he is full of promise and begins his reign
by acting the part of a savior-judge. He is ready to recognize the hand of the
Lord in his victory over the Ammonites (1 Sam 11:12-15). Samuel steps
aside from the leadership but warns the people that it is up to them and
Saul to follow the Lord. If they do, all will be well (1 Sam 12:14-15).

But it is not to be so. Saul's first major blunder is to take upon himself the office of priest, whereupon Samuel tells him that his kingdom will be taken from him (1 Sam 13:8-14). Then the Lord sends him to destroy the Amalekites, whom God puts under the ban. Saul keeps some of the best Amalekite livestock (in order to sacrifice them to God, or so he claims). Thus he shows himself to be the very opposite of the covenant king of Deuteronomy 17. He has rejected the word of the Lord and now the Lord rejects him from the kingship (1 Sam 15:1-23).

■ *Saul*

shows that kingship is God's will for his people, but only if it reflects the cove-nant relationship.

DAVID

While Saul yet lives and reigns as king, a man after God's own heart is being drawn into the leadership through no plan or will of his own (1 Sam 13:14). Samuel is sent to choose David out of all the sons of Jesse (1 Sam 16:13), and to anoint him as king in the place of Saul. The Spirit of the Lord comes upon David but departs from Saul (1 Sam 16:13-14). The role of the savior-judge is never so clearly shown as it is when the young, Spirit-empowered David slays Goliath (1 Sam 17). Here it is evident that the savior-judgeship is the precursor to the emerging savior-kingship. As all Israel retreats in terror from the Philistines and their champion, God's anointed king, who appears weak and insignificant, fights for his people knowing that the battle is the Lord's (1 Sam 17:45-47). David stands alone as the one in the place of the many, and through him God works salvation for Israel.

Understandably David is the toast of the nation. Saul's jealousy grows until he desires only to kill David. Rejected and despised, David flees from society and gathers a band of misfits around him. Yet so overwhelming is his sense of the king being anointed by God, that he refuses on at least two occasions to lift his hand against Saul. He is prepared to leave it to the Lord to remove his anointed from office (1 Sam 24:1-7; 26:6-12). Likewise, in God's time, David will be vindicated in the eyes of the people and will be exalted to the kingship. Saul's grasp on sanity and on the kingdom slips and he dies on Mount Gilboa in a battle with the Philistines (1 Sam 31).

The transition from Saul's rule to David's is not especially smooth. Nevertheless, David is soon proclaimed king at the age of thirty. At the Lord's command he launches a successful campaign against the Philistines and secures the borders of Israel. He also captures the Jebusite stronghold of Jerusalem and makes it his capital (2 Sam 5). He brings the ark of the covenant to Jerusalem (2 Sam 6), and then decides to build a permanent sanctuary for it (2 Sam 7:1-3). However, the prophet Nathan brings the word of the Lord forbidding David to build it.

God's covenant with David is of the utmost importance for understanding the theology that surrounds this most notable of all the kings. God promises to make David's name great and to give his people rest in their land. He will not allow David to build the house of God (a temple) but will himself make for David a house (a dynasty). David shall have a son who shall indeed build the temple and whose throne will be established forever (2 Sam 7:4-12). The continuity of this covenant with the covenant to Abraham can be seen in their respective summaries. "I will be their God, they will be my people" sums up God's purpose in the covenant with Abraham and after him, with Israel (Gen 17:7-8; 26:12; Jer 7:23; 11:4; 30:22). Now the promise concerning David's son, the one who will represent the many, is given as, "I will be his father, and he shall be my son" (2 Sam 7:14). Thus, David's son is also the son of God, and his house, throne and kingdom are established forever (2 Sam 7:16).

Long after he is gone, David is praised for this covenant relationship. An example is found in Psalm 89 (see also Ps 132). The psalmist begins by praising God for his covenant love (Hebrew: *hesed*) and faithfulness which is established forever (verses 1-2). All the hope of Israel now focuses on the prophecies of Nathan to David (2 Sam 7); indeed, this covenant with David is portrayed as the most significant of all God's promises.

> You said, "I have made a covenant with my chosen one,
>   I have sworn to David my servant,
> 'I will establish your line forever
>   and make your throne firm through all generations.'" (Ps 89:3-4)

Then there is an apparent intrusion as the psalmist moves to heavenly regions where God is praised by all creatures and by the hosts of angelic beings. From there God exercises his kingship in the world, controlling nature and showing grace to his people (Ps 89:5-18). But this is no intrusion, for this glorious reign of God is to be represented on earth by the kingship of David and his line. The covenant with David includes all the earlier covenant promises. The psalmist says of God:

> Righteousness and justice are the foundation of your throne;
>   love and faithfulness *(hesed)* go before you. (Ps 89:14)

And of David's son he says:

> My faithful love *(hesed)* will be with him,
>   and through my name his horn will be exalted. (Ps 89:24)

The covenant is both conditional and unconditional:

> If his sons forsake my law . . .
> I will punish their sin with the rod,
>   their iniquity with flogging.
> But I will not take my love *(hesed)* from him,
>   nor will I ever betray my faithfulness.
> I will not violate my covenant or alter what my lips have uttered.
> (Ps 89:30, 32-34)

We have already seen this conditional/unconditional principle operate when a whole generation of the chosen people dies in the wilderness for its sins, yet a new generation continues under the promise. We shall see it repeated more than once in the future. It simply means that the unfaithfulness of the covenant people invites the judgment of God, but is never allowed to annul the covenant faithfulness *(hesed)* of God. Somehow, out of the faithless covenant people, there always emerges a part, a remnant, which is faithful because God is faithful.

■ *David*
receives promises from God which sum up all the previous covenant promises,
and focus them on David's line of descendants.

SOLOMON

Solomon succeeds his father, David, to the throne around the year 961 B.C. He is a complex character who, like his predecessors, shows much promise alongside some significant failings. The narrative in 1 Kings 3—10 concentrates on the good points of this man to whom Nathan's prophecy referred as the son of God and the temple builder. Some negative elements of his

reign, such as mixed marriages and religious disobedience, are hinted at
without direct comment (1 Kings 3:1-2), only after we learn of his virtues.

The notable features of Solomon are narrated in a way that shows him
to be the one who puts the finishing touches to the glories of David's
reign. David was an astute leader and used the counsel of wise men. Solomon is spoken of as the leading wise man of Israel who desires and receives an understanding mind to govern the people (1 Kings 3:6-9; 4:29-
34). The fact that wisdom characterizes his reign demands that we try to
understand the significance of wisdom in biblical theology (see chapter
eighteen). The king who rules wisely is not only concerned with intelli-
gent decisions which promote justice (1 Kings 3:16-28), but he also
achieves prosperity in the good land according to the covenant promise
(1 Kings 4:20-28). He seeks out the relationships that exist between all
parts of the creation (1 Kings 4:29-34). At the heart of his wisdom is the
revelation of God and his covenant. Even the magnificence of the temple
is related to Solomon's wisdom.

David's religious masterstroke was to bring the ark to Jerusalem and to
make the city the focal point of the covenant relationship with God. All the
promises of God concerning his relationship to his people and the land he
gives them are concentrated in Jerusalem, or Zion. Solomon now builds
the temple as the dwelling place of God in the holy city. Its glory is described in detail in 1 Kings 5—7, but the theology of the temple is contained in Solomon's dedicatory prayer (1 Kings 8).

In the first place the temple replaces the tabernacle and functions as a
permanent and fixed sanctuary within the Promised Land. When the ark
is brought to the sanctuary the glory of the Lord fills the house (1 Kings
8:6-10). This is now the place of sacrifice and of reconciliation with God.
When sin clouds the relationship of the nation to God, repentance and
prayer towards the temple secure forgiveness. Through this house and
its ministry the covenant relationship is maintained (1 Kings 8:15-53).
Even the promise to the Gentiles is focused here, for it is at the temple
that foreigners can find acceptance with God. The temple is a witness to
all the nations that God dwells in Israel and that he is found through the
name he has revealed and by which the temple is named. In other words,
a foreigner can be joined to the people of God only by coming to the temple, for it is here that God chooses to deal with those who seek him (1
Kings 8:41-43).

THE PATTERN OF RULE IN THE NEW EARTH

SUMMARY

The combined effect of the reigns of Saul, David and Solomon was to show the pattern of God's rule in the new earth. At the heart of it was the covenant. The king represented the whole nation as the true covenant partner of God. At the same time, he mediated God's rule to the people in conjunction with the temple and its ministry of reconciliation and forgiveness.

KINGDOM	GOD	MANKIND	WORLD
CREATION	GOD	ADAM AND EVE	EDEN
FALL			
FLOOD	GOD	NOAH	ARK
ABRAHAM	GOD	ABRAHAM'S DESCENDANTS	CANAAN
MOSES	THE LORD	ISRAEL	CANAAN
DAVID	THE LORD	DAVID'S LINE	TEMPLE IN JERUSALEM

MAIN THEMES

Judgeship
Kingship
Temple
Davidic covenant

SOME KEY WORDS Covenant love *(hesed)*

THE PATH AHEAD David's line established in Jerusalem—A new David will reign in a new Jerusalem, Jeremiah 23:5-6; Ezekiel 34:20-31—Christ, the new David, Acts 2:29-33; 13:23, 32-34

Of course, Solomon's reign and character are blemished. The biblical history, however, concentrates first of all on the positive points, for it is from these that the theological significance of Solomon can be drawn. He is the covenanted son of God who mediates God's rule in God's land. Together with David he shows the pattern of the rule of the messianic savior-king. The messianic reign is marked by true wisdom, by the glory of the land and of the royal court. It is capped by the house of God, which, for Israel, is the visible center of the universe and the touchstone of reality and truth.

■ *Solomon*

completes the pattern of God's rule which is mediated through the anointed king (messiah).

STUDY GUIDE TO CHAPTER 17

1. From the wider perspective on kingship looked at in this chapter, why was God so hard on Saul? Was it wrong for the Israelites to have wanted a king?

2. Read 2 Samuel 7:1-14. Why do you think some have seen this passage as the theological center of the books of Samuel? See what other biblical writers have said about it: Psalms 89; 132; Isaiah 9:6-7; 55:1-4; Jeremiah 23:5-6; 33:23-26; Ezekiel 34:20-24.

3. How does Solomon fulfill Nathan's prophecy about David's son in 2 Samuel 7:12-14? Given that Israel is ideally God's son, what does it mean that Solomon is God's son?

4. Summarize the biblical theology of kingship over God's people as it has been revealed up to the time of Solomon.

FURTHER READING

1. *GK*, pp. 69-76.
2. *IBD* articles on "David," "Saul," "Solomon," "Temple."
3. *KG*, chap. 1.

18

THE LIFE OF FAITH

Christ the power of God and the wisdom of God. (1 Cor 1:24)

It is because of him that you are in Christ Jesus, who has become for us wisdom from God. (1 Cor 1:30)

"Everything must be fulfilled that is written about me in the Law of Moses, the Prophets and the Psalms." (Lk 24:44)

OUTLINE OF BIBLICAL HISTORY, GENESIS, EXODUS, LEVITICUS, NUMBERS, DEUTERONOMY, JOSHUA, JUDGES, RUTH, 1 & 2 SAMUEL, 1 KINGS 1—10, 1 CHRONICLES, 2 CHRONICLES 1—9

BELIEVING ISRAELITES IN EVERYDAY LIFE

A consistent theme in the books of the Old Testament is that of God as the creator, covenant-maker and redeemer. He is no distant and aloof deity cloaked in obscurity. Rather he has made himself known in such a way that the whole life of his people is caught up in what he does to save them. God is alive and active, exercising his lordship over the history of the whole world to move it inexorably towards the goal he has ordained for it. Within this world-history are to be found the ordinary men and women of Israel who respond to the word and action of God in personal ways as they take hold of the covenant promises and struggle to apply them to their own lives.

The writers of most of the biblical books concentrate on those people and events that are central to redemptive history. This focus on the great events easily obscures the fact that often whole generations are born, grow old and die without them. Life in ancient Israel is not three miracles a day and a new holy war each week. Most people live their lives while God does no new thing. For every biblical hero there are thousands of Israelites who know God only through what is taught by priests and prophets, and seek to be obedient to the law in personal devotion, in home and family life, and in worship of God.

What is the life of faith as lived by ordinary Israelites? Most of the biblical evidence concerns the nation as a whole, the big events and high feast days. We must assume that to some degree those prescribed forms of public worship, observance of the great annual feasts and attention to the required sacrifices, govern the religious thinking and activities of believing Israelites. But how do believing Israelites translate their faith into everyday life?

■ *The saving acts of God*
have a profound meaning for the everyday life of ordinary people.

KNOWLEDGE AND THE FEAR OF THE LORD

The creation narratives remind us that being created human and in the image of God meant very special relationships to God, to other people and to the physical creation. The word of God came to Adam and Eve to enable them to know who and what they were and what their task in the world was to be. The word of God gave them the necessary starting point for true knowledge. It gave them the framework for a right understanding of the universe. By making himself known to them as the Creator, God established every fact of true knowledge as a fact about himself. But he did not tell them those things they could find out for themselves. Within the framework of revelation humans are free to use their God-given brains and senses to gather knowledge, to classify it, to deduce relationships, to invent, to plan and to have dominion over the creation.

Sin, as we saw in chapter ten, involved a rejection of the order of creation and a refusal to accept revelation as the basis of true knowledge. It was the rejection of the principle that underlies the book of Proverbs: "The fear of the LORD is the beginning of knowledge" (Prov 1:7). We saw how important the process of thought was in the human relationship to God and to the creation. Crooked thinking led to crooked relationships. It stands to reason, then, that the process of redemption involves the restoration of the right way of thinking. The human mind is as much the object of regeneration as is the body or the soul.

If the fear of the Lord is the beginning of knowledge (Prov 1:7) and the beginning of wisdom (Prov 9:10), what is it and where does it come from?

According to Solomon's dedicatory prayer, the fear of the Lord is linked with the covenant and the ministry of the temple (1 Kings 8:38-43). This fear is not a terror of God, rather it is a response of reverent awe and trust to the redemptive revelation of God (Deut 4:10; 6:2; 10:12, 20-21). It is the Old Testament equivalent of trusting Christ or believing the gospel. The fear of the Lord is the response of faith to all that God has done to redeem his people, as he himself interprets what he has done by his Word.

As God's redemptive revelation is progressively unfolded through the covenant promises, the law of Sinai, the great redemptive acts of the exodus and the conquest of Canaan, so the framework for understanding reality becomes clearer. From the beginning the people of God struggled to gain true knowledge and understanding. In the early stages, they came under the care and instruction of the law because the picture was not complete enough or clear enough for them to deduce what a life consistent with their covenant status was. But by the time of Solomon the whole structure of redemption and the kingdom was revealed through the way God had dealt with them since the initial promises to Abraham. Thus, within the framework of the law and the prophetic revelation, wisdom comes into its own as a human activity demanded by the grace of God. It is as if God, through his servant Solomon, signals that the framework of redemption is now in place and the believer is free to pursue knowledge and understanding within that framework.

■ *The Word of God*
and his saving acts provide the framework for the response of trust and reverence. The quest for true knowledge and wisdom starts from this "fear of the Lord."

ORDER, DISORDER AND REGENERATION OF ORDER

The original orderliness of creation expressed the proper relationships between God, mankind and the world. Thus, it was harmonious and good (Gen 1:31). The rebellion of Adam and Eve resulted in a measure of disorder in which all relationships were adversely affected. Despite appearances, then and now, this disruption is not a minor malady, rather it is terminal and destructive (Gen 2:17; 3:17-19; Rom 5:12; 8:19-20). Human thought that reflects this rebellion is foolishness, not wisdom, and involves a deliberate and wicked suppression of the truth (Rom 1:18-23; 1 Cor 1:18-25).

From the moment God begins the work of redemption we can see the regeneration process affecting the people of God. At first there are hints of glory and glimpses of what is to come. Regeneration starts with the people that God binds to himself by his unfolding revelation and by their faith. They find themselves an elect few, a special nation in a godless world. The promises of God, as these are filled out by his redemptive activity, point to the future reality of the regeneration of all things. They also highlight the nature of the original order and of the serious degeneration caused by sin.

The intellectual task with which Israel finds itself is that of understanding what its present stage of redemptive experience means for the good life. In what way are relationships being restored, and in what way are they as yet not restored? The Israelite believer had similar problems to those we have as Christians. What is the response of faith to the secular world? How does a believer relate to other believers and to unbelievers in a creation that is yet unregenerate? The wisdom literature of the Old Testament expresses the Israelite quest for knowledge and understanding in a world in which all relationships are confused by the human rejection of God. But it is recognized that God has never let sin totally destroy all relationships, for the world is still orderly and nature is still supportive of human life. It is also understood that only the goodness of God, as he imparts wisdom through his Word, can enable the believer to make progress in his struggle to gain wisdom and knowledge.

■ *The order of creation*
degenerated into disorder because of sin, and is being regenerated into the order willed by God. The regenerated order includes right thinking.

THE WISDOM BOOKS

Proverbs, Job and Ecclesiastes are the main books of the Old Testament that deal with the search for knowledge. They start from the framework of revelation or the fear of the Lord. From the standpoint of believing, covenant-based Israelites they explore the issues of human experience. The world and human life have meaning because God not only preserves his creation from chaos, but also because he has shown that he is restoring all things to right relationships.

The book of Proverbs invites us to assemble our experiences and to examine them for the underlying relationships that make life coherent and meaningful. The wise person tries to understand the real nature of things and to bow to the order that makes for a life with God. The individual proverbs are not detailed expressions of the law of Sinai handed down from God but human reflections on individual experiences in the light of God's truth. Thus, they show that being human as God intends means learning to think and act in a godly way. It means that, in revelation, God gives the framework for godly thinking but he will not do our thinking for us. We are responsible for the decisions we make as we seek to be wise (to think in a godly way) and to avoid being foolish (to think in a godless way). Decisions are wise when they are made in the light of the life which God sets before us as our goal.

But while so much human experience is predictable in the way Proverbs expresses it, there is also mystery. God is great and his ways are often hidden from us (Job 11:7; Is 55:8-9). He does not reveal to us the whole picture of his will; indeed we could not understand it if he did. Thus, the believer may encounter suffering and tragedy that seem to be senseless and a denial of God's care and control of events. The book of Job explores the problem of this hidden order and how wisdom may find its greatest expression in the humble recognition that humans are puny creatures, and that God's loving kindness may be expressed in ways that we simply cannot grasp. Thus we are reminded that wisdom is never a purely intellectual hold on ideas, but involves trust in the sovereign will of a gracious yet mysterious God.

The greatness of God is not the only source of mystery for God's people. Human sin and corruption conspire to confuse the order of things and to make relationships difficult. At times even the pursuit of true wisdom seems to lead up a blind alley. Ecclesiastes shows that not only the pagan but also the Israelite is in danger of developing a rigid way of thinking that distorts and obscures the truth. This means that human sinfulness not only upsets relationships but also renders us, even as believers, prone to misunderstanding and false thinking.

■ *The wisdom books*
express the human quest for knowledge and understanding within the framework of God's revelation. The fact that there is mystery in God's ways compels trust in his goodness.

PRAISING THE LORD

We cannot do justice to the Psalms in one short section, and I will mention only a few of the major characteristics that make this collection of poems theologically important. There are a number of different types of psalms that reflect different situations for which they were used: they show how individuals and congregations think about God and their relationship to him. Like wisdom, the psalms take their starting point from the covenant theology and salvation history. Unlike wisdom, the psalms are much more self-consciously a response to what God has done.

One of the most important of the psalm types is the song of praise. The psalmists praise God as creator, as redeemer, as king and as the one who makes Zion his holy city. Worship of God is typically a recalling of the mighty saving deeds of God within the history of Israel.

Psalms of lamentation often reflect on the apparent disparity between the declared status of the people of God and their actual experience of persecution and suffering. Some of these psalms finish on a note of confidence that God will yet act to save and restore them. There are thanksgivings for the favors bestowed by God on his people, and there are psalms which are intended more for instruction and imparting wisdom than for addressing God.

The Psalms and the works of wisdom show that the history of redemption, the covenant and the prophetic word from God, are not merely religious ideas or statements about the past but encounters with the living God. The great objective facts of God's work for his people to save them can never remain merely out there. They are the foundation for spiritual experience and endeavor. They motivate and shape piety, worship and good deeds. They are the indispensable means by which the Spirit of God regenerates the heart, mind and soul of those whom he calls into fellowship with himself.

■ *Wisdom and psalms*
are expressions of daily fellowship with God by those who know what it is to be redeemed by his loving mercy.

THE REGENERATING OF HUMAN EXISTENCE

SUMMARY   The regenerating power of God, in redemption, works on the lives of the individual people of God. The revelation of redemption provides the framework within which the regenerated mind works to understand reality. The believer expresses fellowship with God by reaching out for true knowledge of God's world, and by returning praise and thanks to the Lord.

KINGDOM	GOD	MANKIND	WORLD	
CREATION	GOD	ADAM AND EVE	EDEN	Order
FALL				Disorder
FLOOD	GOD	NOAH	ARK	
ABRAHAM	GOD	ABRAHAM'S DESCENDANTS	CANAAN	Regeneration of order fore-shadowed
MOSES	THE LORD	ISRAEL	CANAAN	
DAVID	THE LORD	DAVID'S LINE	TEMPLE IN JERUSALEM	

MAIN THEMES   Orderliness of creation
Fear of the Lord
Regeneration of the mind

SOME KEY WORDS   Order
Wisdom
Knowledge

THE PATH AHEAD   The messianic prince will be the truly wise man, Isaiah 11:1-5—Jesus, the source of wisdom, becomes wisdom for us, Matthew 7:24-28; 1 Corinthians 1:30

STUDY GUIDE TO CHAPTER 18

1. God's revelation doesn't simply add to sound knowledge that we already have. Rather it changes every fact we have by relating it to the Creator of the universe and to his purposes for it. Consider or discuss this proposition in the light of the doctrine of creation and of sin.

2. What is the fear of the Lord? Read through 1 Kings 8 and note the relationship of the fear of the Lord to God's revelation and to the temple.

3. The proverbial sentences in Proverbs 10—29 are not general rules based on the Ten Commandments, but individual reflections on experiences in the light of "the fear of the LORD." How does Proverbs 26:4-5 illustrate this point? Can you find other examples to support this notion?

4. Read the following psalms and suggest the possible life situations, either personal or congregational, that they address: Psalms 1; 22:1-18; 93; 122; 136; 137; 150.

FURTHER READING

1. Graeme Goldsworthy, *Gospel and Wisdom* (Exeter, U.K.: Paternoster, 1981).
2. *IBD* article on "Psalms, Book of."

19

THE FADING SHADOW

Remember the height from which you have fallen! Repent and do the things you did at first. If you do not repent, I will come to you and remove your lampstand from its place. (Rev 2:5)

God made him who had no sin to be sin for us, so that in him we might become the righteousness of God. (2 Cor 5:21)

OUTLINE OF BIBLICAL HISTORY, 1 KINGS 11—22, 2 KINGS
Solomon allowed political considerations and personal ambitions to sour his relationship with God, and this in turn had a bad effect on the life of Israel. Solomon's son began an oppressive rule that led to the rebellion of the northern tribes and the division of the kingdom. Although there were some political and religious high points, both kingdoms went into decline. A new breed of prophets warned against the direction of national life, but matters went from bad to worse. In 722 B.C. the northern kingdom of Israel fell to the power of the Assyrian Empire. Then, in 586 B.C., the southern kingdom of Judah was devastated by the Babylonians. Jerusalem and its temple were destroyed, and a large part of the population was deported to Babylon.

THE PROPHETIC WARNING

From the time God establishes Israel as his chosen people under the terms of the covenant, there exists the warning against covenant-breaking disloyalty. It was largely the prophets' responsibility to make this warning clear. Moses may be regarded as the first great prophet whose ministry sets the pattern for all future prophets. As the mouthpiece of God, the human mediator of the Word of God, the prophet reveals God's plans for salvation. We have seen how this plan involves the covenant relationship. Undoubtedly the grace of God is the most remarkable feature of his covenant and saving acts. God chooses absolutely without condition a people who deserve nothing. In the course of their history he unfolds to them a way of salvation that not only applies to them, but that will one day in its fullness have significance for all the nations of the earth. From the beginning there can be no dispute that the grace of God means that election is unconditioned by any virtue in those who are chosen, and that salvation is a free gift received by faith alone.

But free grace and unconditional election must not be allowed to obscure the place of God's judgment. We have already seen how judgment was revealed against all wickedness in the days of Noah, against Babel and the sinful city of Sodom, against a hard-hearted Egyptian king and his nation and against the pagan Canaanites. According to the Bible no such judgment ever falls that is not deserved. Such judgments, especially when their execution appears to us to be especially barbaric, must be understood in the light of the complete biblical picture of human rebellion against God.

What, then, shall we say about judgment on the elect? Once the saving grace of God is effectively displayed in the exodus from Egypt, the prophetic word concentrates on the nature of the covenant relationship. In the book of Deuteronomy particularly there are stern warnings against turning away from the covenant. Israel is saved by grace alone, but to be saved is not merely to be acquitted of guilt. It is a positive restoration to fellowship with the living God. There is always a real choice in front of the people of God: the way of life or the way of death, covenant blessings or covenant curses (Deut 8:11-20; 28:1-48; 30:15-20).

We should be careful to understand election in its Old Testament form. If Israel was elect, does that mean that every Israelite will be in the eternal kingdom? No, it does not. If a whole generation of Israelites perished in the wilderness, does this mean that they are all excluded from the eternal kingdom? Again, the answer is no. Moses died outside the Promised Land, but we know that he is saved. The prophetic word makes it clear that Israel cannot as a nation go on enjoying the blessings of the covenant while it refuses the responsibilities of covenant life.

From time to time God sends prophets to warn the people and to call them back to himself. After Moses the next of the notable prophets is Samuel, who has the task of steering Israel into a correct understanding of the kingship. Many other prophets appear briefly in the biblical history. Gad and Nathan minister particularly to David as the pattern of kingship develops. Elijah and Elisha perform a combined ministry to Israel after the schism from Judah. Jeroboam's move to set up a rival kingdom with its own worship places and priesthood lays him open to Canaanite influences. The reign of Ahab (869-850 B.C.), who married a Canaanite princess, is marked by official apostasy and an attempt to eliminate the worship of Israel's God. Into this grave situation come Elijah and Elisha to summon the people back to the true faith. The famous contest between Elijah and the prophets of Baal on Mount Carmel is a call to return to the God whose grace of forgiveness was revealed through Moses and the covenant (1 Kings 18).

The prophetic office from Moses to Elisha must be understood in relation to God's revelation of salvation. The covenant, as we have already seen, is both conditional and unconditional. The condition is that those who reject the covenant in unbelief will find that the blessings of the covenant are removed from them. There are warnings against such unbelief in individuals who, if they persist, must be cut off from the covenant people (Lev 17:10; 20:1-6; 24:13-17). If there is national unbelief, then the nation forfeits the blessings (Deut 8:1-20; 28:15-68). The unconditional nature of the promise is not at all a contradiction of the conditional. In effect it is saying that God will not allow unbelief to frustrate his purposes to fulfill the promises originally made to Abraham. The prophets testify to the faithfulness of God and warn against unbelief.

■ *The prophets*
warn that the unconditional blessings of the covenant cannot be enjoyed by those who continue to break the covenant.

THE LIMIT IS REACHED

The reversal of Israel's fortunes after Solomon's reign is so obvious that one wonders why the people don't see their condition and do something about it. There are two obvious reasons why things are allowed to get worse. The first is that the sinful nature of the human heart resists the call to continual reformation. The second is that the slide from being a top nation under David to destruction and exile in Babylon actually takes about four hundred years. The Israelites are no different from people today who tend to live for the moment with little thought for the past or the long-term future.

The national decline begins with the rebellion and separation of the northern tribes. The setting up of the northern kingdom with its mixture of Israelite and Canaanite religion is a serious and retrograde move (1 Kings 12:25-33; 16:29-34). But there are also problems in the south. Despite the fact that Judah has the temple, a legitimate priesthood, and the ruling dynasty of David, disobedience to God increases. Sometimes there is an acceptance of pagan practices (1 Kings 14:21-24), and sometimes there is the presumption that outward observance of the worship of God is all that is necessary (Is 1:12-20; Jer 7:1-7). Elijah is sent to challenge the apostasy of the north in the time of Ahab (1 Kings 16:29—17:6; 18:1-40). The implication of his message is that there is still time to return to the Lord.

As time goes on it becomes clear that the limit is being reached. Amos and Hosea fail to move Israel to repentance and, in 722 B.C., the Assyrians devastate the nation (2 Kings 17). The people of Judah, though warned to learn from the fate of Israel (Ezek 23), continue the slide towards destruction. Attempts at reform are made by Hezekiah and Josiah (2 Kings 18:1-8; 22:1-20). But so great is the accumulated effect of unbelief, that these reforms cannot prevent the inevitable end (2 Kings 23:26-27). The Assyrian Empire falls to the Babylonians in 609 B.C. and soon after, in 597, Jerusalem is captured and many of the inhabitants of Judah are taken to Babylon. When Zedekiah, the puppet-king, rebels against Babylon, retribution is swift and terrible. In 586, Jerusalem and the temple are laid waste and more people are exiled to Babylon. The curses of the covenant, so plainly stated in Deuteronomy, are now reality.

■ *The limit*

of God's forbearance is reached in Israel's history after Solomon, and the curses of the covenant become a reality.

THE NEW PROPHETIC MESSAGE

After Elijah and Elisha a new breed of prophet arises. The most obvious thing about them is that, for some reason and by persons often unknown, their sermons and oracles are written down and collected into books. It is not difficult to suggest a reason for this. The five books of Moses (Genesis to Deuteronomy) contain, among other things, the record of the prophetic revelation concerning the covenant, and of God's acts for the salvation of his people. The main task of the prophets that emerge in the period from Samuel to Elisha is to call Israel to faithfulness to the covenant. Samuel and

Nathan also round off the prior revelation by showing the proper place of kingship in God's purposes. Adequate record of these prophetic ministries is given in the historical accounts.

Once the decline of the nation begins, a new perspective emerges. In part, the prophets continue to point to Israel's failure to keep the covenant and threaten the judgment of God upon their sins. But there is also the recognition that Israel is incapable of true repentance, and that God must do a new work of salvation. Thus, in the progressive revelation of the Old Testament, the first hints are given that Israel's experience of the exodus and the possession of the Promised Land is only a shadow of the reality of salvation.

While it is important to observe how the prophets bring charges of Israel's disloyalty to the covenant, this is not their main significance for us. The implications of the covenant for social justice, fidelity in marriage, honesty, compassion for the poor and dispossessed and sincerity in the worship of God are constantly set before us in the prophets. But addressing the ills of our present society in the name of Christianity does not necessarily make our message "prophetic." Within the perspective of biblical theology, we see the prophetic judgment as the clearest indicator of the fact that full salvation has not yet come.

As the nation of Israel disintegrates after the death of Solomon, the faithful might wonder what has gone wrong in God's saving purposes. From our vantage point we can see that nothing has gone wrong with God's plan. The problem is human sin, and it becomes ever clearer that this problem cannot be dealt with by those things that God has done for Israel in her history. Why, then, did God embark on the whole "redemptive" process from the exodus on? Because, in his wisdom he leads his people in a series of distinct stages of revelation towards the fullness of time when salvation will come in power. The prophets serve to show that what has happened up to now is but a passing stage in revelation.

None of this diminishes the importance of Israel's past history. All God's dealings with his people, from Abraham to Solomon, are expressions of real grace while being shadows of a more solid reality to come. In accommodating himself and his revelation to where his elect people are themselves. God leads them through their spiritual infancy by means of tangible realities of captivity by an earthly king in a foreign land, of release from bondage, of conquest of a promised land, and so on. These things

THE DEGENERATION OF THE KINGDOM PATTERN

SUMMARY   The pattern of redemption and the kingdom of God as revealed in the history of Israel from Abraham to Solomon is complete. But now the inability of Israel to be faithful to the covenant leads to a decline in the kingdom. Once again the reality of the fall is shown to such a degree that it is clear that the kingdom of God has not yet come.

KINGDOM	GOD	MANKIND	WORLD	
CREATION	GOD	ADAM AND EVE	EDEN	Order
FALL				Disorder
FLOOD	GOD	NOAH	ARK	Regeneration of order fore-shadowed
ABRAHAM	GOD	ABRAHAM'S DESCENDANTS	CANAAN	Regeneration of order fore-shadowed
MOSES	THE LORD	ISRAEL	CANAAN	shadowed
DAVID	THE LORD	DAVID'S LINE	TEMPLE IN JERUSALEM	

MAIN THEMES   Conditional nature of the covenant
Inevitable judgment
New prophetic perspective

SOME KEY WORDS   Shadow
Reality
Judgment

THE PATH AHEAD   The judgment of God comes to his people, Isaiah 65:1-12—Jesus accepts the judgment of believers, 2 Corinthians 5:21

show the nature of their plight in bondage to sin and death, the structure of salvation and the kingdom of God. But the shadow must fade so that the full light of the solid reality may be revealed in its place. In the meantime, those who by faith grasp the shadow are undoubtedly thereby grasping the reality of salvation in Christ.

■ *The new perspective*
of the prophetic message shows that Israel's historic experience of redemption is only a shadow of the reality yet to come.

STUDY GUIDE

1. How can the covenant be both conditional and unconditional at the same time?

2. Read the account of the last years of Judah in 2 Kings 18—25. Note the attempts at reform and the reasons they were not successful in averting disaster.

3. Using Bible dictionaries and similar helps, research the life and ministry of the prophet Jeremiah and the role he played in the last years of Judah.

4. What elements of a biblical theology of judgment can you now discern in the biblical story from the fall (Gen 3) to the exile in Babylon?

5. Why was the glory of the kingdom of David allowed to fade?

FURTHER READING

1. *BT*, part 2, chap. 6, sections A-C.
2. *GK*, pp. 77-81.
3. *IBD* article on "Prophecy, Prophets."
4. *KG*, chap. 2.

THERE IS A
NEW CREATION

Therefore, if anyone is in Christ, he is a new creation; the old has gone, the new has come! (2 Cor 5:17)

But in keeping with his promise we are looking forward to a new heaven and a new earth, the home of righteousness. (2 Pet 3:13)

Then I saw a new heaven and a new earth, for the first heaven and the first earth had passed away. He who was seated on the throne said, "I am making everything new!" (Rev 21:1, 5)

OUTLINE OF BIBLICAL HISTORY, JEREMIAH, EZEKIEL, DANIEL, ESTHER
The prophets of Israel warned of the doom that would befall the nation. When the first exiles were taken to Babylon in 597 B.C., Ezekiel was among them. Jeremiah was allowed to remain in Jerusalem. Both prophets ministered to the exiles. Life for the Jews (the people of Judah) in Babylon was not all bad, and in time many prospered. The books of Jeremiah and Ezekiel indicate a certain normality to the experience, while Daniel and Esther highlight some of the difficulties and suffering experienced in an alien and oppressive culture.

THE PATTERN OF REDEMPTION

A review of the pattern of redemption is in order. During the period of Israel's history from Abraham to David and Solomon, we have seen a clearly distinguishable set of events that are interpreted by the Word of God. With the covenant promises to Abraham as the background, redemption begins in the captivity in Egypt. Israel's bondage is a denial of the kingdom of God, and a condition of being unsaved.

Israel is brought from the captivity by powerful acts of God into a new experience of freedom. God releases them from slavery and binds them to himself as his people in the covenant of Sinai. This covenant shows that redemption is more than a mere release from bondage. The life of the redeemed is regulated in fellowship with God. It is also shaped by entry into the Promised Land and the establishment of the nation under God's representative ruler. Redemption means exit from bondage and entry into the kingdom of God.

If the covenant with Abraham stands behind the whole process of redemption in Israel, behind the covenant with Abraham stands God's original commitment to the creation. In the end-of-chapter summaries I have emphasized the theme of creation and re-creation. That which God *generated* at the beginning *degenerated* through the fall of mankind. Redemption and salvation are seen as the process of *regeneration*, which affects the whole degenerated creation, including mankind. Thus the captivity in Egypt is a historical experience which underlines the reality of the fall into sin and the ejection from the kingdom of God as it was experienced in the garden of Eden. Redemption from Egypt into the Promised Land, the land flowing with milk and honey, is a picture of a return to Eden. The kingship of David recalls the rule or dominion that God gave to Adam in Eden.

The progressive diagram illustrates the various stages in which the kingdom is expressed. The original pattern

GOD	ADAM AND EVE	EDEN

looks forward to the highest expression of the kingdom in Israel's history.

THE LORD	DAVID'S LINE	TEMPLE IN JERUSALEM

This expression of the kingdom in history fades leaving two options for the people. Either they reject the promises of God as untrue, or they have confidence in their future fulfillment according to the prophetic word.

■ *The pattern of redemption involves*
  captivity
  exodus
  covenant regulation
  entry into and possession of the land
  rule of David, temple, Jerusalem

THE GOD OF SALVATION

The writing prophets all do three things. First, they identify the specific ways in which Israel has broken the covenant. These include social injustice and oppression, insincere worship of God, mixing pagan religion with the true faith revealed by God and even worship of false gods. Second, they pronounce the judgment of God on this unfaithfulness to the covenant. Sometimes the judgment is predicted in specific terms of the destruction of Samaria or Jerusalem. At other times the judgment is more general, and even universal as a degeneration of the whole earth. Whether it is the end of the nation or the end of the world (Jer 4:23-28; Is 24:1-3; Amos 7:4; Zeph 1:2-3) the judgment is coming because Israel rejects God's grace. Third, they speak a message of comfort to the faithful. God will yet save them completely, finally and gloriously.

God has been revealing himself within the whole process of biblical history. His character is not presented as a series of abstract ideas, such as holiness, omnipotence, righteousness and so on. Rather, God reveals himself in the midst of his deeds that he himself interprets by his Word. From his activity as creator, judge, covenant-maker and redeemer, we learn the meaning of words like *holy, almighty* and *righteous* as they apply to God.

It is characteristic of the writing prophets that they take up the events of Israel's prior experience of God and reuse them. Creation, captivity, redemptive exodus, covenant regulation, possession of the Promised Land and kingly rule, all become invested with deeper significance as God promises a new experience of them. This will not be a mere shadow but rather the solid reality of redemption and the kingdom of God. Such consideration of the final events, which herald the coming of the eternal kingdom, is referred to in theological language as *eschatology* (Greek: *eschatos*, last).

The God of the prophets is thus the Creator (Is 40:12-26; 43:1, 15; 44:21-24; 45:7-13, 18; 48:13; 54:5) who is doing a new thing (Is 42:9; 43:18-19; 48:6-7). In this, he shows himself to be absolutely faithful to his original covenant commitment (Is 54:7-10; Jer 33:14-26; Hos 2:16-23; 11:8-11). Grace and faithfulness show the unconditional love of God (Deut 7:7-8; Hos 2:14-20; 3:1; 11:1-9; 14:4; Is 63:9). Such a God is righteous in that he acts consistently with his character even when saving those who rebel against him (Is 9:2-7; 11:1-5; 42:6; 45:13; 51:5-6; 56:1; 59:15-17; 63:1; Jer 9:24; 23:5-6). He is, therefore, the Savior God who restores the kingdom in which he, his people and the created order relate perfectly. Salvation is the whole process by which God restores his people and the creation to the kingdom. This means the regeneration of all things.

■ *God*

revealed himself to his people progressively through his word and deeds. This reve-lation reaches a climax in the oracles of salvation spoken through the later prophets.

THE PEOPLE OF GOD

There has also been a progression in the revelation of the people of God, which I have summarized in the middle column of the progressive diagram (p. 188). The placing of God, his people and the created order in columns side by side implies the revealed relationships that God intends should exist between them. We know God as he reveals himself in relation to his people and the creation. And we know ourselves truly only in relation to God who created and redeemed us.

The purpose of God that initially focused on Adam and Eve in Eden, comes to be concentrated on the son of David. A theological problem of immense proportions for the people of God apparently arises when the son of David, Solomon, fails to live up to expectations. Not that anyone before him had done any better in this regard, but Solomon's failure eventually led to the undoing of all the outward, historical marks of the kingdom of God in the life of Israel. What, then, is the prophetic view of this catastrophe? Israel and Judah are condemned for breaking the covenant, and the judgment of God is pronounced. Yet, there is hope based upon the unconditional nature of God's commitment and his faithfulness to it.

There are many prophetic themes relating to the people of God and their restoration. A number have to do with national restoration and the gathering of the exiles into the Promised Land once more. Sometimes this is depicted as a remnant, a faithful few who wait for the Lord (Is 10:20-23; 11:11-12; 14:1-4; 40:1-2; 46:3-4; 51:11; 61:4-7; Jer 23:1-8; 29:10-14; 30:10-11; 31:7-9; Ezek 34:1-16; 36:22-24; 37:15-22; Mic 2:12). The gathering of the exiles will also mean that salvation comes to the nations as foreigners are somehow caught up in the return of Israel to the Promised Land (Is 2:2-4; Mic 4:1-4; Zeph 3:9; Zech 8:20-23). In some places the return is described as a second exodus (Is 40:1-5; 43:1-7, 15-21; 48:20-21; 49:24-26; 51:9-11; Jer 23:7-8).

In the place of a second Moses there are at least two key figures representing Israel and mediating the saving presence and work of God. These are David (or a descendant of David) and the suffering servant of the Lord.

The glorious rule of God through David is central to the coming kingdom (Is 9:2-7; 11:1-5; 16:5; 55:3-5; Jer 23:1-6; Ezek 34:20-24; 37:24-28; Amos 9:11). It does not matter whether the prophecies think of a return of David, or of one of his descendants to fulfill the role. Any lack of clarity is dispelled in the New Testament as it identifies Jesus as the true king of David's line, both son of David and Son of God.

The suffering servant is a figure presented in four passages in Isaiah (Is 42:1-4; 49:1-6; 50:4-9; 52:13—53:12). He is an unobtrusive, humble and compassionate character who suffers rejection, shame and death. By this he brings salvation to Israel and light to the nations. He is finally vindicated and exalted by God, apparently through resurrection. The identity of the servant is a vexed question, for he is Israel (Is 49:3) and his mission is to Israel (Is 49:5-6). Yet there is no problem in this when we recall that David's son is the representative Israelite, that is, he is true Israel while serving Israel (2 Sam 7:14). Knowledge of the suffering messiah does not depend on Isaiah's four so-called servant songs. There is a constant theme of those chosen by God as mediators of salvation to Israel being humiliated and rejected by those they are sent to help. The most obvious of these are Joseph, Moses and David. It is no accident that David's messianic role is indicated long before he is actually made king (1 Sam 16:13), and that he suffers much before he is vindicated. Had the disciples on the road to Emmaus understood this better they would have known that the Christ must suffer before entering his glory (Lk 24:26).

■ *The people of God*
are finally represented in the prophets by a suffering messiah prince. This is the one who fulfills all God's will for the many and, in so doing, brings salvation to the many.

THE PROMISED LAND

The third element of the kingdom of God, after God and his people, is the place in which the people live in fellowship with God. The Old Testament does not lay a foundation for the popular idea of some vague heavenly realm "above the bright blue sky" where disembodied souls live. God related to Adam and Eve, who were physical people, in Eden on earth. He set Israel in the Promised Land of Canaan. Now the prophets portray the kingdom of God coming on the earth.

First, there are prophecies of a renewed creation, a new heaven (the sky above) and a new earth (Is 65:17; 66:22). As God created the present universe for his people (Is 51:13-16), so he will destroy it (Is 51:6) in order that he might re-create it (Is 51:3, 11). This involvement of the whole universe in the final salvation of God's people most probably lies behind the calls to the created order to rejoice in the saving acts of God (Is 44:23; 49:13; Ps 98:7-9; 148:1-14). Then there are those prophecies which focus on the new land to which Israel returns, and at the center of which is the new Jerusalem, or Zion, and the restored temple. This is the new Eden, the land of fruitfulness and of harmony between all living things, and of perfect healing (Is 2:2-4; 11:6-9; 32:1-20; 35:1-10; 65:17-25; Ezek 34:11-16, 25-31; 36:35-38; 47:1-12).

Here then, is the Old Testament foundation for the New Testament understanding of regeneration and new birth. While the regeneration of the individual child of God usually comes first to people's minds, we need to remember that regeneration is as wide as the universe itself.

■ *The Promised Land,*
which was first expressed as Eden, and then as the Promised Land of Canaan,
is finally portrayed as a renewed Canaan in a new earth. At its center is the new
temple in the new Jerusalem.

THE COVENANT

The principal expression of the relationship between God and his people is the covenant. A biblical theology of the covenant takes note of its unity and diversity. There is only one commitment of God to his purpose to establish his kingdom. Thus there is one covenant which has a number of different expressions in the course of redemptive history. The first of these is the initial commitment of God to the creation. But the rebellion of mankind, the chief covenant partner with God, throws all relationships into confusion. Thereafter, God's commitment to redemption is expressed in a series of covenant statements. Thus far we have noted the covenants with Noah, Abraham, Israel (at Sinai) and David.

The eschatology of the prophets picks up the themes from Israel's past and thus implies the continuation of God's faithfulness to the one covenant. All the restoration themes relate to one or the other of the covenant expressions.

THE REGENERATION OF ALL THINGS PREDICTED

SUMMARY   The prophets now fill the gap left by the failed historical kingdom of Israel. They speak of a future fulfillment of all God's purposes. Israel's historical experience of God's saving work is shown to be a shadow of the final and true work of salvation. In this all things, including the heavens and the earth, will be regenerated.

KINGDOM	GOD	MANKIND	WORLD	
CREATION	GOD	ADAM AND EVE	EDEN	Order
FALL				Disorder
FLOOD	GOD	NOAH	ARK	Regeneration of order foreshadowed
ABRAHAM	GOD	ABRAHAM'S DESCENDANTS	CANAAN	
MOSES	THE LORD	ISRAEL	CANAAN	
DAVID	THE LORD	DAVID'S LINE	TEMPLE IN JERUSALEM	
PROPHETS	THE LORD	FAITHFUL REMNANT	NEW TEMPLE AND JERUSALEM	Regeneration predicted

MAIN THEMES   The pattern of redemption in Israel's history
Revelation of God through his word and saving acts
Prophetic revelation of the kingdom yet to come

SOME KEY WORDS   Eschatology

THE PATH AHEAD   The prophetic promises of the kingdom—Jesus claims to fulfill prophecy, Luke 24:27, 44—Apostolic message that Christ fulfills all prophecy, Acts 13:32-33; 2 Corinthians 1:20

But as the coming kingdom will be perfect, glorious and permanent, so something must happen to enable the people to be faithful to the covenant. The prophets predict not only a return of the people to the renewed land, but also a renewal of the people themselves. One remarkable passage speaks of a renewed covenant written on people's hearts so that they will truly know the Lord and perfectly keep his will (Jer 31:31-34). Another prophecy portrays the spiritual renewal of the heart so that there is reality to the covenant summary: "You will be my people, and I will be your God" (Ezek 36:28).

■ *The one covenant*
that stems from God's original commitment to creation, is expressed redemptively in the covenants with Noah, Abraham, Israel, David and in the new covenant of the prophets.

STUDY GUIDE TO CHAPTER 20

1. By now you should be familiar with the idea of the pattern of redemption being worked out in Israel's history. We have considered only some of the main events in this regard, but every event in Old Testament history must relate to this pattern in some way. Try relating the following events to redemptive history:
   a. The fall of Jericho (Josh 6)
   b. The death of Sisera (Judg 4)
   c. David spares Saul (1 Sam 24)
   d. The visit of the Queen of Sheba (1 Kings 10).

2. Read the following major passages of prophetic eschatology and note all the themes of restoration which are based on Israel's past history: Isaiah 11; 35; 61; 65; Ezekiel 34; 36; 37; Joel 2; Zephaniah 3.

3. Starting with creation and the covenant with Abraham, suggest an outline of a biblical theology of mission including the relevant aspects of prophetic eschatology.

FURTHER READING

1. *BT*, part 2, chap. 6, section D.
2. *GK*, pp. 81-86.
3. *KG*, chaps. 3, 4, 5.

21

THE SECOND EXODUS

Two men, Moses and Elijah, appeared in glorious splendor, talking with Jesus. They spoke about his departure (Greek: exodos), which he was about to bring to fulfillment at Jerusalem. (Lk 9:30-31)

OUTLINE OF BIBLICAL HISTORY, EZRA, NEHEMIAH, HAGGAI
In 539 BC, Babylon fell to the Medo-Persian empire. The following year Cyrus, the king, allowed the Jews to return home and to set up a Jewish state within the Persian Empire. Great difficulty was experienced in reestablishing the nation. There was local opposition to the rebuilding of Jerusalem and the temple. Many of the Jews did not return but stayed on in the land of their exile. In the latter part of the fourth century BC, Alexander the Great conquered the Persian Empire. The Jews entered a long and difficult period in which Greek culture and religion challenged their trust in God's covenant promises. In 63 B.C., Pompey conquered Palestine and the Jews found themselves a province of the Roman Empire.

RETURN TO DISAPPOINTMENT

From the viewpoint of the Jews[1] exiled in Babylon, the prophecies concerning the return to the Promised Land apply to their present situation. One can imagine how many of them would interpret the prophecies of the return. They would be expecting a world upheaval that would leave the Jews as the top nation. Instead, the overthrow of Babylon leaves them still under the thumb of a foreign power. When Cyrus the Persian lets them return to reestablish the nation, the city of Jerusalem and the temple, they are resisted by local groups of foreigners now inhabiting the Promised Land. The books of Ezra, Nehemiah and Haggai should be read for an understanding of the problems of the new community. These include opposition from without to reconstruction and carelessness within with regard to the law of God.

The positive aspects of the setting up of the new Jewish state must not be overlooked. The people are set free to return to the Promised Land. For a while, leadership is held by a descendant of David, a man named Zerub-babel (Ezra 2—5; Hag 1—2; Mt 1:13; Lk 3:27). An autonomous state within the Persian Empire is established, and eventually a new Jerusalem and a new temple are built.

The problem is that although the structure of the kingdom portrayed by the prophets is there in outline, the substance is not. There is no glorious return, no magnificent temple set in the midst of the regenerated earth. It is clear also that the people have still not undergone that spiritual transformation that makes them perfectly the people of God. There is no magnificent reign of the Davidic prince.

■ *The return from exile*
results in only a pale shadow of the predicted glorious kingdom for the people of God.

PROPHECY AND VISIONS

The three prophets of the postexilic period, Haggai, Zechariah and Malachi, help us to understand what is happening. From the human point of view, the Jews are largely unrepentant. The prophets continue to charge them with covenant-breaking and to warn of judgment. They also look towards the future fulfillment of the covenant blessings. But from the divine point of view, the time is not yet right for the coming of the kingdom, and the believing people must continue to live in hope of the future.

These prophets, together with the narratives of Ezra and Nehemiah, make it plain that the restored nation is not the kingdom of God. What, then, is its purpose? We can only surmise that it reminds the people that God is still active in the history of salvation, and at the same time it invites true faith to look beyond the present experience to some greater fulfillment. Thus, each of these prophets points to the glory yet to come (Hag 2:6-9; Zech 8:20-23; 14:1-21; Mal 4:1-6).

This later period of prophecy also sees the emergence of a particular form of prophetic writing. Apocalyptic is a word used to describe the kind of vision that we find in Daniel 7—8, and in Zechariah 1:7—6:15. Most Jewish apocalyptic does not occur in the Bible, but was written in the period between the two Testaments. The apocalyptic style of writing involved symbolic visions that centered less on Israel and more on the purpose of God for the whole universe.

■ *The postexilic prophets*
interpret the nature of the restored community and point beyond it to the real fulfillment of the promises.

THE UNFINISHED STORY

So we come to the end of the Old Testament and find that it is a book without an ending. In the Jewish community, even though it is back in the Promised Land, nothing has been resolved. The people either wait in hope of God's future saving acts or, so we must assume, they give up on the whole idea of the covenant being fulfilled. The evidence relating to the history of the Jews after the Old Testament period ends (about the close of the fifth century B.C.) shows that they had many more difficulties to face. Most of our information about the period between the Testaments comes from the collection of Jewish writings called the Apocrypha.[2] From these writings we can gain a reasonably accurate picture of life under Persian, Greek and Roman rule.

Let us now summarize the main stages by which the theology of the kingdom of God in the Old Testament has developed. First, God revealed his kingdom in the *creation*, or generation, of the heavens and the earth, with Eden as the focal point:

CREATION	GOD	ADAM AND EVE	EDEN

Second, after the fall, or degeneration, God revealed his redemptive purpose for the restoration of his kingdom in two main stages (although we have also considered a preliminary revelation in Noah and the flood). The first main stage of redemptive revelation takes place in the *history of Israel* from Abraham to David and Solomon. There are three parts to this: the promises originally given to Abraham, the redemptive events of the exodus and the final shape of the kingdom in the Promised Land. Thus the promises are given, they are acted upon in redemption and they are fulfilled:

ABRAHAM	GOD	ABRAHAM'S DESCENDANTS	CANAAN	Promises given
MOSES	THE LORD	ISRAEL	CANAAN	Promises acted on
DAVID	THE LORD	DAVID'S LINE	TEMPLE IN JERUSALEM	Promises fulfilled

Third, after another historical experience of fall, exile or degeneration, *prophetic eschatology* promises a final day of actual and absolute fulfillment that is yet in the future. This is the second main stage of redemptive revelation. This actual regeneration of all things never comes to pass in the Old Testament period:

| PROPHETS | THE LORD | FAITHFUL REMNANT | NEW TEMPLE AND JERUSALEM | Promises restated |

Having this plan of Old Testament revelation in view, we are now in a position to discern many of the overtones that exist in the text of the New Testament. The New Testament unfolds the story of Jesus, the Christ, who has come to fulfill all the expectations of the Old Testament. Much of the terminology of the gospel is drawn directly from these preparatory shadows. While the gospel will reveal the final significance of all God's promises to Israel, the redemptive revelation in the Old Testament will deepen our appreciation of what it means for Jesus to be the Christ.

■ *The Old Testament*
concludes without the promises of God being fulfilled.

STUDY GUIDE TO CHAPTER 21

1. Read the books of Ezra (don't be put off by the long lists of names) and Nehemiah in the light of the prophetic promises. Note particularly the reasons for a sense of disappointment among the returning exiles who believe.

THE REGENERATION REMAINS A FUTURE HOPE

SUMMARY The restoration of the Jews to the Promised Land looked as if it would be the fulfillment of God's promises. In fact, the expected regeneration of all things did not come to pass. The only hope now is that at some future time God will act to bring about his kingdom and the salvation of his people.

KINGDOM	GOD	MANKIND	WORLD			
CREATION	GOD	ADAM AND EVE	EDEN	**Kingdom pattern established**		
ABRAHAM	GOD	ABRAHAM'S DESCENDANTS	CANAAN			
MOSES	THE LORD	ISRAEL	CANAAN	**Kingdom revealed in Israel's history**		
DAVID	THE LORD	DAVID'S LINE	TEMPLE IN JERUSALEM			
PROPHETS	THE LORD	FAITHFUL REMNANT	NEW TEMPLE AND JERUSALEM	**Kingdom revealed in prophetic eschatology**		

MAIN THEMES Return from exile
Disappointment of prophetic hope

SOME KEY WORDS Apocalyptic
Apocrypha

THE PATH AHEAD Temple of God to be rebuilt by the Spirit, Zechariah 4:6-7—Jesus the new temple, John 2:19
A new Elijah to herald the Lord's coming, Malachi 4:5-6—John the Baptist the new Elijah, Matthew 11:12-14

2. Read the visions of Zechariah (Zech 1—6). Note the function of the interpreting angel. Try to understand what these visions would convey to a people who were expecting the restoration of Israel and the temple.

3. Summarize the biblical theology of covenant and regeneration as it has emerged in the Old Testament.

FURTHER READING

1. D. S. Russell, *Between the Testaments* (London: SCM Press, 1960).
2. *KG*, chap. 6.
3. John Bright, *History of Israel* (Philadelphia: Westminster Press, 1959), chaps. 11 and 12.
4. Joyce Baldwin, *Haggai, Zechariah, Malachi*, TOTC (Downers Grove, Ill.: InterVarsity Press, 1972).
5. Leon Morris, *Apocalyptic* (Grand Rapids, Mich.: Eerdmans, 1972).

NOTES

1. The name "Jew" means a member of the tribe of Judah. It is incorrect to refer to the whole of Israel as the Jews. When the kingdom of Israel split with the secession of Jeroboam, the southern kingdom was correctly called Judah and its people the Jews. Thus, the exile into Babylon and the return involved the Jews.
2. The Apocrypha was not part of the recognized canon of Scripture for the Jews or the Christians. Some Bibles have the Apocrypha printed between the Old and New Testaments. It is an important collection of Jewish religious writings and is our main source of information for the history and religion of the Jews in the period between the Testaments.

22

THE NEW CREATION
FOR US

Jesus answered them, "Destroy this temple, and I will raise it again in three days."
(Jn 2:19)

OUTLINE OF BIBLICAL HISTORY, MATTHEW, MARK, LUKE, JOHN
The province of Judea, the homeland of the Jews, came under Roman rule in 63 B.C.
During the reign of Caesar Augustus, Jesus was born in Bethlehem, probably about
the year 4 B.C. John, known as the Baptist, prepared the way for the ministry of Jesus.
This ministry of preaching, teaching and healing began with Jesus' baptism and last-
ed about three years. Growing conflict with the Jews and their religious leaders led
eventually to Jesus being sentenced to death by the Roman governor Pontius Pilate.
Jesus was executed by the Romans just outside Jerusalem, but he rose from death two
days later and appeared to his followers on a number of occasions. After a period with
them, Jesus was taken up to heaven.

UNITY AND DIVERSITY IN THE BIBLE

In attempting to highlight a unifying theme across the entire span of biblical revelation, I have not wanted to obscure the great diversity that also exists. It is, however, extremely important that the different perspectives and
approaches adopted by the various biblical authors not be regarded as
somehow ruling out the existence of unity in the Bible. The authors of the
individual books each leave something of themselves and their way of
thinking in their works. But, as I pointed out in chapter six, the Bible is a
divine book as well as a human one. The Holy Spirit, using a diversity of
human authors, has produced one single work that says exactly what God
intends it to say.

In an introductory work such as this, we must concentrate only on the
one message of the Bible. This does not mean that we ignore the diversity
in the presentation of the message by the various authors. Note carefully,
however, that many writers and commentators make the unwarranted

and false assumption that diversity means that there must also be a conflict of ideas.

There is also a tendency to separate the Old Testament from the New. There is no divine direction for printing them separately with a new table of contents between them. Of course, there are important distinctions between the two Testaments, as we have already seen throughout this work. Unfortunately, these distinctions often seem more obvious to us than the unity of the Bible. Let us remind ourselves that there is continuity between the Old and New Testaments in that the New fulfills the Old and the Old testifies to the Christ of the New. There is discontinuity between them in that the Old must give way to the New, and the people of God must embrace the solid reality of Christ and let go of the shadows in the law of Moses and the worship of Israel.

There is also diversity within the New Testament. The four Gospels tell essentially the same story but with different emphases, and by selecting different details in the life and ministry of Jesus. The epistles show a variety of concerns, often in response to particular needs in the life of the congregation being addressed. Again, this in no way detracts from the one central message of Jesus Christ as the unifying element. There is no teaching in the New Testament that is inconsistent with the person and work of Jesus Christ.

■ *Unity and diversity*
in the Bible are seen in the single theme of revelation, which centers on Jesus Christ, and in the variety of emphases with which this theme is presented.

JESUS IS TRUE GOD

Remember that I have chosen to emphasize the new creation or regeneration as one of the unifying themes in the Bible. Coupled with it is the idea of the kingdom involving God, his people and the created order, all perfectly related. Thus, the original creation, or generation, resulted in the revelation of God's kingdom in Eden.[1] The fall, or degeneration, resulted in the obliteration of the kingdom of God by confusing the relationships between God, people and the world. Redemptive revelation has shown the progress towards the regeneration or restoration of the kingdom of God.

The importance of the new revelation in Jesus Christ cannot be overstated. I pointed out in chapter six that Jesus Christ is God's final and fullest revelation. You might find it helpful to read that chapter again at this stage. The disciples should have understood from the Old Testament the nature of the gospel (Lk 24:25-27). This is because Jesus fulfills Old Testament expectations. But in another sense he fulfills them in such a surprising way that no one could have fully predicted the way he would bring in the kingdom.

Prophetic eschatology involved a whole range of pictures and images, some highly symbolic, others sitting much closer to Israel's actual historical experience, which presented the coming of the kingdom from many different angles. It is, however, understandable that most Jews would form an idea of the fulfillment as God suddenly coming in power to restore his still scattered people to the Promised Land, to drive out the Romans and other enemies, to reestablish Jerusalem and the temple in unsurpassed splendor, to gather people from out of every nation of the earth into the kingdom, to judge the wicked and unbelieving and, above all, to set up the glorious rule of his kingdom through a Davidic prince ruling Jerusalem. Thus, Jerusalem would become the center of the new earth in which all peoples, creatures and things exist in perfect harmony.

Given that kind of expectation, we can begin to understand the Jews unreadiness for their God to come as Mary's baby boy. Any claims that Jesus made to be God drove the Jewish religious leaders into a frenzy of hatred (Mt 26:63-68; Mk 2:5-12; Jn 8:48-59; 10:29-31; see also Ezek 34:17-21). John reflects on the Creator joining the human race and not being received by those whom he had prepared for the event (Jn 1:1-18). The incarnation (becoming flesh) of God is at the very center of the gospel event by which God restores the true relationship between himself and the human race.

The early church came to accept the deity of Jesus as an essential element of the gospel. Thus, we may inquire into the necessity of the incarnation for our salvation (Jn 1:1-3; Phil 2:5-7; Col 1:16-17; 2:9; Tit 2:13; Heb 1:8; Rev 22:13).

■ *Jesus Christ*
is true God, the Creator of the universe.

JESUS IS THE TRUE PEOPLE OF GOD

The New Testament indicates that not only Christ's deity but also his perfect and complete humanity is necessary for the gospel of our salvation. While he is God the Creator, the God of Adam, of Abraham, of David and of the prophets, he is also the truly created man, the last Adam, the seed of Abraham, the son of David and the true prophet (Mt 21:9; Lk 4:16-24; Rom 1:3; 5:19; 1 Cor 15:22, 45; Gal 3:16; Col 1:15).

Again, a situation foreshadowed in the Old Testament proves to be unexpected by the Jews of Jesus' time. Significant figures, such as priests and kings, who mediated salvation for the many in Israel, point to the One who comes as the true Israelite representing the many. On the basis of this interpretation of the prophetic promises, the Jews were waiting for a return of a great crowd of people to the Promised Land. Even the remnant would be a considerable group. They were not prepared for the true people of God to be one man. They could not see that everything that God had intended for Adam and then for Israel was being fulfilled in the perfectly sinless human existence of Jesus.

Adam was the first head of the human race but he failed to keep his race in the right relationship to God. He was tempted and fell through rebellion against his Creator. He was sent out of the garden so that all human existence since then takes place outside of Eden. Now the last Adam emerges to be head of a new human race. He fulfills Adam's tasks perfectly. He is tempted in like manner, so that by overcoming he might bring his new people back into the garden, into fellowship with God. The temptation narratives (Mt 4:1-11; Mk 1:12-13; Lk 4:1-13) are to be read in light of both Adam and Israel as sons of God who failed the test. In his baptism, Jesus identifies with the human race and receives divine approval as the true Son of God. Note how Luke's family tree of Jesus links him, through the generations of Israel, all the way back to Adam, son of God (Lk 3:23-38). Again our summary diagram (p. 208) illustrates this progression of the people of God from Adam (a failure), through the Israelites (failures), to Jesus, the only fully pleasing Son of God since before Adam sinned.

Sonship is linked with the role of servant. The true son is the one who serves the Father (Ex 4:23; Heb 3:6). The Father's approval of Jesus at his baptism echoes the messianic promise of Psalm 2:6-7 and the suffering compliance of the servant of the Lord in Isaiah 42:1. The first temptation of Christ in the wilderness contains the challenge, "If you are the son of

God . . ." Note that the Scriptures used by Jesus to defeat the devil's attack (Deut 8:3; 6:13, 16) are drawn from Moses' commentary on Israel's failure during the wilderness testing. The meaning is clear. At his baptism, Jesus is declared to be true Adam, true Israel. Immediately after this, the same Spirit that descended on him in baptism now leads him to the test. He emerges unscathed as the true and faithful Israel of God.

In the Old Testament, the key offices that represent the people were prophet, priest, king and wise man. In reading the New Testament it becomes obvious that the various writers understood the person and work of Jesus to be fulfilling these roles.

First, Jesus is the true prophet heralding God's kingdom (Mk 1:14-15; Lk 4:16-21; Heb 1:1-2). Not only does he preach the prophetic word, he *is* the Word (Jn 1:1-3, 14-18; 14:6). The whole work of Jesus in revealing the truth about God and the kingdom may be seen as the climax to the prophetic office of the Old Testament.

Second, Jesus fulfills the role of priest. This is indirectly referred to by Jesus' own words about his death as a sacrifice and a ransom for many (Mk 10:45; Lk 22:19-20; Jn 10:11, 15). In the epistle to the Hebrews the theology of Christ's priesthood is worked out in greater detail, both in continuity with Israel's priesthood and in superiority to it as the perfect fulfillment of it (Heb 3:1; 4:14—5:10; 7:24—10:25). Here the link with the covenant theme is clearly shown, for Christ establishes a new and better covenant in his own blood. It emerges from these texts that Jesus is both the true priest and the one, perfect and acceptable sacrifice for sin. He is thus the true passover lamb (1 Cor 5:7), the sinless offering for sin (2 Cor 5:21; 1 Pet 2:24). His priestly work is to take upon himself the curse which God declared on all who break his covenant (Deut 11:26-28; Gal 3:10-14).

Third, the kingship of Christ begins with the fact that he is quite literally a descendant of David and that he fulfills the prophetic expectations of the Davidic messiah (Mt 1:17-20; 20:29-31; Lk 1:30-33; Rom 1:3). The resurrection and ascension of Jesus are seen as a proclamation of his lordship and a fulfillment of the covenant promises to Israel. Jesus is declared Son of God at his resurrection (Rom 1:4). Not only is a new Israel raised from death, but the king of Israel is also proclaimed (Acts 2:30-32, 36; 13:22-23, 32-37). The kingship image refers back not only to Israel's king, but also to the dominion over creation given to Adam (Gen 1:26-28). The miracles of Jesus point to the restoration of human dominion as well as to God's conquest over Satan. Thus, Jesus is identified as Son of Man, a reference to the son of man in Daniel 7, who restores dominion to the people of God. The coming of the Son of Man in great power and glory will signal the final restoration of the human race (Lk 21:27-28).

Finally, we note the fulfillment of the wise man theme in Jesus. Solomon was both son of David and wise man of Israel. Now one greater than Solomon has come (Lk 11:31). Wisdom is characteristic of the Davidic king-messiah (Is 9:6; 11:2). Jesus shows superior wisdom to that found in the temple (Lk 2:46-52). He uses the speech forms of a wisdom teacher (parables) and claims to be the source of true wisdom (Mt 7:24-29). Christ has become wisdom for us and is the means by which we are rescued from the false wisdom of the world (1 Cor 1:20—2:16).

■ *Jesus Christ*
is true human being. He is the last Adam, the true Israel.

JESUS IS THE NEW CREATION

The temple in Israel was the focal point of the Promised Land. It was the place where God and his people met, where reconciliation and restoration took place. We have seen how the dealings of God with these people were concentrated in the temple because the mediating work of the priest was necessary if there was to be fellowship between a person and God. The prophetic hopes of a new creation consistently involve a new and glorified temple as the center of the earth. John tells us that the coming of Christ was the coming of the Word in the tabernacle of human flesh to dwell among us (Jn 1:14). Thus, the dispute over Jesus cleansing the temple led him to identify himself as the true temple (Jn 2:13-22). But if Jesus is the focal point of the new creation, he must somehow embody that creation. The New Testament makes indirect reference to this by linking the new creation with the redemption of our bodies (Rom 8:19-23; 2 Pet 3:11-13).

The divine strategy of salvation now emerges with greater clarity. All that God has promised in the Old Testament is fulfilled in Christ, especially in his resurrection from the dead (Acts 13:32-33). The message of Christ is the affirmation that all God's promises are fulfilled in him (2 Cor 1:20). The matters raised in this chapter make it necessary for us to understand that *all* of God's promises are indeed fulfilled by the birth, life, death and resurrection of Jesus. The promises of the Old Testament add up to the re-generation of all things. This is a re-creation of the kingdom in which God, his people and the created order exist in perfect harmony, perfectly fulfilling their respective roles. The strategy of salvation then is that God restores the kingdom by Christ, through the work of Christ, and actually *in the person* of Christ. In a representative way, Christ the God-man is the regeneration of all things. He is true God, true man and true created order, dwelling together perfectly. "God with us" (Hebrew: *immanuel*, Mt 1:20-23) is not merely God living in our world among human beings, but God dwelling with the true and representative man in the person of Jesus of Nazareth. The consistent message of the New Testament is that what Jesus was, he was *for us*. The new creation has come for us, on our behalf, in him.

In chapter six, I raised the subject of typology. The *type* is the historical foreshadowing of the future reality, or *antitype*, which is Christ. We may now propose the use of the term *prototype* to refer to the original kingdom as it existed before the fall. Prophetic eschatology, using as it does the historical events of the past to describe the future, confirms the typology of that history (see summary diagram, p. 208).

■ *Jesus Christ*
is the new temple and embodies the new created order. He is the regeneration of all things in himself.

STUDY GUIDE TO CHAPTER 22

1. Make sure that you have really understood the concept of Jesus fulfilling *all* the promises of the Old Testament in himself.

2. Trace the theme of God dwelling with his people as it is developed in the Old Testament and fulfilled in the incarnation of Jesus.

3. In what sense are the covenant curses and threats of judgment in the Old Testament fulfilled in Christ?

4. Can you think of any Old Testament promise that is not fulfilled in the first coming of Christ? Would you agree that there are prophecies that refer only to his second coming?

THE REGENERATION COMES IN JESUS FOR US

SUMMARY   The regeneration in the Old Testament was revealed as a re-creation of the people of God and of the created order. The New Testament reveals that this first comes about in a representative way in the person of Jesus. He is true God, true human being, and true world in which God meets his people.

KINGDOM	GOD	MANKIND	WORLD	
PROTO-TYPE	GOD	ADAM AND EVE	EDEN	Kingdom pattern established
ABRAHAM	GOD	ABRAHAM'S DESCENDANTS	CANAAN	Kingdom revealed in Israel's history
MOSES	THE LORD	ISRAEL	CANAAN	
DAVID	THE LORD	DAVID'S LINE	TEMPLE IN JERUSALEM	
PROPHETS	THE LORD	FAITHFUL REMNANT	NEW TEMPLE AND JERUSALEM	Kingdom revealed in prophetic eschatology
ANTITYPE	JESUS CHRIST			Kingdom revealed in Jesus

MAIN THEMES   Jesus as God, mankind and world
Jesus is the regeneration for us

SOME KEY WORDS   Unity and diversity
Incarnation

THE PATH AHEAD   Christ, the regeneration—Our recognition in him, 2 Corinthians 5:17—The regeneration of all things consummated, Revelation 21:1-5

FURTHER READING

1. *IBD* articles on "Incarnation," "Jesus Christ, Tiles of," "King," "Kingdom of God," "Prophets" and "Priests."
2. *KG*, chap. 7.
3. Graeme Goldsworthy, *Gospel and Wisdom* (Exeter, U.K.: Paternoster, 1987), chap. 11.
4. John Calvin, *Institutes,* book 2, chaps. 10-17.

NOTES

1. The actual term "kingdom of God" is unknown in the Old Testament and has its origins in the period between the Testaments. I am reading back the name and applying it to the concept in the Old Testament that lies behind the New Testament teaching on the kingdom.

23

THE NEW CREATION
IN US INITIATED

And everyone who calls on the name of the Lord will be saved. (Acts 2:21)

Believe in the Lord Jesus, and you will be saved—you and your household.
(Acts 16:31)

OUTLINE OF BIBLICAL HISTORY, ACTS
After Jesus had ascended, his disciples waited in Jerusalem. On the day of Pentecost,
the Holy Spirit came upon them and they began the task of proclaiming Jesus. As the
missionary implications of the gospel became clearer to the first Christians, the local
proclamation was extended to world evangelization. The apostle Paul took the gospel
to Asia Minor and Greece, establishing many churches as he went. Eventually a
church flourished at the heart of the empire at Rome.

OUTLINE OF REDEMPTIVE ACTION

Up to this point I have made frequent references to the relationship between the Old Testament and the New Testament. Just as the Old Testament has its own internal structure, so also does the New. We have seen
how the Old Testament foreshadows the New in two main stages: the history of Israel from Abraham to Solomon and the prophetic promises of the
future kingdom. Likewise, the New Testament sets out the fulfillment in
stages that we must carefully observe.

In the previous chapter I argued that the New Testament understands
the person of Jesus Christ, come in the flesh, to be the fulfillment of the Old
Testament promises. Jesus' life, death, resurrection and ascension are the
means of that fulfillment. Jesus is now at the right hand of the Father. He
is the perfect man in perfect relationship with the Father. But he does all
that he does, and he is all that he is, for us. He can be our representative,
our savior, only if what belongs to him is somehow shared with us. It is not

a lot of use to us if the kingdom of God, the new creation, remains exclusively in the person of Jesus Christ.

While Jesus is with them, his disciples sense that they are in contact with the kingdom of God. There is a great deal they do not understand and, indeed, they cannot understand until the entire picture is revealed. Thus, they find it difficult to cope with the news that Jesus will not always be physically with them (Jn 13:31-38). Jesus deals with this situation by telling the disciples that this is the only way for them to receive the blessings of God. It is entirely to their advantage that he leave them and the Holy Spirit take his place with them. In this way, he will actually remain with them, though not with his bodily presence (Jn 14:1-3, 18-20; 15:26-27; 16:4-7).

The confusion in the minds of the disciples is understandable. After all, the Old Testament has not really presented a picture of a kingdom in which the king would be bodily present for only a short while. Jesus thus introduces a new dimension to the existing revelation. There will be a period of discipleship in which the Lord, in his human form, will be absent. Why should this be to the advantage of God's people and how is it related to their doing even greater things than those already done by their Messiah (Jn 14:12; 16:7)? The answers to these questions become plain when we understand what follows the earthly existence of Jesus.

■ *The kingdom of God*
which was foreshadowed in the Old Testament, comes to reality in the person of Jesus Christ. Yet he remains with his people for only a short time.

HOW THE KINGDOM COMES

Luke and Acts make up a unique part of the Bible. Luke's Gospel has much in common with the other three Gospels. But only Luke tells us about the transition from the period when Jesus was here in the flesh, to the period when he is physically absent but present in the Spirit. Jesus' last discourse, recorded in John 14—16 tells us what is to happen. Luke and Acts tell us how it actually does happen.

As I noted in chapter eight, Luke 24 depicts two disciples whose hopes for the kingdom have been dashed by the death of Jesus. The expectations of the sudden and glorious coming of God's kingdom on earth are totally unfulfilled. The enemies of the kingdom have apparently triumphed over it (Lk 24:17-21). A lesson in biblical theology, given by the Master himself, begins with a reference to the correct interpretation of the prophets. The Christ must first suffer and only then enter his glory (Lk 24:25-27). His death was entirely predictable, and he had been trying to prepare them for it (Mk 8:31-33; 9:9-13; 10:35-45).

Once the disciples are convinced that Jesus is alive again, their hopes for the coming of the kingdom are revived (Lk 24:31-35). The suffering of the Messiah is apparently over and all that remains is for him to enter his glory. This can only mean, so they think, that the glory of the prophetic kingdom is about to burst upon them. Hence their question, "Lord, are you at this time going to restore the kingdom to Israel?" (Acts 1:6).

The answer that Jesus gives to this question is extremely important for understanding the way the kingdom of God comes. First, he rejects their perception that the matter can be resolved in purely temporal terms. "It is not for you to know the times or dates," he says (Acts 1:7). Second, he redirects their thinking about their involvement in the process by which the kingdom will come. "But you will receive power when the Holy Spirit comes on you; and you will be my witnesses in Jerusalem, and in all Judea and Samaria, and to the ends of the earth" (Acts 1:8). In effect he is saying that the kingdom is being restored now, but not in the way they had expected it. It comes through the preaching of the gospel under the influence of the Holy Spirit. The power of the kingdom does not lie in the Holy Spirit's work alone, nor does it lie in the word of Christ alone, rather it lies in both working together. Jesus thus gives the definitive interpretation of the Old Testament prophecies concerning the day of salvation.

We recall how Israel was commissioned to be a light to the nations, and yet there was never any call to go into the world to proclaim the kingdom to the Gentiles. We also recall those great prophecies, such as Isaiah 2 and Zechariah 8, which speak of the Gentiles coming to Jerusalem when the kingdom is established. Now Jesus, the true Israel and the new temple, is telling his disciples that the Holy Spirit takes his presence into the entire world through the preaching of the gospel. In this way the nations will be gathered to Christ, who takes the place of the old Israel and Jerusalem.

A similar perspective appears in the "great commission" of Matthew

28:17-20. Jesus' claim to have all authority in heaven and earth is nothing short of a claim that he is the one who brings the kingdom of God. At this point, the disciples may well expect a word about the Gentiles rushing in to Jerusalem from all over the world. But Jesus is actually saying that Jerusalem and the temple have been superseded. The focal point of the kingdom is no longer a building in the land of Judah, rather it is himself, wherever his presence is to be found. After he exchanges his bodily presence for his presence by the Spirit, the Gentiles will be brought to the new temple that is created by that Spirit wherever the gospel is preached. "Therefore go and make disciples of all nations," means that they can no longer stay in geographical Jerusalem, instead they will go out and make disciples.[1] Wherever the Holy Spirit takes the word of Christ and gathers people to the Savior, there is the new temple. The disciples do greater things than Jesus did in the sense that their ministry will be worldwide. It is to their advantage that he leaves them because only then can they know him by his Spirit and be united to him in a new way.

■ *The kingdom comes*
by the Holy Spirit taking the word about Christ into all the world, through the
preaching of the disciples.

THE NEW CREATION IN US

Acts shows us the transition from the situation described in the Gospels to that addressed in the epistles. On the one hand Jesus is here in the flesh. He gathers his disciples and instructs them in the things of the kingdom. While he is with them, the gospel events happen in their presence. Both John the Baptist and Jesus are said to preach the gospel (Lk 3:18; Mk 1:14).[2] Yet they did not proclaim the full gospel at that time, for it was not completely revealed. Only when Jesus' death, resurrection and ascension are realities is the full gospel available.

The disciples were undoubtedly believers in Jesus. Yet John says that the disciples had not yet received the Holy Spirit: "Up to that time the Spirit had not been given, since Jesus had not yet been glorified" (Jn 7:39). It is unlikely that this giving of the Spirit took place on the day Christ rose, even though he said to them, "Receive the Holy Spirit" (Jn 20:22). The statement in John 7:39, coupled with the Pentecost narrative in Acts 2, gives us a firm clue to understanding this situation. The giving of the Spirit is related to the person and work of Christ. Just as Jesus undoubtedly had the Spirit before his baptism, so the disciples had the Spirit before Pentecost. At his baptism, the Spirit came on Jesus with respect to his task as the Savior. The disciples, if they were believing Jews, had the Spirit with respect to the foreshadowing of Jesus in the Old Testament covenant. As disciples of Jesus, their faith in him as their Master was a divine gift and therefore of the Spirit. At Pentecost the Holy Spirit comes upon them for the first time with respect to the fully revealed Christ. This can happen only after he is glorified (Jn 7:39).

Pentecost, then, involves an experience unique to the disciples, for it marks a point of transition. It is a fact of history that no one except the apostles has ever had this experience. No one since that time has come from knowing Jesus face to face, in the flesh, to knowing him by his preached Word and by his Spirit. Therefore, no one can have the same, two-stage experience of the Holy Spirit that they had. A believing Jew, who became a disciple of Jesus and then received the Spirit at Pentecost, would have had a three-stage experience of the Spirit.

Once we recognize what is not repeatable about the Pentecost experience, we are in a better position to understand what remains as part of the Christian experience. Clearly, the gospel proclaims that the enabling power of the Spirit is what converts us. Acts 2:38 explains what normally happens for Christians: the unbeliever, whether Jew or Gentile, who hears the gospel and believes it, receives forgiveness of sins and the gift of the Holy Spirit. This is the baptism of the Spirit that John the Baptist referred to in Luke 3:16.

■ *The Holy Spirit*
was always present in relation to the work of salvation. At Pentecost it was given for the first time in relation to the finished work of Christ.

BIBLICAL THEOLOGY OF THE HOLY SPIRIT

Acts, together with what has gone before, is important for the construction of a biblical theology of the Holy Spirit. An outline of this topical theology includes the place of the Spirit in the creation of the world. The human race, created in God's image, is under the influence of the Spirit of God, but sin leaves the race deprived of this good impulse until the grace of God begins the work of salvation. Thus, we are justified in saying that the people of God are the people of the Spirit, while rebellious sinners are people without the Spirit.

As redemption is progressively revealed in Israel, so the work of the Spirit is also progressively revealed. In the period of Israel's history from Abraham to Solomon, the Spirit's work is seen primarily as a special endowment of representative people for the work of mediating God's salvation, including giving prophetic utterance. During this period there is some indication of the possession of the Spirit by all the people of God.

In prophetic eschatology the Spirit appears active primarily in relation to the saving deeds of God and in the lives of the human agents of these deeds. The suffering servant, the true prophet and the messianic prince are all people upon whom the Spirit is said to come mightily. The Spirit of God is also the regenerative power in the lives of all the people of God. It helps them become true covenant partners of God. A mark of the new age will be that the Spirit will be given in full to all the people of God (Joel 2:28-29).

Only in the New Testament is there a true fulfillment of this eschatological hope. It happens first in the man, Jesus of Nazareth, who is the Spirit-filled man, the regenerate Israelite, the anointed prophet, priest and king. While for us the focus is on Jesus as the new creation, the emphasis for Jesus is on the Holy Spirit.

The ascension of Jesus and Pentecost mark the point of transition. The focus is never removed from Jesus, but it is now widened to include people being united with him and sharing in his relationship with God and the kingdom. As the gospel is preached, people are drawn into the kingdom through repentance and faith. In this conversion experience, the regeneration that exists in Christ starts to become a reality in us.

■ *The theology of the Spirit*
leads, through the endowment of the representative saving figures in Israel's history and prophetic eschatology, to Christ. At Pentecost Christ's Spirit is shared with his people.

THE REGENERATION BEGINS IN GOD'S PEOPLE

SUMMARY The regeneration that first came in the person of Jesus Christ now becomes a reality in the lives of God's people. The Holy Spirit takes the place of the bodily presence of Jesus. At Pentecost he comes, for the first time, to relate believers to the regeneration as it is fully revealed in Christ.

KINGDOM	GOD	MANKIND	WORLD	
PROTO-TYPE	GOD	ADAM AND EVE	EDEN	Kingdom pattern established
ABRAHAM	GOD	ABRAHAM'S DESCENDANTS	CANAAN	Kingdom revealed in Israel's history
MOSES	THE LORD	ISRAEL	CANAAN	
DAVID	THE LORD	DAVID'S LINE	TEMPLE IN JERUSALEM	
PROPHETS	THE LORD	FAITHFUL REMNANT	NEW TEMPLE AND JERUSALEM	Kingdom revealed in prophetic eschatology
ANTITYPE	JESUS CHRIST			Kingdom revealed in Jesus
	FATHER, SON, HOLY SPIRIT	BELIEVERS	THE NEW TEMPLE	

MAIN THEMES Jesus reinterprets the kingdom
Transition to age of the Spirit

SOME KEY WORDS Baptism
Conversion

THE PATH AHEAD The One (Jesus) comes for the many—The One unites the many to himself by his Spirit so that where the One is, there also the many will be

STUDY GUIDE TO CHAPTER 23

1. Read the sermons of Peter and Paul in Acts (Acts 2:14-40; 3:12-26; 4:8-12; 10:34-43; 13:16-41). Note how they apply the Old Testament to the ministry of Jesus. What can you learn from the apostles about interpretations of the Old Testament?

2. Read Stephen's speech to the Jews in Acts 7:2-53. Note the structure and the recurring themes. How does the accusation in verses 51-53 follow from the reference to the tabernacle and temple in verses 44-50? What is the main point of the speech?

3. What aspects of the events in Acts can be regarded as normative for all Christians and for all time? What aspects are unique to the period?

FURTHER READING

1. *IBD* article on "Spirit, Holy Spirit."
2. I. H. Marshall, *Acts*, TNTC (Grand Rapids, Mich.: Eerdmans, 1980).
3. F. D. Bruner, *A Theology of the Holy Spirit* (Grand Rapids, Mich.: Eerdmans, 1970).
4. Morris Inch, *Saga of the Spirit* (Grand Rapids, Mich.: Baker, 1985).

NOTES

1. The command is to make disciples. The word *go* appears in some English translations where the original Greek has a participle: "going," or "as you go." It may seem to be a fine distinction, but the emphasis is on the making of disciples. The "go" may simply be a means of directing the disciples to the fact that the Gentiles won't be coming to geographical Jerusalem but that the new Jerusalem will be wherever they go.
2. The Greek word *euangelizesthai* is often taken to mean "preach good news." Taken with its Old Testament Hebrew equivalent, *basar*, we must recognize that the good news is the serious news of the kingdom. It is not possible to preach the kingdom without some reference to judgment.

24

THE NEW CREATION
IN US NOW

Since, then, you have been raised with Christ, set your hearts on things above, where Christ is seated at the right hand of God. Set your minds on things above, not on earthly things. For you died, and your life is now hidden with Christ in God. When Christ, who is your life, appears, then you also will appear with him in glory. (Col 3:1-4)

OUTLINE OF BIBLICAL HISTORY, NEW TESTAMENT EPISTLES
As the gospel made inroads into pagan societies it encountered many philosophies and non-Christian ideas which challenged the apostolic message. The New Testament epistles show that the pressure to adopt pagan ideas that had existed for the people of God in Old Testament times were also a constant threat to the churches. The real danger to Christian teaching was not so much direct attacks upon it, but rather in the subtle distortion of Christian ideas. Among the troublemakers were the Judaizers, who added Jewish law-keeping to the gospel. The Gnostics also undermined the gospel with elements of Greek philosophy and religion.

GOD'S STRATEGY FOR SALVATION

At some time or other you may have been instructed that the Christian's response to the question "Are you saved?" should refer to the past, the present and the future. "Yes, I have been saved; I am being saved; I will be saved," expresses the way salvation is experienced. The past reference is to Christ's perfect and finished work *for us*. The present reference is to the ongoing work of the Holy Spirit *in us* as he applies the gospel to our lives and conforms us more and more to the image of Christ. The future reference is to the consummation when what is happening in us will conform perfectly to what exists for us, and when all things are made new in themselves. Many Christians will recognize the words *justification, sanctification* and *glorification* as applying to these three aspects of our salvation.

The New Testament, then, shows that God's saving purpose is to restore all things to their proper relationships. The strategy, or method, he uses to achieve this goal is the actual person of Christ and his saving work. He unites his people to Christ by faith, attributing to them the perfection that is in Christ. On the basis of what they are accounted as being in Christ, God, by his Spirit and gospel, begins the work of restoring the true relationships in them and in the whole community of believers. Finally, the consummation of the whole creation is reached when Christ returns in glory.

Salvation or Regeneration		
Past	Present	Future
What took place perfectly in Christ for us.	What is taking place in us, but not yet perfected.	What will take place in us and the whole creation.
The grounds of our acceptance with God, or justification.	The result of our acceptance with God, or sanctification.	The final result of our acceptance with God, or glorification.
All the promises of the Old Testament have been fulfilled for us in Christ.	All the promises of the Old Testament are being fulfilled in and among us.	All the promises of the Old Testament will be fulfilled in us and the whole creation.

UNION WITH CHRIST

One of biblical theology's chief tasks is to point out the relationships between the various stages of redemptive revelation. An area of great confusion in many Christians' thinking, which church history shows has always been an issue, is how the work of Christ for us relates to the work of Christ by his Spirit in us. In other words, how does the gospel relate to Christian living, or how does justification relate to sanctification? Some New Testament epistles show that the problem for Jewish Christians was the relationship of the gospel to the law. We may also express it as the relationship of grace to good works.

Few would argue with the statement that we are converted by believing the gospel. But how does the gospel figure into Christian growth or sanctification? Examination of the New Testament documents shows that growth is not stepping out from the gospel, but rather stepping out with the gospel. Many of the problems dealt with in the epistles arise from a failure to apply the gospel to some aspect of life. The solution to this problem is to restore the gospel to its rightful place at the center of our thinking and doing.

The New Testament describes, in various ways, the relationship between what God did for us in Christ and what he is currently doing in us. John's Gospel emphasizes believing in Christ and having eternal life through him (Jn 20:31). Peter speaks of coming to Christ to be built into the new temple as living stones, and to be part of a new Israel (1 Pet 2:4-10). Paul has his own distinct ways of dealing with this relationship, and he focuses on our union with Christ.

Paul's use of the phrases "in Christ" and "with Christ" to describe the believer's relationship to Jesus needs careful examination. These are some of the clearest expressions correcting the misconception that the essence of Christianity is following the precepts of Jesus. Now, of course, there is an important sense in which we are to follow his teachings and imitate his human existence. But what some people mean by this is observing the moral teachings of Jesus, such as the "golden rule" (Mt 7:12). This leads to the popular idea that we can work our way into heaven by our good deeds.

Paul argues strongly against all tendencies to see our acts as the basis of our acceptance with God. His teaching on justification by faith points to the heart of the gospel's significance for us. What God has done for us in the life, death and resurrection of Jesus Christ, is the only basis of our acceptance with God (Rom 3:21—4:25; Gal 3:14-29). By faith in Christ's person and work for us we receive salvation and acceptance as a free gift. Justification by grace through faith alone raises immediate questions about the justified sinner's future lifestyle. For some people, it is pleasant to think of justification by grace as making no demands and implying no change of lifestyle.

Paul's answer to this wrong thinking is to point out that justification and forgiveness are part of the process by which we are brought back to the kingdom of God. Through faith we enter into a union with Jesus Christ which is cemented by the presence of the Holy Spirit in our lives. This union is not to be seen as a mystical joining of our being to the being of Jesus so that he merges with us and lives his life in us. Certainly the Spirit dwells in us, but he does so to maintain our faith-union with Christ. This union, which is signified by baptism, is described as effecting something quite amazing. It means that what took place in Christ in his life, death and resurrection, God now regards as having involved us. The merits and perfection of Christ are applied to us so that what belongs to him as the true Son of God, belongs to us who are caught up "in him."

Christ, then, becomes our other identity, our *alter ego*. We possess and know this other self only by faith, hence we "live by faith, not by sight" (2 Cor 5:7). Consequently, we have died with Christ and have been buried with him (Rom 6:3-11; Gal 2:19-20; Col 2:12, 20), we have also been raised with him (Rom 6:4-5, 11; 1 Cor 15:22; Eph 2:5) and we have ascended to the right hand of the Father with him (Eph 2:6). In Christ we are a new creation (2 Cor 5:17). None of these things are goals for us to achieve for they already exist perfectly in Christ on our behalf.

Paul's use of "in Christ" and "with Christ" is a direct application of the Old Testament idea of the representative mediator of salvation. The believer is "in Christ" in the same way that the believing Israelite was "in" the priest or king who represented him. A main thrust of Paul's theology of our union with Christ is to destroy the false notion that justification by faith alone allows a believer to live a godless life. It is inconceivable that anyone united to the most durable of all realities, the new creation in Christ, can go on living as if it were a fiction. Since it is the Holy Spirit who applies the reality of Christ to us, life in Christ is also life in the Spirit (Rom 8:1-25; Eph 5:18-20; cf. Col 3:16-17).

■ *Believers*
are united to Christ by faith in such a way that God attributes to them everything that belongs to Christ as the perfect human being.

THE UNAVOIDABLE WAR

Since it is very easy to become preoccupied with matters of our personal lives, let us stand back and survey the larger view. The Old Testament prophets foretell the coming day of salvation, in which the glorious kingdom will be fully revealed and the people of God finally saved and perfected. There is no clear indication in the prophets of how this kingdom will come or how long the process will take. If anything, the achievement of final glory seems to be expected to happen in an instant. Even if there are some suggestions of protracted time, the kingdom comes openly and universally. The New Testament, however, qualifies this by showing that the kingdom comes first in the person of Jesus, then it comes through the progress of the gospel in the world; only after these does it come openly and universally.

In the period between the first and second comings of Christ, Christians battle against the old, alien order in the world (Rom 12:2; Jas 1:27), the flesh (Gal 5:17) and the devil (1 Pet 5:8-9). Warfare and struggle exist only when two opposing realms are competing. We are in this struggle until we are removed from the world by our death or by the second coming of Christ. Thus, we live in a period in which the two ages overlap. When the regeneration or new age came perfectly in Jesus Christ and the old age or degeneration continued to exist. It still exists, even while the regeneration is being formed in the people of God throughout the world. Only at the second coming will the old age be destroyed with all that belongs to it. We belong to the new age because, by faith, we are fully acceptable to God and have been united to Christ who embodies the new age. Thus, we must accept that in God's eyes we are just or righteous. At the same time, we acknowledge that we are not fully saved because we are still sinners. When we understand the overlap of the two ages, we also understand the nature of the struggle within and around us.

The first time Christ came, the regeneration invaded the realm of the degeneration. But this regeneration was in his bodily existence. Now that he is absent in the flesh, the regeneration comes as his Spirit applies the gospel to people throughout the world. At the personal level the regeneration in Christ is applied to us by the Spirit and grows in us as our thinking and actions become more and more conformed to what is in Christ. Since this process involves our minds and human responsibility, there is a constant appeal in the New Testament to conform to Christ. Because we have died with Christ, the appropriate regenerate response is to put to death whatever belongs to our sinful earthly nature (Col 3:3-5).

It should be noted that the exhortations in the New Testament call us to conformity with Christ, not with the law of Moses. It is striking that the Ten Commandments are not set forth as the standard of Christian conduct. This is a vexed topic, about which there is much difference of opinion. Perhaps there is a way to recognize a distinction between God's lawful rule of his kingdom and the law of Sinai. The latter was a temporary expression suited to that period of revelation. Since Christ has come, we are no longer under that expression of kingdom rule because Christ is the perfect revelation of it (Rom 6:14; Gal 3:21-25). In the light of Christ we see that some aspects of the Sinai law have enduring validity yet we are free from the total rule of the law.

■ *The overlap of the ages*
means that Christian existence is characterized by the warfare between them.

REGENERATION OF THE BELIEVER

There is an ongoing argument among some Christians about the relationship of faith and the initiation of personal regeneration. It is put in terms of *when* regeneration occurs, before or after faith. The New Testament does not really raise the question of order. Thus, the *when* question should probably be evaded in the same way that Jesus dealt with the disciples' "when" question about the coming of the kingdom (Acts 1:6-8). There can be no doubt that God's Spirit alone can overcome any willful suppression of the truth and give faith. Therefore, it cannot be true to say that when I freely believed, and because I did, God gave me the gift of regeneration. However, in preserving the sovereignty of God in our salvation, we must not fall into the trap of believing that the Spirit acts independently of the preaching of the gospel. Remember that the regeneration in Christ is the basis for the regeneration in us.

When we examine the variety of regeneration passages in the New Testament we see two main perspectives. One is concerned with the objective, historical facts of Jesus and the other with the subjective element of our faith. When Nicodemus twice asked how one could be born again (Jn 3:4, 9), Jesus' first response pointed to the sovereign movement of the Spirit, and the second to the response of faith in the gospel events (Jn 3:5-8, 10-15). Peter says that we are born anew by the resurrection of Jesus, and then he says that we are born again through the gospel that is preached to us (1 Pet 1:3, 23). The necessity of the gospel for a new birth is also expressed by Paul (Gal 3:2) and James (Jas 1:18).

Paul's well-known statement in 2 Corinthians 5:17 is probably deliberately ambiguous: "If anyone is in Christ, he is a new creation; the old has gone, the new has come!" Notice Paul does not say "If Jesus is in anyone," as it is so often interpreted. The emphasis is on the new creation that is in Christ. But Paul does not leave the objective "in Christ" without the subjective outworking. The reason for pointing out that the believer is linked to the new creation in Christ is so that we might be aware of what is now being formed in us. Regeneration has its effects in terms of changed lives (Tit 3:1-7).

Since this subjective regeneration, being born again, is the fruit of the

THE REGENERATION GROWS IN GOD'S PEOPLE

SUMMARY   That which believers possess by faith, the regeneration for us in Christ, becomes that which begins to be formed in them. The personal regeneration of the believer is the fruit of the regeneration in Christ. Both are related to the final regeneration of all things, which will take place when Christ returns.

KINGDOM	GOD	MANKIND	WORLD	
ORIGINAL GENERATION	GOD	ADAM AND EVE	EDEN	Kingdom pattern established
Regeneration foreshadowed	GOD	ABRAHAM'S DESCENDANTS	CANAAN	Kingdom revealed in Israel's history
	THE LORD	ISRAEL	CANAAN	
	THE LORD	DAVID'S LINE	TEMPLE IN JERUSALEM	
Regeneration in prophecy	THE LORD	FAITHFUL REMNANT	NEW TEMPLE AND JERUSALEM	Kingdom revealed in prophetic eschatology
Regeneration for us and in us	JESUS CHRIST			Kingdom revealed in Jesus
	TRINITY	THOSE WHO ARE "IN CHRIST"	WHERE CHRIST IS	

MAIN THEMES   Regeneration of the believer and its relationship to the gospel
Struggle due to overlap of the two ages

SOME KEY WORDS   Justification, Sanctification, Glorification
Consummation

THE PATH AHEAD   The new age has been formed in Christ—The new age is being formed in God's people—The new age will be formed in the whole of creation

gospel, to proclaim the necessity of the new birth is not in itself a proclamation of the gospel. The gospel is not "You must be born again!" The significance of the doctrine of personal regeneration in the New Testament is
not the main thrust of the evangelist's message to unbelievers. It is a doctrine primarily for believers so that they might understand what a radical
and life-changing thing faith in Jesus Christ really is.

■ *Regeneration*
begins in Christ who is the embodiment of the new age. When people are united
with Christ, the regeneration begins to be formed in them.

STUDY GUIDE TO CHAPTER 24

1. Read Ephesians 1:1-14 and note the use of the phrase "in Christ" or "in
   him." Which statements refer to God's past work for us in Christ, and
   which to God's ongoing work in us by the Spirit?

2. Using a concordance and a Bible dictionary, work out a statement on
   the meaning of the terms *justification, sanctification* and *glorification.*
   How would you explain the relationship between them?

3. Read Ephesians 6:10-18. How does the gospel figure in the Christian warfare? Check out the ideas that are borrowed and even quoted from the
   Old Testament concept of God as the warrior who fights for his people.

4. Are the terms *regeneration, new birth* and *new creation* interchangeable?
   Why is it insufficient to deal with the relationship of faith and regeneration in terms of which comes first?

FURTHER READING

1. G. E. Ladd, *The Pattern of New Testament Truth* (Grand Rapids, Mich.:
   Eerdmans, 1968).
2. Herman Ridderbos, *Paul* (Grand Rapids, Mich.: Eerdmans, 1975).
3. *IBD* articles on "Justification," "Sanctification."
4. James Buchanan, *The Doctrine of Justification* (Edinburgh: Banner of
   Truth, 1961).
5. Robert Horn, *Go Free* (London: Inter-Varsity Press, 1976).

25

THE NEW CREATION CONSUMMATED

And I heard a loud voice from the throne saying, "Now the dwelling of God is with men, and he will live with them. They will be his people, and God himself will be with them and be their God. He will wipe every tear from their eyes. There will be no more death or mourning or crying or pain, for the old order of things has passed away." He who was seated on the throne said, "I am making everything new!" (Rev 21:3-5)

OUTLINE OF BIBLICAL HISTORY, THE NEW TESTAMENT
God is Lord over history and therefore, when he so desires, he can cause the events of the future to be recorded. All sections of the New Testament contain references to things that have not yet happened, the most significant being the return of Christ and the consummation of the kingdom of God. No clues to the actual chronology are given, but it is certain that Christ will return to judge the living and the dead. The old creation will be undone and the new creation will take its place.

UNIVERSAL REGENERATION

Many Christians think of the new birth or regeneration almost exclusively as the moment when spiritual life begins in the individual coming to faith in Christ. There is no doubt that this is a biblical concept, and that the image of a birth reinforces the idea of initiation to new life. I have attempted to show that this initiation or new birth by the Spirit of God is part of a wider rebirth which ultimately takes in the whole of creation.[1] The New Testament doctrine of regeneration stands firmly on the foundation of the Old Testament view of creation and new creation. In the Old Testament the regeneration came to be perceived mainly in terms of the Spirit-endowed representative such as the judge, prophet, king-messiah, or servant of the Lord (for example, Is 42:1; 61:1-4; note the connection between the Spirit-filled messiah in Is 11:1-5 and the regeneration of nature in verses 6-9). But there is also an expectation that the people of God, as a whole, will be renewed by the Spirit in the new age (Ezek 36:25-28, which is linked to the regeneration of nature in verses 33-35. See also Ezek 37:1-14). Then, finally, there is the renewal of the whole created order (Is 32:15-20; 35:1-10; 65:17-25).

We have observed how the New Testament shows the fulfillment of these expectations, first as they *all* take place in Christ. Then what takes place in Christ, who is the representative new creation, has its outworking in us and, ultimately, in the whole of creation. We are thus able to speak of regeneration in three ways: an objective regeneration in Christ, a subjective regeneration in us, and a comprehensive regeneration in the whole universe. The three are inseparably bound together, which is why a preoccupation with one at the expense of the others can lead to distortions of biblical truth.

As we consider the consummation (bringing to final perfection or completion), we note that not only the idea but also the word regeneration is applied to it in the New Testament. The word which literally translates as *regeneration* (Greek: *palingenesia*) is used only twice: in Titus 3:5 and in Matthew 19:28. In the latter, Jesus refers to the new age as the regeneration. Other terms used to describe entry into new life include new birth or birth from above.

■ *Regeneration has three aspects:*

objective regeneration in Christ; subjective regeneration in us; comprehensive regeneration in the universe.

THE RETURN OF CHRIST

In the Old Testament, the day of the Lord or the day of salvation was portrayed as a single event, even if it was a potentially lengthy one. We have no real evidence in the prophetic promises of more than one coming of the Lord. I have already dealt with the way the New Testament restructures the Old Testament promises so that the age of the Spirit and of Christian mission emerges as part of the events of the day of the Lord. Jesus himself described an aspect of this in the discourses with the disciples in John 14—16 and in Luke 24—Acts 1. He must suffer, go away and come again. It is as if the prophetic promises add up to a basic bird's-eye view of the events, looking mainly at the results of God's saving acts but not at the details.

Being present as the events actually occur, the disciples discover that there are a few surprises, some of which they should have anticipated, and others that result from further revelation. Thus (and this is important), the end of the old age occurs when Jesus comes the first time because he is the embodiment of the new age. Yet the old age continues to exist along with the new age so that the two overlap. The idea that the end has come and the fact that the end is not yet come, corresponds to the Christian being saved and still waiting to be saved. Jesus comes into conflict with the old age because he invades it to destroy it. In this conflict he is rejected, suffers and dies. The suffering ministry of Christ as the servant lies at the heart of the gospel. The suffering Christ, who invaded the old age while here in the flesh, goes on invading the old age through the message if his servant role proclaimed in the gospel. The church as Christ's body suffers because it is the instrument of Christ's invasion.

The effects of Christ's resurrection are largely hidden. His reappearance from the dead does not of itself convey the whole meaning of this event. It had to be proclaimed that this event brought about certain things that are as yet invisible. The disciples' question in Acts 1:6 indicates that they expected the kingdom would be a visible result of the resurrection. Instead, the gospel summons people to faith in the risen and now invisible Savior. In the resurrection Jesus is proclaimed the true Son of God who, because of God's unbreakable covenant, cannot remain cut off from God by death (Rom 1:4). The resurrection fulfills God's covenant commitment to his people in general, and David in particular (Heb 13:20; Acts 2:29-35; 13:32-35). Thus, the resurrection means that Jesus is Lord and Christ (Acts 2:36). Yet these are all matters that must be received by faith.

The fact that the age of the gospel is one in which the kingdom of God is not visible, points to the necessity of Christ's return. Even among the first generation of Christians, the delay in Christ's glorious return became a problem (2 Pet 3:3-13). Although we experience time differently than God, the overlap of the two ages cannot go on forever. The warfare, which was decisively won in the death and resurrection of Jesus, must end. Thus, the New Testament writers constantly refer to the day when Christ will appear in glory, for without it the whole redemptive revelation would be meaningless.

■ *The return of Christ*
ends the overlap of the ages and makes the reality of the kingdom universally visible.

THE NEW CREATION

The bodily resurrection of Jesus dominates the New Testament under-standing of the gospel. In no way does this emphasis detract from the death of Jesus as the perfect offering, which covers our sins. The resurrec-tion is central because it presupposes his death and because it stands as the new beginning of the human race. It may be for this reason that the birth of Jesus as the new creation is not a theme that is developed in the New Testament. The new humanity rises in the resurrection of Jesus; and in our own bodily resurrection, our participation in the kingdom will cease to be one that is experienced by faith alone and will become a fact of our total experience. Thus, we are born again by Christ's resurrection (1 Pet 1:3). Through his resurrection we enter into newness of life (Rom 6:4-11).

The consummation is perceived as being the event that takes place when Christ is revealed in glory. The life in the Spirit, which is the life of faith, continues for a time. It is a life of suffering (Rom 8:18). At the same time the whole creation, which has been subjected to futility, waits with longing for the final redemption of our bodies (Rom 8:11, 19-23). The res-urrection of the children of God will signal the final redemption and re-newal of the whole creation. This involvement of the physical body along with the physical creation in the regeneration is one reason why re-generation should not be thought of exclusively as God giving new life to our spirits. The New Testament constantly repudiates the Greek Gnostic[2] notions of salvation of the immortal soul alone. Texts dealing with the soul between death and resurrection are very scarce. But texts dealing with the resurrection of the whole person abound throughout the whole New Testament.

By now it should be obvious that Old Testament references to the king-dom being on earth and populated by people with bodies cannot be spiri-tualized away. Once we accept that Jesus rose bodily, even though his resurrection body was not exactly as it has been before, the physical com-ponent of the kingdom is clear. Those texts that support the idea of souls going to heaven (for example, 2 Cor 5:1-10) see it as a purely temporary sit-uation. Peter's description of the new heaven and the new earth is drawn directly from Isaiah 65:17 (2 Pet 3:13), which is based on Genesis 1:1. Like-wise, the marvelous description of the kingdom in Revelation 21—22 is based on a number of Old Testament passages. But there is no suggestion that it is mere symbolism that must be interpreted in a spiritualized way.[3]

For John, the consummation is the open fulfillment of the Old Testament hope. There is a new heaven and a new earth, and a new Jerusalem coming down out of heaven (Rev 21:1-2). Some may think of the heavenly Jerusalem as a place *in* the heavens. But John describes it as *from* heaven and coming down onto the new earth. That which the tabernacle and temple pointed to, the dwelling of God with his people, becomes a reality (Rev 21:3). The regeneration is now complete (Rev 21:5), and there is no longer any need for "government outposts and agencies," such as the temple, which is the symbol of God's presence, for he is present and is also the source of all light (Rev 21:22-23). The old images of Eden are joined with those of the holy city and throne (Rev 22:1-2; cf. Ezek 47:1-12).

No doubt all sorts of questions spring to mind regarding what the new earth will be like. Most of them will have to remain unanswered in this life since Scripture provides little information. One thing is sure: the biblical view of the total regeneration of all things really beats the popular pagan view of an eternity spent as disembodied souls with only the odd cloud or two for support!

■ *The bodily resurrection*
of Jesus points us to the fact of our own bodily resurrection and to the restoration of the whole physical creation.

MEANWHILE LIFE GOES ON

The last words of the book of Revelation bring us back to our present existence and remind us of the continuing struggle as we wait for Jesus to come. In a number of ways, the New Testament refers to those things that structure the Christian life in this world. The first is, of course, the gospel event. The second, which results from the gospel event, is the consummation. An important passage summarizing the relationship of our present to these past and the future events is Colossians 3:1-5. An analysis of this passage shows that the past gospel facts and the future consummation of the gospel both shape the directives that are given about Christian living in the present. Notice how words so often overlooked, such as *therefore, since* and *for*, actually point to these relationships.

GOSPEL EVENT	CHRISTIAN LIFE	CONSUMMATION
Colossians 3:1-5 Since, then, you have been raised with Christ,		
	set your hearts on things above, where Christ is seated at the right hand of God. Set your minds on things above, not on earthly things.	
For you died, and your life is now hidden with Christ in God.		
		When Christ, who is your life, appears, then you also will appear with him in glory.
	Put to death, therefore, whatever belongs to your earthly nature.	

Two other comments are in order. First, the consummation can take place only because of the gospel. It is the opening to a universal view of the results and significance of the gospel in a way that will compel recognition. It will then be too late to receive the offer of salvation since Christ returns this time to judge. Nevertheless, for the Christian, the motivation to holy living provided by the hope of his coming is not fear of judgment, but the desire to be like him. Second, the return of Christ also motivates us in the same way the gospel does because of its relationship to, and dependence on, the gospel event. What we already are in Christ, we shall be in ourselves and, in the meanwhile, we move towards the goal by the Holy Spirit at work within us.

Given the intimate connection between the gospel event of the past and our continuing struggle in the present, there is a great danger in separating the two. The New Testament contains many passages of command and exhortation to live holy lives. When we remove these from the wider context

THE FINAL PERFECTION OF THE NEW CREATION

SUMMARY   That which believers possess by faith, the regeneration for us in Christ, becomes that which begins to be formed in them. At the return of Christ the regeneration of believers is completed, and the whole creation is renewed. The kingdom of God, first revealed in Eden, is consummated for eternity.

KINGDOM	GOD	MANKIND	WORLD	
ORIGINAL GENERATION	GOD	ADAM AND EVE	EDEN	Kingdom pattern established
Regeneration foreshadowed	GOD	ABRAHAM'S DESCENDANTS	CANAAN	Kingdom revealed in Israel's history
	THE LORD	ISRAEL	CANAAN	
	THE LORD	DAVID'S LINE	TEMPLE IN JERUSALEM	
Regeneration in prophecy	THE LORD	FAITHFUL REMNANT	NEW TEMPLE AND JERUSALEM	Kingdom revealed in prophetic eschatology
Regeneration for us and in us and in the whole of creation	JESUS CHRIST			Kingdom revealed in Jesus
	TRINITY	THOSE WHO ARE "IN CHRIST"	WHERE CHRIST IS	
	TRINITY	GOD'S PEOPLE IN HIS PRESENCE	NEW HEAVEN AND NEW EARTH	

MAIN THEMES   Regeneration of the whole creation and its relation to the gospel

Second coming of Christ and the consummation of the kingdom

of the already perfect status before God that we possess through faith in Christ, then we reduce Christian living to a form of legalism quite foreign to the New Testament. The corrective to this is to keep firmly in our minds that the whole of Christian existence is the application of the gospel to every part of our lives. We start with Christ as the new creation for us, and we move towards the goal, which is to be made like him in the universal new creation. As in biblical theology, so in Christian living, Christ is Alpha and Omega, the first and the last, the beginning and the end.

■ **Christian existence**
is shaped and motivated by the gospel and by the consummation of the gospel.

STUDY GUIDE TO CHAPTER 25

1. There is a considerable difference of opinion among Christians about whether or not the formation of the state of Israel in 1948 is a fulfillment of prophecies concerning the return of the Jews to their land. In the light of our study, consider your position on this issue.

2. Read 1 John 3:1-3 and analyze it in terms of the past, present and future elements of salvation. Note that verse 1 can be seen in terms of both the past basis of our sonship and the present experience of it.

3. List the events that you believe the Bible teaches will occur at Christ's return, and check them to be sure the Bible does teach them. Now consider whether anything will happen universally at his second coming that has not already happened in him or to him at his first coming.

4. Why is the bodily resurrection of Jesus so essential to the gospel?

FURTHER READING

1. Stephen Travis, *The Jesus Hope* (Leicester, U.K.: Inter-Varsity Press, 1980).
2. Graeme Goldsworthy, *The Gospel in Revelation* (Exeter, U.K.: Paternoster Press, 1984).
3. Leon Morris, *Revelation*, TNTC (London: Tyndale Press, 1969).
4. *IBD* article on "Eschatology."

NOTES

1. Universal regeneration refers to the renewal of the whole of creation. This does not imply the unbiblical doctrine known as universalism, which states that every human being that ever existed will eventually be redeemed. Such a doctrine has no place for final judgment or hell.

2. *Gnosticism* is a rather broad term. Essentially it refers to the Greek idea which regarded all matter as inherently evil while good lies in the spirit or soul of man. The Gnostics thus taught that salvation did not include the physical body. Their highest aspiration was to be released from their imprisonment in the body so that the soul could be free. Gnostic thought affected Christianity by denying that Jesus had come in the flesh. 1 John 4:1-3 is almost certainly aimed against Gnostics.

3. It should be evident by now that "spiritual" in the New Testament is not in opposition to "physical" or "bodily" (see 1 Cor 15:42-44). Paul opposes "spirit" and "flesh," but it is clear that he is not denying the regeneration of the physical creation but rather opposing the old age of the flesh to the new age of the Spirit.

B I B L I C A L
T H E O L O G Y —
W H E R E ?

Finally, and very briefly, we ask where the content and method of biblical theology can be applied. Once we have grasped some kind of biblical theological overview, it will permanently change our understanding of the Bible in general. But there are also specific matters that can be opened up in a way we may never have thought possible. Here are a couple of examples.

26

KNOWING GOD'S WILL

AN OUTLINE BIBLICAL THEOLOGY OF GUIDANCE

THE PROBLEM

Getting guidance, or knowing God's will for our lives, is a concern for every Christian. The Bible says a lot about the will of God and about his rule in our lives. What kind of guidance can we expect and how do we get it? We know that there are matters of behavior where the choice is between doing good or doing evil. But not all choices are such clearly moral ones. Does God guide us in things like what we have for dinner today, where we go for holidays or by which route we take the dog for a walk? Or does he only guide us in big issues such as what career we choose, whether or not we should get married and to whom?

SOME PITFALLS

It is amazing how easy it is for Christians to develop an idea or an approach to some aspect of Christian living without really testing it against Scripture. Traditions can grow and become firmly fixed and yet have absolutely no basis in the Bible. When these traditions are surrounded by pious or "spiritual" language they are even harder to shake. So it is with the subject of guidance. There are some evangelical traditions concerning guidance that are accepted by many without questioning. A further pitfall is the use of proof texts to support an idea. Proof texts are often texts taken out of their biblical-theological context and applied in a way that is not true to Scripture.

A SUGGESTED APPROACH

The subject relates to no one specific word in Scripture. Looking up *guidance* in a concordance will not yield very much. A certain amount of creativity is required to pin down relevant words, which can then be looked up in a concordance. But we must go wider than that and be alert to the ideas of Scripture that relate to the theme of guidance. Here are some steps that the method of biblical theology suggests.

1. *Make some general contact with the subject at the level of the gospel.*
   What kind of guidance did Jesus seek in his life and work? What guidance did he promise to his disciples?

2. *Select key words and themes to be investigated at the various levels of redemptive revelation.*
   For example: *guide, lead, path, way, calling, show the way, will of God, God's purpose and ultimate goal.* This requires a lot of hard work in checking texts within their contexts. We must be careful to ask:
   a. What does the text actually say?
   b. What is its meaning in its theological and historical context?

3. *Now investigate each of the strata of biblical theology for these things.*
   How does God guide people towards his ultimate goal for them at each level of redemptive revelation? Our results might include the following:
   a. *Adam and Eve* (Gen 2:16-17): They are free to eat anything except one forbidden fruit.
   b. *The patriarchs* (Gen 12:1; 24:27-38; 45:5-7): Guidance is related to the covenant and its operation for the salvation of God's chosen people.
   c. *The exodus* (Ex 13:17, 21; 15:13; Deut 1:33; 8:2, 15; 29:5; 32:12; Neh 9:12, 19; Ps 77:20; 78:53; 106:9; Is 43:21; 63:12-13): Guidance equals the way of salvation. The law contains specific aspects of the will of God.
   d. *Canaan-monarchy*: Guidance is given concerning entry into the land, the possession of it and the settlement of it. Guidance is also given in matters of the leadership of the people of God. This is part of the revelation of the kingdom of God. There is no evidence of God guiding ordinary people in the specific decisions of their private lives.
   e. *Prophecy*: Guidance is there in the law for all to follow. Future guidance will mean God leading his people finally into his kingdom (salvation) (*e.g.* Is 42:16; 48:17; 49:10; 58:11).
   f. *Personal piety*: Knowing God's will in the Psalms is a matter of the law and the way of salvation. In the wisdom literature it is the fear of the Lord (trust in God's covenant promises and saving acts). Beyond that we must learn to act responsibly by making decisions that

are consistent with the fear of the Lord. God gives us the necessary guidelines, but he does not make our decisions for us.

g. *The Gospels*: The goal of the Old Testament is in Jesus Christ as the perfectly guided man for us. Yet, he is never a puppet of the Holy Spirit. The gospel is the goal of guidance, thus, when we come to Christ, we have arrived at God's goal for us.

h. *Acts*: Care is needed here that we do not make events required by this transitional age normative for us now. The gospel is the essential guidance for the apostles.

i. *Epistles*: There are a number of dimensions here:

   i. Divine providence in retrospect; we look back on our decisions and see how God has led us (e.g., Phil 2:12-13).

   ii. Christ did the perfect will of God for us.

   iii. God's will for us is our sanctification, that is, to live consistently with the gospel (e.g., 1 Thess 4:3).

CONCLUSIONS

This investigation in outline suggests a number of conclusions that should be carefully checked out:

1. God's goal for us is to make us like Christ and restore us to his presence in glory.

2. Christ has already reached this goal for us and, by faith, we are united to him and have reached the goal in him.

3. Between conversion (justification) and glorification our lives are to be governed by the gospel (sanctification).

4. When we are faced with decisions, the choice of evil or godless alternatives are ruled out by the gospel.

5. When there are a number of possible good alternatives, a responsible decision must be made. Since certain decisions will affect the life of the congregation, consideration should be given to how other Christians should share in the decision-making process.

6. There is no real basis for the idea that there is only one possible choice out of the many alternatives by which we can do the will of God.

7. There is no basis for the idea that the Holy Spirit takes over our responsibility for making wise and godly decisions, or that some kind of inner peace is the criterion for knowing that the right decision has been revealed to us.

QUESTIONS TO THINK ABOUT

1. Many ideas about being called by God to a particular ministry or to be a missionary in some particular place have little biblical basis. Work out a biblical theology of "calling." Pay special attention to what kinds of ministry people in the Bible are called to. What does the New Testament say about the way people are appointed to the various ministries in the church?

2. Consider the following assessment of the evidence: The Bible gives no grounds for the belief that God guides us in everyday decisions other than by revealing the gospel, its fruit in our lives and its final goal.

27

LIFE AFTER DEATH

AN OUTLINE BIBLICAL THEOLOGY OF RESURRECTION

THE PROBLEM

There is a universal fear of death that seems to breed a fascination with the subject. This being the case, it is often a matter of disappointment, especially amongst those engaged in the Christian ministry, to find that so many Christians are confused about how the gospel addresses the question of death and what follows it. Bible students also find the theology of life after death perplexing since the Old Testament seems to have so little to say on the matter. Why does the New Testament come out so strongly for a unique doctrine of the resurrection of the body in opposition to the popular idea of the immortality of the soul?

SOME PRACTICAL CONCERNS

Understanding death and the hereafter is important for a number of reasons. For example, we might suggest the following issues:

1. Can we be sure of eternal life?
2. What happens when we die?
3. What shall we say about spiritualism that claims to contact the dead?
4. Is cremation an option for Christians?
5. How can I minister to relatives when the deceased was not a believer?
6. Why is the Old Testament so vague about life after death?
7. What is the role of grief for bereaved Christians?
8. Is there any place for a doctrine of reincarnation?

A SUGGESTED APPROACH

Again some imagination is needed in deciding where to search for the relevant biblical data. Word-studies and the investigation of certain ideas are part of the process required by biblical theology. In this suggested approach we shall concentrate on the idea of life after death although we cannot avoid some consideration of the subject of death itself.

1. *Our starting point is the very heart of the gospel: the resurrection of Jesus.*
   The bodily resurrection indicates that the humanity of Jesus is rescued from death and that the event is not purely a result of Jesus being God. Although the Gospels say little about the general resurrection of believers it is clearly a doctrine that was known at that time and seen to be consistent with the Old Testament (*e.g.* Jn 11:23-24).

2. *Some of the words to be investigated will be fairly obvious.*
   For example: *die, sleep, death, grave, sheol,* in the Old Testament, and *resurrection, eternal life, heaven, hell,* in the New Testament. But there are also some more broadly based themes that are linked to resurrection in the New Testament that may give us some important clues. For example, Jesus' resurrection fulfills Old Testament promises to Israel (Acts 13:32-33) and is therefore a covenant theme (Acts 2:30-31; Heb 13:20).

3. *Now investigate the various strata of biblical theology.*
   Look at them in turn for the way life after death occurs and, in the Old Testament, watch out for what might fill the gap when life after death is hardly in evidence.
   a. *Adam and Eve*: Death is due to sin, thus eternal life seems to have been the original intention.
   b. *The patriarchs*: The blessings of God are promised in terms of this life. Death is regarded rather neutrally, especially when one dies in old age. Sheol is the place of the departed but not the ultimate bliss.
   c. *The exodus*: The promises are for a long life in the land given by God. Life after death is not promised.
   d. *Canaan-monarchy*: Same as for c.
   e. *Prophecy*: The blessings of God are seen in some future age. The nation will be restored (Ezek 37) to a renewed land. However, once the kingdom of God is portrayed as an age not entirely continuous with the present, the question arises as to how past generations can share in it. The first indications of resurrection occur in relation to the covenant (Is 26:19; 52:13; Dan 12:2; and possibly Job 19:26). Not all prophecy has this perspective on resurrection to eternal life (Is 65:20).
   f. *The Gospels*: Jesus' ministry of healing and raising the dead does not

of itself indicate general resurrection. However, when it is coupled with his teaching on the kingdom and his own resurrection, it is difficult to escape that implication.

g. *Acts*: The apostolic preaching centers on the resurrection of Jesus as the fulfillment of the covenant and the promises of the kingdom.

h. *Epistles*: The resurrection of Jesus is again central. Theologizing on this event, especially by Paul, shows the unbreakable link between the resurrection of Jesus and that of the believer who is *in Christ*. Jesus is shown, by his resurrection, to be the head of a new race of God's people. There is no room for reincarnation.

CONCLUSIONS

The following suggested conclusions from our study should be checked out:

1. Creation shows God's original and permanent commitment to a creation that includes the physical universe.
2. Death enters because of sin, but God will not forgo his original commitment.
3. This commitment is expressed in the covenant of redemption.
4. While the covenant promises are given in terms of the present age, there is no indication of life beyond this age. Yet Sheol shows that death does not obliterate us.
5. Once the covenant promises are framed in terms of a future age, life after death becomes an issue. However, the future age is never described as anything other than bodily existence in the physical world. Resurrection is the only possible way for people dying in this age to share in the future age.
6. The resurrection of Jesus is demanded by God's faithfulness to his covenant promises. The Old Testament view of the new earth is maintained in the New Testament.
7. Christians dying in this age are with the Lord, but the New Testament emphasis is on the resurrection to life. This takes place at the second coming of Christ along with the renewal of the physical universe.

QUESTIONS TO THINK ABOUT

1. There is much mythology about the human soul. Part of the problem is that the word is used with a number of meanings in both Old and New

Testaments. With the aid of a concordance, investigate the biblical usage of the word. What biblical data can you bring to bear on the question of whether or not the dead consciously enjoy the presence of Christ while awaiting their resurrection?

2. How could you minister biblically to a child bereaved of his or her pet, who asks, "Will my dog go to heaven?"

3. Are there any biblical grounds for why a Christian should prefer burial to cremation?

Subject Index

Abraham, 36, 56, 64-69, 80, 84-85, 88, 120-26, 128-31, 136, 139-41, 146, 158-59, 161, 167, 174, 182, 184-85, 187-88, 192, 194, 197, 204, 210, 215

biblical theology, 7, 9-12, 15, 17-19, 27, 29, 32, 35, 43-45, 47, 55, 60, 71, 73-74, 76-79, 82, 95, 111, 114, 121, 163, 169, 171, 184, 186, 192, 194, 200, 212, 214, 219, 233, 235, 238, 240, 242

blessing, 115-16, 121, 124-25, 127-28, 141, 149-50, 155, 159

captivity, 131, 133, 136-39, 160, 184, 187-89

consummation, 218-19, 226-27, 229-33

covenant, 36, 56, 73, 77, 85, 96, 114-19, 121-29, 131-33, 135-46, 151-53, 155, 157-70, 172, 174, 177, 180-90, 192, 194-97, 200, 205, 207, 214-15, 228, 238, 242-43

creation, 7, 11-12, 40-42, 49, 60, 71, 75-77, 80, 84-85, 90-100, 103, 106, 110-13, 115, 118-20, 142-43, 150, 161, 163, 169, 173-75, 178-79, 188-90, 192, 194, 197, 202, 205-6, 214, 219, 221, 223-24, 226-27, 229-30, 232-34, 243

creation, order of, 173, 175

curse, 106, 117, 154, 205

David, 25, 51, 56, 80-82, 84-85, 88, 127, 159, 161, 164, 166-71, 181-83, 186-88, 190-92, 194, 196-97, 204-6, 228

election, 116-19, 122-23, 125-26, 134, 153, 181

eschatology, 189, 192, 194, 198-99, 203, 207-8, 215-16, 224, 232

exegetical theology, 32-33, 35

exodus, 80, 131, 134, 136-38, 143-44, 151-53, 160, 163, 174, 181, 184, 188-90, 197, 238, 242

faith, 18, 21-22, 30-31, 36, 44-45, 47-48, 73, 81, 83, 87, 107, 112, 114, 119, 121-23, 128, 130-32, 135, 137, 140-41, 152, 154, 159, 161, 173-75, 181-82, 186, 189, 196, 214-15, 219-26, 228-29, 232-33, 239

fall, 11, 39-42, 59, 75, 85, 96, 103, 105-6, 110-11, 118, 154, 158, 161, 185-86, 188, 194, 197-98, 202, 207, 223

gospel, 7, 31, 42, 47-50, 55-56, 60, 66-67, 71-74, 76, 81-84, 86-88, 90, 92, 103, 106, 116, 123, 142-43, 146, 148, 158, 174, 198, 203-4, 210, 212-15, 218-25, 228-33, 238-42

Gospels, the four, 7, 13, 46, 70, 84-85, 87-89, 179, 209, 211, 220, 233

grace, 50, 60, 93, 106-9, 111, 114, 116-19, 122-26, 128-29, 141-43, 147-48, 150-51, 153, 158, 161, 167, 174, 180-82, 184, 189, 215, 219-20

history, 11, 22, 30-35, 38, 42, 44, 48, 50, 52, 56, 59, 61-68, 70-72, 74-75, 77, 80, 82, 84, 87, 91-93, 100, 102-3, 109, 116, 119-20, 122-23, 127, 129, 133, 135-36, 146, 152-53, 160-61, 163, 171-72, 177, 180-81, 183-85, 187-89, 192-94, 196-97, 199-200, 207-8, 210, 214-16, 219, 224, 226, 232

holiness, 145, 148, 157, 159, 189

Holy Spirit, 18, 37, 43, 45, 47-50, 60, 63-64, 66, 82-83, 85, 201, 210-18, 220-21, 231, 239

image of God, 41-42, 45, 62, 95-98, 107, 151, 173

incarnation, 63, 66, 74, 203, 207

interpretation, 23-25, 32, 37, 41, 43, 50, 52, 54, 59-60, 64, 66-71, 77, 84, 92, 103, 130, 204, 212

Israel, 19-20, 22, 24, 50, 52, 56, 67-69, 74, 80, 82, 84-85, 88, 91, 93-94, 110, 118, 125-27, 130-62, 164-67, 169, 171-72, 175, 177, 180-94, 197-200, 202-6, 208, 210, 212, 215-16, 220, 224, 232-33, 242

Jerusalem, 22, 69, 108, 164, 167, 169-70, 180, 183, 187-89, 192, 195-96, 201, 203, 210, 212-13, 217, 230

Jesus Christ, 7, 9, 21-24, 29, 45, 47, 50, 53, 56-57, 59-64, 68, 72-73, 75-77, 79-81, 84-85, 87-88, 90, 103, 161, 202-3, 206-7, 209-11, 216, 220, 222, 225, 239

judgment, 40, 102, 105-13, 116-17, 131, 135-37, 151, 161, 168, 181, 184-86, 189-90, 196, 207, 217, 231, 234

kingdom of God, 11, 22, 47, 71-73, 77, 94-95, 99, 110-11, 113, 130-31, 136, 140, 143, 150, 153, 157, 161, 185-91, 196-97, 202, 209, 211-13, 220, 226, 228, 232, 238, 242

kingship, 161, 163-67, 171, 181, 184, 188, 205

knowledge, 9, 18, 27, 29, 31, 37-40, 42-43, 45-47, 55, 87, 97-99, 112, 122, 144, 153,

173-76, 178-79

law, 22-24, 140-43, 145-49, 157, 161, 165, 168, 173-74, 176, 195, 202, 218-19, 222, 238

literalism, 67-68

Lord, fear of, 173-75, 179, 238-39

meditation, 92

Moses, 24-25, 53-54, 80, 86, 91, 130, 132-37, 139-41, 144, 149-52, 155-56, 159, 161, 172, 180-83, 190-91, 195, 202, 205, 222

name of God, 133, 150

nations, 85, 88, 115-16, 121, 123-24, 126, 128, 141, 149-50, 159, 161, 165, 169, 181, 190-91, 212-13

new Creation, 11-12, 77, 100, 146, 153, 187, 202, 206-7, 211, 215, 221, 223, 225-27, 229, 233

Old Testament, 7, 12-14, 17, 21-23, 36, 47, 50-57, 62, 64-69, 71-73, 76, 78, 82-88, 91-92, 95, 114, 117, 123, 131-32, 141-42, 157-59, 161, 172, 174-75, 181, 184, 191-92, 194, 197-98, 200, 202-12, 214, 217-19, 221, 225-27, 229-30, 239, 241-43

overlap of the ages, 223, 228

people of God, 31-32, 67-68, 78, 82-83, 85, 96, 99-100, 116-17, 127-28, 133, 136, 141, 143, 145, 149, 153-54, 156, 162, 169, 174-75, 177-78, 181, 190, 191, 196, 202, 204, 206, 208, 215, 218, 221-22, 226, 238

presuppositions, 44-46, 48, 55, 60, 69, 74

Promised Land, 121, 124-26, 128, 130, 136, 147, 149, 151-52, 154-55, 157-58, 160,

164, 169, 181, 184, 188-92, 195, 197, 199, 203-4, 206

promises of God, 52, 54, 56, 64-66, 68-69, 76, 82-85, 114, 120-33, 136-38, 141, 146, 149, 151-52, 155-59, 161, 167-69, 172, 174-75, 182, 187-89, 193, 195, 197-99, 204-7, 210, 219, 227, 238, 242-43

prophecy, 50-51, 56, 127, 168, 171, 193-94, 196, 224, 232, 242

prophets, 22, 50, 52-53, 57, 63, 69, 81, 86, 113, 143, 146, 161, 172, 180-84, 187, 189-94, 196-97, 204, 212, 221

redemption, 49, 59, 62, 73, 77, 96, 116-17, 119, 131, 133, 135-43, 145-47, 149, 153, 163, 173-75, 177-78, 185-89, 192-94, 197, 206, 215, 229, 243

regeneration, 173, 175, 188-89, 192, 198-200, 202, 207-8, 215-16, 222-27, 229-30, 232, 234

resurrection, 43, 47, 53, 60, 66, 81-82, 191, 205-7, 210, 213, 220, 223, 228-30, 233, 241-44

revelation, 10-11, 24, 32, 35, 37, 39-41, 43, 45, 52, 55-57, 59-60, 64-77, 79, 91, 93, 99-100, 107, 119, 123-24, 126-27, 130-32, 135, 142-45, 151, 160, 169, 173-76, 178-79, 182-84, 190, 193, 197-98, 201-3, 211, 219, 222, 228, 238

salvation, 29, 36-37, 47-49, 51, 56, 63, 67, 69, 72, 81-82, 84-85, 100, 109, 111, 113-14, 126-27, 132, 134, 136, 142, 148, 153, 158-61, 163, 166, 177, 180-84, 186, 188, 190-93, 196, 199, 203-4, 206-7,

212, 214-15, 218, 220-21, 223, 227, 229, 231, 233-34, 238

second coming of Christ, 18, 207, 222, 233, 243

signs and wonders, 132-34

sin, 37, 41-42, 46, 49, 59-61, 83, 90, 93-94, 96, 100, 102-7, 109, 111-12, 115, 117, 131, 137, 143-46, 151, 158, 168-69, 175-76, 179-80, 184, 186, 188, 205, 215, 242-43

Solomon, 80, 127, 161, 164, 168-71, 174, 180, 182-85, 187, 190, 197, 206, 210, 215

Son of God, 53, 61, 81-82, 84, 88, 102, 108, 138, 141, 149, 191, 204-5, 220, 228

systematic theology, 30, 32

tabernacle, 140, 144-45, 147-48, 150-51, 169, 206, 217, 230

temple, 22, 69, 147, 164, 167-70, 174, 179-80, 183, 188, 192, 195-96, 199-201, 203, 206-7, 212-13, 217, 220, 230

temptation, 53, 85, 103-4, 106, 110, 204

theism, Christian, 41-44, 46, 48-49, 51, 72

Trinity, 82

truth, 10, 18, 21, 32, 37, 40, 42-45, 48-52, 59-61, 63-66, 69, 71-72, 74-76, 91-92, 103-4, 131, 156, 171, 174, 176, 205, 223, 227

typology, 59, 67-69, 161, 207

unity and diversity, 7, 20, 23-24, 34, 56, 76-78, 116, 163, 192, 201-2, 208

wisdom, 7, 17, 23, 82, 169, 171-78, 184, 206, 238

Word of God, 10, 17-18, 24, 31, 43, 47-48, 52, 58-61, 63-64, 72, 75, 94, 97, 174, 180, 187

Scripture Index

Genesis
1, *55, 90, 92, 93, 94*
1—2, *91, 96, 101*
1—11, *119*
1:1, *229*
1:10, *93*
1:11-13, *93*
1:12, *93*
1:14-19, *93*
1:18, *93*
1:21, *93*
1:24-25, *93*
1:25, *93*
1:26, *95, 96*
1:26-28, *97, 205*
1:26-30, *93*
1:27, *95, 96*
1:28, *98*
1:28-30, *41*
1:31, *93, 112, 174*
2, *92, 93*
2:15-17, *94*
2:16, *98*
2:16-17, *238*
2:17, *42, 103, 174*
3, *85, 102, 103, 111, 186*
3:5, *104*
3:7, *104*
3:10, *105*
3:12-13, *105*
3:14-24, *105*
3:15, *106*
3:15-24, *42*
3:16, *106*
3:17-19, *174*
3:17-24, *106*
3:22, *104*
4, *107, 113*
4—11, *117, 119*
4:1, *107*

4:11-12, *107*
4:15, *108*
4:17-24, *108*
4:24, *113*
4:25, *107*
4:26, *113*
5, *113*
6, *108*
6—9, *114*
6:1-4, *108*
6:5-7, *109*
6:8, *114*
6:18, *114*
8:21, *115*
9:1-3, *115*
9:6, *95*
9:8-17, *115*
9:18-28, *116*
9:19, *115*
9:20-27, *115*
10, *115, 116*
11:1-9, *116*
11:4, *117*
11:10-32, *116*
12:1, *238*
12:1-3, *121, 129*
12:2, *121*
12:3, *141, 159*
12:7, *124*
12:11-20, *122*
13—21, *122*
13:14-18, *121*
15:2-3, *123*
15:4-6, *122*
15:6, *123*
15:13-16, *131*
17, *85*
17:1-8, *85*
17:1-14, *121*
17:1-21, *122*
17:7-8, *167*
18:16-19, *122*
20:1-18, *122*
21:5, *123*
24:1-7, *124*
24:27-38, *238*
25:21, *124*

26:1-6, *124*
26:7-16, *124*
26:12, *167*
27, *124*
28:3, *125*
28:13-15, *125*
32:9-12, *125*
32:22-32, *125*
35:9-15, *125*
37—50, *126*
45:5-7, *238*
48:3-6, *127*
48:5, *127*
48:8-14, *127*
49:8-10, *165*
49:10, *127*
50:20, *127*

Exodus
1, *131*
1—14, *137*
1—15, *139*
2, *25*
2:21, *159*
2:23-25, *132, 136*
3:1—4:17, *132*
3:6, *132*
3:7-9, *132*
3:13, *132*
3:13-15, *136*
3:14, *133*
3:14-16, *132*
3:16-17, *155*
3:19-20, *136*
4:1, *132*
4:1-9, *133*
4:21, *134*
4:22, *85*
4:22-23, *133, 135, 138*
4:23, *57, 204*
4:27-31, *133*
5:21, *133*
6, *139*
6:1-6, *136*
6:1-8, *133*
6:2-5, *136*

6:6-7, *134*
6:6-8, *136*
7:3, *134*
7:3-5, *136*
7:5, *134*
8:15, *134*
9:12, *134*
9:34, *134*
9:34—10:1, *134*
10:1, *134*
10:1-2, *136*
10:20, *20*
11:4-5, *135*
12:1-13, *135*
12:14-20, *135*
13:17, *238*
13:17-18, *136*
13:21, *238*
14:1-4, *136*
14:4, *136*
14:8, *136*
14:13-14, *136*
14:14, *136*
14:31, *137*
15:1-3, *136*
15:1-18, *137*
15:13, *137, 139, 238*
15:17-18, *155*
16, *140*
17, *140*
19:4-6, *141, 142, 148*
19:8, *141*
20:2, *142*
20:8, *19*
23:19, *20*
25—30, *144, 148*
32, *151*
35—40, *144*

Leviticus
1—6, *145*
11, *145*
11:44-45, *146*
16, *145*
17:10, *182*

19:2, *146*
19:18, *143*
19:34-36, *146*
19:34-37, *146*
20:1-6, *182*
22:31-33, *146*
23:43, *146*
24:13-17, *182*
25:38, *146*
25:42, *146*
25:55, *146*
26, *146, 148*
26:1-13, *146*
26:12, *146*
26:12-13, *146*
26:14-39, *146*
26:40-45, *146*
26:45, *146*

Numbers
6:24-26, *150*
6:27, *150*
10:35-36, *150*
12:1, *159*
12:1-2, *151*
12:3-15, *151*
13:30, *151*
14:6-9, *151*
14:11, *151*
14:13-20, *151*
14:21-35, *151*
20:10-13, *161*
21:4-9, *152*

Deuteronomy
1—3, *152*
1:33, *238*
2:4-5, *126*
2:9, *126*
2:19, *126*
4—26, *152*
4:10, *174*
4:20, *153*
4:34, *134*
4:37-40, *153*
5:15, *153*
6:2, *174*

6:4-5, *152*
6:5, *143, 148*
6:6-9, *153*
6:13, *205*
6:16, *205*
6:20-25, *153, 158*
7:6-11, *153*
7:7-8, *189*
8, *85*
8:1-20, *182*
8:2, *238*
8:3, *97, 205*
8:7-9, *110*
8:7-10, *153, 155*
8:11-20, *181*
8:15, *238*
9, *161*
9:1-24, *153*
10:12, *174*
10:12-16, *153*
10:20-21, *174*
10:20-22, *153*
11:26-28, *205*
17, *166*
17:14-20, *157, 165*
28, *153*
28:1-48, *181*
28:10, *133*
28:15-68, *182*
29:5, *238*
30:15-20, *181*
32:12, *238*
33—34, *155*
33:22, *20*

Joshua
1:1-9, *157*
1:9, *157*
2:8-14, *159*
3:1-17, *157*
3:10, *158*
4:21-24, *158*
5:13—6:7, *158*
6, *194*
6:17, *159*

6:17-21, *158*
6:25, *159*
7:1-5, *158*
7:6-26, *158*
10:13, *20*
10:40, *20*
23:1-13, *157*
23:4-5, *157*
23:14, *157*
24:14, *131*

Judges
1:27-36, *160*
2:2-3, *160*
2:11-13, *160*
2:11-23, *160*
2:14-23, *160*
3:10, *160*
4, *194*
6:34, *160*
6:36-40, *161*
8:22-23, *164*
9, *164*
11:29, *160*
13:25, *160*
14:19, *160*
15:14, *160*
15:19, *160*
21:25, *164*

Ruth
4:1-11, *137*

1 Samuel
8:4-8, *165*
8:10-18, *165*
11:12-15, *165*
12:14-15, *165*
13:8-14, *166*
13:14, *166*
15:1-23, *166*
16:13, *166, 191*
16:13-14, *166*
17, *25, 166*
17:45-47, *166*
24, *194*
24:1-7, *166*

26:6-12, *166*
31, *166*

2 Samuel
5, *167*
6, *167*
7, *85, 167*
7:1-3, *167*
7:1-14, *171*
7:4-12, *167*
7:12-14, *85, 171*
7:14, *167, 191*
7:16, *167*

1 Kings
3—10, *168*
3:1-2, *169*
3:6-9, *169*
3:16-28, *169*
4:20-28, *169*
4:29-34, *169*
5—7, *169*
8, *169, 179*
8:6-10, *169*
8:15-53, *169*
8:38-43, *174*
8:41-43, *169*
10, *194*
12:25-33, *183*
14:21-24, *183*
16:29-34, *183*
16:29—17:6, *183*
18, *182*
18:1-40, *183*

2 Kings
17, *183*
18—25, *186*
18:1-8, *183*
22:1-20, *183*
23:26-27, *183*

Ezra
2—5, *196*

Nehemiah
9:10, *134*

9:12, *238*
9:19, *238*

Job
11:7, *176*
19:26, *242*

Psalms
1, *179*
8:5, *96*
22:1-18, *179*
77:20, *238*
78:53, *238*
89, *171*
89:3-4, *167*
89:5-18, *167*
89:14, *168*
89:24, *168*
89:30, *168*
89:32-34, *168*
93, *179*
98:7-9, *192*
104:24-30, *97*
106:9, *238*
122, *179*
132, *167, 171*
136, *179*
137, *179*
137:8-9, *20*
148:1-14, *192*
150, *179*

Proverbs
1:7, *173*
9:10, *173*
10—29, *179*
26:4-5, *179*
30:15, *20*

Song of Solomon
7:4, *20*

Isaiah
1:12-20, *183*
2, *212*
2:2-4, *190, 192*
9:2-7, *189, 191*

9:6, *206*
9:6-7, *171*
10:20-23, *190*
11, *194*
11:1-5, *178, 189, 191, 226*
11:2, *206*
11:6-9, *192*
11:11-12, *190*
14:1-4, *190*
14:12-15, *102*
16:5, *191*
24:1-3, *189*
26:19, *242*
32:1-20, *192*
32:15-20, *227*
35, *194*
35:1-10, *192, 227*
40:1-2, *190*
40:1-5, *190*
40:12-26, *189*
42:1, *204, 226*
42:1-4, *191*
42:6, *85, 189*
42:9, *189*
42:16, *238*
43:1, *189*
43:1-7, *190*
43:7, *133*
43:15, *189*
43:15-21, *190*
43:18-19, *189*
43:21, *238*
44:21-24, *189*
44:23, *192*
45:7-13, *189*
45:13, *189*
45:18, *189*
46:3-4, *190*
48:6-7, *189*
48:13, *189*
48:17, *238*
48:20-21, *190*
49:1-6, *191*
49:3, *191*
49:5-6, *191*
49:10, *238*

49:13, *192*
49:24-26, *190*
50:4-9, *191*
51:3, *192*
51:5-6, *189*
51:6, *192*
51:9-11, *190*
51:11, *190, 192*
51:13-16, *192*
52:10, *85*
52:13, *242*
52:13—53:12, *191*
54:5, *189*
54:7-10, *189*
55:1-4, *171*
55:3-5, *191*
55:8-9, *176*
56:1, *189*
58:11, *238*
59:15-17, *189*
61, *85, 194*
61:1-4, *226*
61:4-7, *190*
63:1, *189*
63:9, *189*
63:12-13, *238*
65, *194*
65:1-12, *185*
65:17, *12, 100, 192, 229*
65:17-25, *192, 227*
65:20, *242*
66:22, *192*

Jeremiah
4:23-28, *189*
7:1-7, *183*
7:23, *167*
9:24, *189*
11:4, *167*
23:1-6, *191*
23:1-8, *190*
23:5-6, *170, 171, 189*
23:7-8, *190*
29:10-14, *190*
30:10-11, *190*
30:22, *167*

31:7-9, *190*
31:31-34, *147, 194*
32:20-21, *134*
33:14-26, *189*
33:23-26, *171*

Ezekiel
23, *183*
23:19-21, *131*
34, *194*
34:1-16, *190*
34:11-16, *192*
34:17-21, *203*
34:20-24, *171, 191*
34:20-31, *170*
34:25-31, *192*
36, *194*
36:8-12, *162*
36:22-24, *190*
36:25-28, *226*
36:28, *194*
36:35-38, *192*
37, *194, 242*
37:1-14, *227*
37:15-22, *190*
37:24-28, *191*
47:1-12, *110, 192, 230*

Daniel
7, *206*
7—8, *196*
12:2, *242*

Hosea
2:14-20, *189*
2:16-23, *189*
3:1, *189*
11:1, *57, 138*
11:1-9, *189*
11:8-11, *189*
14:4, *189*

Joel
2, *194*
2:28-29, *215*
2:32, *113*

Amos
7:4, *189*
9:11, *191*

Micah
2:12, *190*
4:1-4, *190*

Zephaniah
1:2-3, *189*
3, *194*
3:9, *190*

Haggai
1—2, *196*
2:6-9, *196*

Zechariah
1—6, *200*
1:7—6:15, *196*
4:6-7, *199*
8, *212*
8:20-23, *190, 196*
14:1-21, *196*

Malachi
4:1-6, *196*
4:5-6, *199*

Matthew
1:1, *84*
1:13, *196*
1:17, *57*
1:17-20, *205*
1:20-23, *207*
2:14-15, *130*
3:17—4:4, *57*
4:1-11, *53, 204*
4:3-4, *149*
5:17, *140, 147*
7:12, *220*
7:15-23, *110*
7:24-28, *178*
7:24-29, *206*
11:12-14, *199*
16:15-17, *63*
19:4-5, *53*

19:28, *227*
20:29-31, *205*
21:9, *204*
22:34-40, *143*
24:37, *112*
26:63-68, *203*

Mark
1:1-2, *84*
1:12-13, *204*
1:14, *213*
1:14-15, *205*
1:15, *72*
2:5-12, *203*
8:31-33, *212*
9:9-13, *212*
10:35-45, *212*
10:45, *205*
12:24, *53*

Luke
1:17, *85*
1:27-32, *85*
1:30-33, *205*
1:31-32, *164*
1:32-33, *56*
1:46-55, *57*
1:54-55, *85*
1:70-75, *85*
2:29-32, *85*
2:46-52, *206*
3:16, *214*
3:18, *213*
3:22-28, *85*
3:22-38, *138*
3:23-38, *204*
3:27, *196*
4:1-12, *85, 110*
4:1-13, *53, 204*
4:3, *138*
4:3-4, *102*
4:16-21, *85, 205*
4:16-24, *204*
9:30-31, *195*
11:31, *206*
21:27-28, *206*
22:19-20, *205*

23:43, *156*
24, *211, 227*
24:17-21, *212*
24:25-26, *86*
24:25-27, *53, 203, 212*
24:26, *191*
24:27, *50, 51, 86, 193*
24:31-35, *212*
24:44, *50, 172, 193*
24:44-45, *54, 86*
24:45, *50*

John
1:1, *61, 84*
1:1-3, *50, 60, 90, 203, 205*
1:1-18, *203*
1:3, *84, 91, 92*
1:14, *50, 61, 84, 206*
1:14-18, *205*
1:18, *50*
2:13-22, *206*
2:19, *164, 199, 201*
3:4, *223*
3:5-8, *223*
3:9, *223*
3:10-15, *223*
3:14-15, *57, 149, 152*
3:16, *83*
4:22, *127*
5:39, *50*
5:39-40, *54*
7:39, *213, 214*
8:48-59, *203*
8:56, *64, 120*
8:58, *120*
10:11, *205*
10:15, *205*
10:29-31, *203*
10:35, *53*
11:23-24, *242*
13:31-38, *211*
14—16, *211, 227*
14:1-3, *211*
14:6, *49, 205*
14:12, *211*

14:18-20, *211*
15:26-27, *211*
16:4-7, *211*
16:7, *211*
16:13, *49*
20:22, *213*
20:31, *85, 220*

Acts
1, *227*
1:6, *212, 228*
1:6-8, *223*
1:7, *212*
1:8, *212*
2, *87, 213*
2:14-39, *86*
2:14-40, *217*
2:16-39, *57*
2:21, *210*
2:29-33, *170*
2:29-35, *228*
2:30-31, *51, 56, 242*
2:30-32, *205*
2:36, *205, 228*
2:38, *214*
3:12-26, *217*
3:13-26, *86, 88*
4:8-12, *217*
4:10-12, *86, 88*
5:30-32, *86, 88*
7:2-53, *217*
7:2-56, *57*
10:34-43, *217*
10:36-43, *86, 88*
13, *87*
13:16-33, *56*
13:16-41, *217*
13:16-43, *57*
13:22-23, *205*
13:23, *170*
13:32-33, *50, 51, 193, 206, 242*
13:32-34, *170*
13:32-35, *228*
13:32-37, *205*
16:31, *210*
17:22-31, *86*

Romans
1:1-4, *50, 81*
1:3, *51, 204, 205*
1:4, *205, 228*
1:16, *47, 72*
1:18-23, *174*
1:18-25, *42*
1:18-32, *46*
3:21—4:25, *220*
4, *128, 129*
5:12, *103, 174*
5:19, *204*
6:3-11, *221*
6:4-5, *221*
6:4-11, *229*
6:11, *221*
6:14, *147, 222*
6:23, *42*
8:1-25, *221*
8:11, *229*
8:17, *72*
8:18, *229*
8:19-20, *174*
8:19-23, *96, 206, 229*
8:20-22, *42*
9:6, *126*
9:14-18, *134*
9:19-24, *122*
12:2, *48, 222*
16:20, *106*

1 Corinthians
1:18-25, *174*
1:20—2:16, *206*
1:24, *172*
1:30, *172, 178*
5:7, *130, 138, 205*
10:1-13, *154, 155*
15:1-11, *88*
15:22, *204, 221*
15:42-44, *234*
15:45, *12, 100, 204*

2 Corinthians
1:20, *193, 206*
5:1-10, *229*
5:7, *140, 221*
5:17, *12, 100, 187, 208, 221, 223*
5:21, *180, 185, 205*

Galatians
2:19-20, *221*
3, *128, 129*
3:2, *223*
3:10-14, *205*
3:14-29, *220*
3:15-29, *56*
3:16, *204*
3:21-25, *222*
3:23-25, *143*
3:24-25, *140*
3:29, *120*
4:4, *106*
5:17, *222*

Ephesians
1:1-14, *225*
1:3-10, *118*
1:11, *42*
2:1-3, *42*
2:5, *221*
2:6, *221*
5:18-20, *221*
6:10-18, *225*

Philippians
2:5-7, *203*
2:12-13, *239*

Colossians
1:15, *204*
1:16, *49, 60, 90, 91*
1:16-17, *203*
1:17, *97*
2:9, *203*

2:12, *221*
2:17, *68*
2:20, *221*
3:1-4, *218*
3:1-5, *230, 231*
3:3-5, *222*
3:16-17, *221*

1 Thessalonians
4:3, *239*

1 Timothy
2:5, *72*

2 Timothy
2:8, *88*
3:15, *51*

Titus
2:13, *203*
3:1-7, *223*
3:5, *227*

Hebrews
1:1-2, *50, 51, 57, 205*
1:3, *97*
1:8, *203*
3:1, *205*
3:6, *204*
4:1-13, *154, 162*
4:9, *156*
4:14—5:10, *205*
4:15, *102*
7:24—10:25, *205*
10:1, *68*
11:3, *91, 92*
11:4, *107*
11:7, *112*
13:20, *228, 242*

James
1:18, *223*
1:27, *222*

1 Peter
1:3, *223, 229*
1:10-12, *50*
1:23, *223*
2:4-10, *220*
2:24, *205*
3:20-21, *118*
5:8-9, *222*

2 Peter
3:3-13, *228*
3:5-7, *91, 92*
3:11-13, *206*
3:13, *12, 100, 187, 229*

1 John
3:1-3, *233*
4:1-3, *234*

Revelation
1:8, *87*
1:17-18, *81, 87*
2:5, *180*
2:7, *113*
7:9, *116*
12:9, *102, 110*
20:2, *102*
20:11-15, *110*
21—22, *229*
21:1, *12, 100, 187*
21:1-2, *230*
21:1-5, *208*
21:3, *230*
21:3-5, *226*
21:5, *187, 230*
21:22-23, *230*
22:1-2, *230*
22:1-6, *110*
22:13, *87, 203*